# THE SQUARED CIRCLE

# THE SQUARED CIRCLE

## Life, Death and
## Professional Wrestling

# David Shoemaker

GOTHAM BOOKS

**GOTHAM BOOKS**
Published by the Penguin Group
Penguin Group (USA) LLC
375 Hudson Street
New York, New York 10014

USA | Canada | UK | Ireland | Australia | New Zealand | India | South Africa | China
penguin .com
A Penguin Random House Company
Copyright © 2013 by David Shoemaker

LIBRARY OF CONGRESS CATALOGING-IN-PUBLICATION DATA

Shoemaker, David.
The squared circle : life, death and professional wrestling / David Shoemaker.
pages cm
ISBN 978-1-592-40767-5 (hardcover)
1. Wrestling.   2. Wrestling—Social aspects.   I. Title.
GV1195.S46 2013
796.812—dc23
2013007230

Printed in the United States of America
1 3 5 7 9 10 8 6 4 2

Set in Chronicle Text
Designed by Sabrina Bowers

*To Mom and Dad,*
*who never made me turn the channel when this junk was on.*

# CONTENTS

# THE WRESTLEMANIA ERA

# INTRODUCTION

In modern professional wrestling, the really compelling shows start with what they call a "cold open"—they skip the theme song, skip the formality, and get right to the meat. So let me try to do that here:

This is a book about dead wrestlers.

It was supposed to be, anyway. But along the way, it became a history of professional wrestling told through the stories of people who made the myths and who thereafter died. It's the story of a mythology populated not by gods but by real men, fallible mortals who served as vessels for a larger truth, men who lived the lives of kings and who suffered to be our idols. This is the ultimate fakery of wrestling—that the emperor has no clothes, that the gods are mortals. But in reliving their lives, what became clear is that the mythology is what matters the most. We make our own gods for our own purposes. And we love them, and that's the whole point.

☆ ☆ ☆

Dad took me to a wrestling show in 1987 at Freedom Hall in Louisville, Kentucky. Dad was no wrestling fan himself, but he knew how much it meant to me to see Hulk Hogan square off against the nefarious Killer Khan. My only concrete memory of the night was that the Hogan-Khan "main event" went on halfway through the card. When Hogan dispatched the Mongolian monster, I felt for a moment like it was time to leave; that was the main event, after all. It was a bit off-putting until my dad suggested that they must have done it that way because Hogan had a flight to catch. Even as a nine-year-old, I knew that this made sense, that there were perfectly good real-life situations that took precedence over wrestling "reality"; even as we were screaming along to the matches as we were supposed to, as the WWF matchmakers choreographed the night for us to, everybody in the arena knew this. Which is to say, we were in on the joke.

That's the first thing most people get wrong about wrestling fans. We can whoop for the good guys, hiss at the heel antics, and still know that the show is, well, a show. It was a year prior to that Hogan-Khan match when I was first awakened to the complexities of pro wrestling, when a group of good-guy wrestlers showed up in the WWF calling themselves the Machines. There were two of them at first: a burly, nondescript guy called Super Machine (I was too young at the time to recognize him as Bill Eadie, who would later go on to great fame as Ax of the tag team Demolition—his moniker here was a play off of his previous gimmick as the Masked Superstar, a headliner in the Mid-Atlantic territory), and an enormous, stoop-necked monolith called Giant Machine. Even as a child I could see that Giant Machine was Andre the Giant.

Andre had been suspended earlier that year when he failed to show up for a match with two wrestlers from wicked manager Bobby "The Brain" Heenan's troupe. Now he was back, in disguise, and ready to resume his feud with the Heenan Family. As a kid, this was delicious comeuppance for Heenan, who had used every trick in the book to try to steer his wrestlers to victory over the good guys I idolized. Despite Heenan's loud insistence that Giant Machine was Andre, there was nothing the WWF officials could do, the mask being sacred territory in the wrestling world. (Almost every time a masked wrestler has wrestled, his opponents have tried to unmask him. That's the law of the jungle, though—opposing wrestlers can prove their point by unmasking him in the course of a match, but that's the only way it will happen.) Eventually the Machines (and their manager, Captain Lou Albano) were joined by other teammates. First came Big Machine (who was really Blackjack Mulligan, but to me he was another generic behemoth), then later Animal Machine (indisputably George "The Animal" Steele), then Hulk Machine (Hulk Hogan, he of the most identifiable copper-tanned physique in the business), and later Piper Machine (who was so intent on being identified as "Rowdy" Roddy Piper that he was wearing a kilt). With every new partner, I cheered and laughed at the Heenan Family's misfortune.

Of course, the whole point was that we could see what Heenan could see, but nobody else—not the announcers, not the referees, not the WWF front office—could tell. The entire joke was that we were in on the joke.

My grandfather used to tell a story about a wrestling show in small-town North Carolina. A reporter from the local newspaper was assigned to cover the event, but he had someplace else to be on the night of the event, so he went by the arena the day of, watched the guys warming up, took some notes, and then asked the promoter who was going to win each match so that he could file his story ahead of time. He did. But, the story goes, there was a terrible storm that night, and the show was canceled. When the newspaper came out the next day with all the results listed, the townsfolk were infuriated and, in my grandfather's words, just about ran the reporter out of town with pitchforks and torches.

Note that the townsfolk didn't run the wrestlers out of town; they went after the journalist. They knew full well what the reality of wrestling was—they were in on the joke. They just expected that the journalist would stay complicit in the enterprise. That a writer writing about wrestling would be a fan first and a critic second. Anyway, that's where I'm coming from.

☆ ☆ ☆

A quick note about "facts." Not long after the Machines storyline, Andre turned to the dark side and was set against Hulk Hogan in a battle for the centuries. He beat Hogan on a dire episode of *Saturday Night's Main Event* that I watched with my whole family on my parents' bed. I really have no idea why we were all watching; nobody else was a wrestling fan, and that was the only time it happened. But that night, with my parents and my sister bearing witness, the "Million Dollar Man" Ted DiBiase—Andre's partner in crime—stole the WWF title away from Hogan by furtively putting Earl Hebner in as the referee in place of his brother, Dave, who was the referee of record. The story goes that he paid for Earl to have plastic surgery to look just like Dave, so the two were indistinguishable except for their morals and motives. (In reality, the two were identical twins, and Earl—himself a longtime WWF ref—had only briefly been removed from television prior to the *Main Event* match in hope fans would forget about him.)

As a young fan, I was irate. The lesson, though, was the same as it had been with the Machines: Nothing in the world of pro wrestling is what it seems to be, and to assume that it is is to watch at your heart's own peril.

In researching this book, the main thing I realized about pro wrestling is that the offscreen world is almost as fantastical as the one on-screen. "History" is mostly quartered to the realm of wrestler reminiscence, which would be factually problematic on its own, but couple that with the industry's desire to mythologize everything and to keep up the facade of fakery that undergirds the sport and you end up with a lot of facts that contradict each other. What follows is my best effort to sift through them, organize them, break them down, and put them back together in something approaching truth. If all that follows isn't true in the plainest sense of the word, it's an honest effort at it. And at a minimum it's a look at reality through the distorted lens of pro wrestling unreality. It's the truth about a century of misdirection and lies.

☆ ☆ ☆

*Mundus vult decipi, ergo decipiatur.*

*(The world wants to be deceived, so let it be deceived.)*

—PETRONIUS

*It's a life that leaves you lopsided.*

—LANSING McCURLEY

☆ ☆ ☆

# THE
★ GOLDEN ★
# ERA

Wrestling was a bastard art form from the start. You can trace its history back to "catch wrestling,"[1] a mutt form of organized grappling that incorporated aspects of Greco-Roman wrestling, Irish collar-and-elbow, Indian styles, and the famously violent brand of English fighting called Lancashire wrestling.[2] As the catch wrestling fad took hold in America, in New York and in traveling carnivals that toured the growing nation in the late nineteenth century, it continued to evolve with an increased emphasis on submission holds—"hooking," they called it—as well as combative techniques from every corner of the country—and every corner of the world, really, since masses of new immigrants populated the audiences.

Like all the other sideshow acts, these carnival wrestling acts were a fully interactive sham. Here's a description of the setup, recounted in 1935 in *Collier's*:

> "Easy money, boys," the barker shrills. "Step up and get it, boys. You get a dollar for every minute you stay with one of these rasslers. You get a dollar, a clammo, a buckeroo, boys, for even one minute. You get fifty—yes, fifty—large dollars, boys—if you can throw any of these wrestlers. Who'll try his strength and skill for fifty dollars, a half hundred—enough to buy a plow, a horse or a winter coat for the little woman?"

From the outskirts of the crowd a cabbage-eared, dough-nosed shill raises a hand and starts to elbow his way forward. The act calls for him

----

1 Also widely known as "catch as catch can."

2 The "backyard wrestling" of its day.

to go up and throw one of the wrestlers, a maneuver calculated to give confidence to those who might want to try.

The wrestlers were mostly legitimate fighters, but the exhibition was imbued with shtick from the start for entertainment purposes. There are any number of stories of how the troupe would guard against defeat from particularly stout locals. It was one reason why wrestlers became well versed in hooking—there's nothing like a nice toehold to bring a tough guy to his knees—but more duplicitous means were also developed. The earliest days are full of legends about how the wrestler, when he began to feel overmatched, would wrangle his opponent back against the curtain abutting the back of the stage, whereupon an accomplice hidden behind it would clock the local through the curtain with a blackjack, unnoticed by the audience. The local guy would stagger to the ground, and the wrestler would pin him "fairly." And on to the next contestant, and the next town.

☆  ☆  ☆

The counterparts to the sideshow acts were the big-time matches that pitted top grapplers against one another, in large venues with larger crowds. This brand of "professional wrestling," as it came to be known, was more or less *real*, although of course the outcomes of bouts were sometimes fixed—which is to say that wrestling was real in those early days exactly to the extent that boxing was real. Wrestling and boxing existed in a sort of symbiosis for much of the twentieth century; oftentimes their respective popularity would rise and fall in inverse proportion. Wrestling was often the respite for disaffected boxing fans and vice versa, though over the decades the sports shared venues, management, and sometimes even athletes. So, yes, like boxing, wrestling started off as a legitimate sport. It just wasn't a very entertaining one.

Those early championship matches were frequently multihour slogs wherein the combatants rarely stood up off the mat or even moved enough for an audience member past the eighth row to notice. Sure, wrestling drew crowds, but it was not the sort of immersive spectacle that boxing was; it's true that in those days boxing bouts would often last hours as well, but if given the option, the average sports fan will choose the punch over the waist-lock ninety-nine times out of one hundred.

In the wrestling mainstream of those early days, though, even when one did not find rigged fights and predetermined endings, the industry was nonetheless marked by misdirection and mythology. Take the story of Frank Gotch, the sport's first iconic champion. It's said that in June 1899, a young Gotch agreed to wrestle a furniture salesman from the next town on a racetrack. Gotch lost, but as the fight dragged out to nearly two hours, it was clear that both men were grapplers of the highest order. As the furniture salesman left, he gave Gotch his card, revealing himself only then to be Dan McLeod, the Canadian-born American Heavyweight Champion of the wrestling world.[3]

The motif of gods and heroes coming to earth disguised as average peasants has a footing in Greek mythology—see Zeus and Hermes taking shelter with Baucis and Philemon, Odysseus as the beggar, Odysseus as "Noman," and so on—and it's the central metaphor of the Christian faith today. When a historian encounters a scene such as the one told of Gotch above, his eyebrows instinctively rise. Even if there is historical reality to that racetrack match, the metaphorical reality—the reason why the story persisted in popular memory—is more significant: that Gotch was visited by a demigod in the rags of the masses who conveyed upon Gotch the imprimatur through which he himself would ascend to the level of the immortals.

The son of German immigrants settled in Iowa, Gotch was paradigmatic right out of the gate: Wrestling would be the sport of choice for all variety of new immigrants through much of the rest of the century, and Iowa would come to be a hotbed for collegiate wrestling to this day. That latter fact, it should be said, was largely due to the influence of Martin "Farmer" Burns, a world-famous wrestler[4] and himself an American

......................................................................................................

**3** As will become clear, until Lou Thesz, no championship was particularly meaningful (and I guess that one could argue that in the fully staged era that Thesz presided over, no championship has ever been particularly meaningful in a combat competition sense), no matter how profound the honorific sounds.

**4** He got his nickname when he appeared at a carnival in Chicago to challenge the then-champion in the overalls of his day job and the announcer dubbed him "Farmer" on the spot—an inversion of the mythological narrative of Gotch.

champion, who founded wrestling schools in Omaha, Nebraska, and Rock Island, Illinois, and trained a generation of future grapplers, including Earl Caddock,[5] future game-changer Joseph "Toots" Mondt, and Rudy Dusek of the Dusek Riot Squad, a mob of four brothers that took over the wrestling scene in the Midwest and then New York City.

When Gotch defeated the "Russian Lion" George Hackenschmidt in Chicago's Dexter Park in 1908 in an epic two-hour battle, wrestling reached its first real national prominence. In most matches in those days, you had to beat your opponent in two out of three falls—usually by "tossing" him to the mat after a lengthy period of grappling for dominant position—but that day in Chicago, the first fall lasted two hours, and then it only ended because Hackenschmidt surrendered the fall; he didn't return to the ring thereafter, forfeiting the title to Gotch. Hackenschmidt is reported to have withdrawn graciously—"[Gotch] is the king of the class, the greatest man by far I ever met," he was quoted as saying in the American press—but two days later, to the London *Daily Mail*, his story changed: "The tactics by which I was defeated on American soil would not have been tolerated in England. Gotch's body was literally soaked in oil to prevent my holding him. All the world knows this to be unfair and against the rules of wrestling. He dug his nails into my face, tried to pull my ear off, and poke his thumb into my eye."[6]

It wasn't necessarily an issue of Hack changing his mind; the discrepancy is as likely to be because one—or both—of the quotes was created by someone other than the Russian Lion. Such was sometimes the nature of the sports writing world in those days; wrestling immediately evinced itself as the perfect vessel for such fictional storylines. It's notable that both Gotch and Hackenschmidt were performers as much as they were fighters; Gotch appeared in stage plays over the years, and Hack was a

---

**5**  A future world champion, and the original "Man of 1,000 Holds."

**6**  The oil was the main point of contention, but lest one think Hack was fibbing about the other illegal tactics, here's the match recap from the Gotch-sympathetic *New York Times*: "For two hours he [Gotch] eluded every attempt of the Russian to fasten a grip on him. Gotch side-stepped, roughed his man's features with his knuckles, and butted him under the chin, and generally worsted Hackenschmidt until the foreigner was at a loss how to proceed."

vaudeville strongman. In their fight, they played the roles of opposing national heroes, and though the ending was not predetermined, it was left in such a way so as to give credence to each wrestler's constituency. In a sense, even in these comparatively pure days of pro wrestling, it didn't even matter who won. When two fighters come to blows, each representing a different continent, it's not surprising that the perception of the ending will be different depending on what side of the world you're on. Gotch vs. Hackenschmidt may have been a genuine wrestling match—Gotch's suspect tactics aside—but its story would be legend.[7]

When Gotch and Hackenschmidt met for their rematch at Comiskey Park three years later, Gotch was the undisputed world champion and the sport's biggest star, and 30,000 people attended, which was the biggest crowd any athletic event had ever attracted in America. But the match was a dud. Hackenschmidt was injured going in, and Gotch took him down in short order. Rumors abounded that Gotch had paid one of Hack's training partners to "accidentally" injure him before the match, and indeed latter-day champ Lou Thesz long claimed that the infamous hooker Ad Santel told him that he had been paid $5,000 to do the deed. Nobody other than Santel himself puts Santel in Hack's training company, though, and the Hackenschmidt camp always maintained that Dr. Roller[8] caused the knee injury, and that it was actually an accident. Nevertheless, the media of the day picked up on the more scandalous version of the story. "Their return match carried too many phony and lopsided features," recalled Grantland Rice in

........................................................................................

7   The perception of Gotch as a dirty fighter was not limited to that bout. As latter-day world champion Lou Thesz once said, Gotch was widely known to be underhanded in the ring. "The picture that emerged of Gotch from those conversations," Thesz recalled, "was of a man who succeeded at his business primarily because he was, for lack of a kinder description, a dirty wrestler. That's not to say that he wasn't competent, because everyone I ever talked with said he was one of the best. But those same people described him as someone who delighted in hurting or torturing lesser opponents, even when they were supposed to be working out, and he was always looking for an illegal edge when he was matched against worthy ones. One of the old-timers I met was a fine man named Charlie Cutler, who knew Gotch very well and succeeded him as world champion. . . . Gotch would gouge, pull hair and even break a bone to get an advantage in a contest, and he was unusually careful to have the referee in his pocket, too, in case all else failed."

8   Benjamin Roller was a preeminent wrestler in his day who pops up in just about every notable story in the sport's early history, always referred to as "Dr. Roller" or the "Esteemed Doctor" like some sort of seer of pulp literature. He was an actual doctor, by the way.

1931. "The result was one of the loudest and longest squawks in sport and the doom of wrestling in most of the big cities." Whether the fans were dissatisfied with the perceived shenanigans or simply peeved at the anticlimactic match is probably a fair question. Regardless, the wrestling industry was thereafter thrown into widespread disrespect for the first time.

It was just as well that they get used to it. There would be a lot more of that to come over the decades.

For a while it was back to the small venues and sideshows for the grapplers. The New York scene, run by Jack Curley and his posse of heavyweights, remained as the center of the American wrestling universe. But for much of the rest of the country, the touring carnivals were the primary source of wrestling in particular and entertainment in general in those days before cities grew up enough to host their own full-time means of spectacle. The carnivals were a natural fit for wrestling, and as wrestling evolved over the decades, it would never leave behind the insider vocabulary of the sideshow circuit: terms like *mark, work, schmozz, kayfabe*—this is the slang of the carny, not the professional athlete. Many men who would go on to be nationwide stars of the ring, wrestling for championship titles in big cities, came out of those small-time beginnings: guys like Farmer Burns; William Muldoon, who dressed as a Roman gladiator (and was canonized in song as "Muldoon the Solid Man" by composer Ed Harrigan, and later in fiction by Theodore Dreiser as "Culhane, the Solid Man"); and a future icon named Ed "Strangler" Lewis.

☆ ☆ ☆

"The wrestling game became the smelliest sport in the world," said Marcus Griffin in his excellent 1937 history of the wrestling world, *Fall Guys*. After the Gotch-Hackenschmidt debacle, the sport passed out of vogue—and, moreover, into laughingstock territory. If the matches were exciting, they seemed fixed (even when they weren't), and if they were boring, well, they were interminable. Here's *The New Yorker*: "[The wrestlers] would go to the mat and stay there for hours and hours, a mass of mute meat. Matches lasted sometimes as long as a third of a day. As practiced by the old school,

# A BRIEF GLOSSARY OF WRESTLING LINGO

As with any microcosmic world, a wrestling language developed over the years to mark the insiders from the outsiders. What separates wrestling lingo from some other similar industry dialects is how the insider terms have become widespread terms of art with the emergence of the Internet era. Some of the words are derived from carny back-speak or pig Latin, while others grew from the early days of the Territorial Era, with terms moving freely around the country as wrestlers traveled.

A few that come up over the course of the book:

**babyface (often shortened to "face"):** A good-guy wrestler.

**booker:** The backstage head writer and decision-maker.

**bump:** A planned fall after a hit.

**gimmick:** The character a wrestler portrays, or the storyline in which one is taking part.

**heat:** A reaction from the crowd, usually negative, that measures the success of an act.

**heel:** A bad-guy wrestler.

**kayfabe:** The wrestlers' adherence to the big lie, the insistence that the unreal is real—the rule that you have to play your character all the time, even outside the ring, to make sure you don't ruin it for anyone. For decades, this was the abiding dogma of the pro wrestling industry. The term is thought to be an old carny term—perhaps a slangy, bastardized form of "be fake"—borrowed in wrestling's embryonic stages on the sideshow.

**mark:** A wrestling fan not clued in to the sham of the enterprise.

**over:** Popular with the fans. (To *put someone over* is to make one's opponent look good in the ring.)

**pop:** A big cheer; a positive response from a crowd.

**promo:** An interview or monologue given by a wrestler.

**rib:** A prank between wrestlers, usually backstage.

**schmozz:** A match that ends in chaos rather than in a decisive finish, or as Roland Barthes described the art: "Some fights, among the most successful kind, are crowned by a final charivari, a sort of unrestrained fantasia where the rules, the laws of the genre, the referee's censuring and the limits of the ring are abolished, swept away by a triumphant disorder which overflows into the hall and carries off pell-mell wrestlers, seconds, referee and spectators."

**shoot:** An instance of reality in wrestling, be it in a "shoot fight" or in a "shoot interview."

**smart:** Having intimate backstage knowledge of the wrestling world.

**stiff (also "working stiff"):** Using actual force in a wrestling match rather than the standard, more pantomimed technique; as in "a stiff punch."

**swerve:** A shocking left turn in a storyline.

**work:** The act of the wrestling world. As a noun, it's usually the opposite of "shoot"—as in, "I know it looked real, but that match was a work"—and as a verb, it's usually a measure of fooling fans—as in, "He was working the crowd."

wrestling was one of the most unexciting spectacles a person could pay money to see: a race between two century plants."

Even as the carnival men started settling down into offices in the bigger cities, from where they organized loose troupes of mastodons, the wrestling world didn't get much respect in the wider sporting world; with failed boxing managers and former sideshow barkers now acting as the "promoters" of the sport, it's little wonder.

Those wrestling promoters on the East Coast had little use for Robert Friedrich, a teenager from Wisconsin who was going around under the rather presumptuous name Ed "Strangler" Lewis—a moniker given him by a sportswriter who thought he resembled Evan "Strangler" Lewis, the first American Heavyweight Champion. Even though this new Lewis had achieved success on the carnival racket and toured the world honing techniques, like his signature stranglehold (also borrowed from the original "Strangler"), that weren't legal in the "mainstream" American wrestling world (the carnival circuit had fewer rules and more of an emphasis on thrilling the crowd, both aspects that would eventually be taken up by the mainstream as it evolved into its modern form), he was given no warm welcome by the New York promoters—or, rather, he was unwelcome precisely because of his skill. The last thing those increasingly theatrical promoters needed around was a guy who could actually win any match he wanted to win. It wasn't that the matches were all predetermined; it was that a wrestler that good could take the title, take over the territory, and, if he were so inclined, cut the promoters out of the take.

Unemployable in the wrestling mecca, Lewis[9] headed back toward home and settled down in the Midwest. One night, the legend has it, a manager named Billy Sandow threw a wrestling event in Louisville, Kentucky, on the night before the Kentucky Derby. He hired Lewis to take on the "Terrible Turk" Yussif Hussane.[10] It was a fixed bout, and

........................................................................................

**9** From here on out, this new Lewis, the Robert Friedrich one, is the only one who will matter, so if there's any doubt, that's who I'm referring to.

**10** Not to be confused with the original "Terrible Turk," Yusif Ismail, a certified international sensation who won the world championship from Evan "Strangler" Lewis and then died when the ship he was traveling on sank on his return trip to Europe.

Lewis was booked to lose; and as both a man in need of a paycheck and a product of an increasingly fabricated wrestling world, he was fine with it. The breaking point came when Sandow told him to lose in twenty minutes so that he and the Turk could catch the last train out of town. Lewis declined. Sandow said it hardly mattered, that the Turk could beat him in well under twenty minutes if he wanted to, and Lewis said he was happy for him to try. Of course, this being a part of the fabric of wrestling mythology, the two men supposedly then had a legitimate match and Lewis won handily.

Three days later, Sandow[11] was back in Chicago with a new protégé he intended to set loose on the world of wrestling: the very Ed "Strangler" Lewis. They teamed up with Toots Mondt,[12] who was recommended to Sandow by Farmer Burns and who would become the group's enforcer and, more important, the wrestling visionary. Sandow handled the money, Mondt handled the staging—at first in combat style, and later in match choreography—and Lewis handled the wrestling. Over the years they came to be known as the Gold Dust Trio, likely for both their money-making ability and the seeming magic that they were able to orchestrate in the ring.

☆ ☆ ☆

That period of wrestling in the 1920s—the higher-profile championship-level matches in particular—had its share of fixed bouts, sure, but they were in the service of a more fascinating reality. Mondt was hired by Sandow to be Lewis's sparring partner and enforcer. He would take on opponents before they got in the ring with Lewis to make sure they were "worthy" foes, but in reality, Mondt—sometimes regarded as a better

......................................................

11 As was the case with many promoters of the day, Sandow was himself an ex-wrestler. His real name was Wilhelm Baumann; his public name was borrowed from old-time muscleman Eugen Sandow (and, decades later, has been appropriated by incoming WWE wrestler Damien Sandow), just as he had previously appropriated the ring name "Young Muldoon" from the aforementioned "Solid Man" in his early wrestling days.

12 "Mondt" is the only name of the trio that was written on any birth certificate, for those who are keeping record.

pure grappler than Lewis—would soften them up for his colleague. Perhaps it was the fatigue from this role as the heavy lifter in the outfit that led to him rethinking the whole thing, or maybe he was purely a futurist, which is how he's usually painted. Regardless, Mondt could see what nobody else could, that the sports fans weren't just tired of wrestling—they were oblivious to it. They couldn't appreciate the minute maneuvers that made up a marathon heavyweight match. So Mondt conceived of a new style of wrestling that would combine classical Greco-Roman and freestyle catch wrestling with boxing and the sort of brawling that was popular on lumberyard campsites to birth a new hybrid that was wholly entertaining and, as such, the direct antecedent of what we know today as professional wrestling. Mondt created submission holds—some seemingly from thin air, many of which are still used today—that were meant to project out to an audience member thirty rows back. Moves, in other words, that were meant as much to impress onlookers as to inflict agony on opponents. He also conceived of the idea of a touring show, in which a stable of wrestlers would travel together from town to town, mixing and matching opponents or just repeating matchups, night after night. This would allow the promoters full control over the card and cut out the need for local fighters to be hired and wages negotiated at every venue. It would allow managers to set prices more definitively. And it would allow wrestlers the relative luxury of sparring with comfortable partners, in bouts with predictable endings.

An implicit part of this new method was the fixed match. In order to appeal to the fans' sense of drama and spectacle, the matches had to build powerfully to the endings, and the endings had to be fulfilling.[13]

Wrestlers were brought in to the Gold Dust confederacy to face Lewis or to fight on the undercard of the shows they were now promoting nationwide. If they went off the script, as some purists were wont to do in the early days, they would soon find themselves facing the enforcer Mondt (or later John Pesek), who would beat the logic of the new system

---

13 And thus wrestling diverged from its longtime cohort, boxing, which eventually went the route of greater legitimacy, probably to the detriment of the sport. But that's an argument for another day.

into them. The plan was to keep Lewis on top, and to dramatize his reign as much as possible.

The trio quickly realized, however, that a single champ with a never-ending reign was bad for business; to keep things fresh (and believable), they had to supply Lewis with some legitimate competitors, and to legitimize them, Lewis was going to have to lose to them. So began the process of trading wins: You win this match, I'll win the next one. Lewis was the proverbial ace card in this new system. He was widely considered to be the actual best and toughest wrestler in the world—with the occasional dissenter claiming it was Mondt, who allowed his considerable talents to take a backseat to Lewis's and, moreover, to the larger conquest of the trio—so there was little fear that an opponent would be able to abscond with the belt since Lewis could win it back at will. This new system doubled down on the contract with the audience that Mondt's new wrestling vision had signed: The promise of perfectly honed entertainment could now be spread over weeks and months instead of just across the span of one match.[14]

Winning and losing mattered, of course, insomuch as everyone wanted to be on top. The significant fact was that winning and losing—even in that era of perceived legitimacy of the sport, and in a world of rough fellows who were all supremely protective of their own reputations—was subjugated for the greater good of entertainment. When Lewis did occasionally wrestle real "shoot" matches, he confirmed the potency of the Mondt model. "The Strangler once wrestled Joe Stecher in what the boys in the trade call a 'shooting match,'" wrote Arthur Daley in *The New York Times*. "They started at 4 o'clock in the afternoon and Lewis was the winner at 9:30 that night. It wasn't exciting but it was the best brand of wrestling anyone would want to witness." That Lewis could win this sort of drudging bout—that he was a legitimate combatant—was necessary for this transformation to occur. If he hadn't been a legitimate tough guy, it

--------

**14** If this is starting to sound something like an echo of Vince McMahon's rechristening of the industry as "sports entertainment," it's worth noting that at the tail end of his career, Mondt was a close adviser of McMahon's father, the original owner of what was then called the WWWF. More on that later.

would have been impossible to remake the industry. His authenticity married with Mondt's artificiality confirmed that the best brand of wrestling is the exciting brand. What mattered now wasn't who won but *how* they won, and how the crowd would respond. What mattered was how one match would get the fans to pay money for the next one.

Within a few years, the Gold Dust Trio was in control of almost all the wrestling in the United States. Their cartel—really, that's the word, as they were employing almost all of the high-profile wrestlers in North America—spanned multiple houses the country over on multiple nights a week. If it wasn't exactly a majestic sport on par with boxing, it was still a big draw.

★ ★ ★

One of the regional promoters who aligned himself with the Gold Dust Trio in the early 1900s was a Boston-based man named Paul Bowser. Bowser was a central figure in the dissolution of reality in the sport—not because he had a hand in reimagining it like Mondt, but because he presided over some of the last "real" fights in the field. Some of the last ones, anyway, that were supposed to be fake and ended up real. He supposedly told John Pesek to go off script and defeat Nat Pendleton, who was managed by the New York City promoter Jack Curley, who had formed a sort of guerilla operation along with old-school grappler Joe Stecher that ran in opposition to the Gold Dust regime. Curley got his revenge when he paid off Stanislaus Zbyszko (who had previously achieved fame on the Gold Dust circuit) to shoot and upend Gold Dust–approved champ Wayne Munn on April 15, 1925.

These were the death throes of the legitimacy movement in the wrestling world. Even the athletes like Stecher who claimed to be interested in the sport's authenticity were eventually motivated more by fame and profit than purely by victory. When so much uncertainty was set against the potential for money to be made, it was only a matter of time before the dinosaurs died off and the capitalists reigned.

Perhaps the most significant thing that happened under Paul Bowser's watch was the introduction of Gus Sonnenberg. Sonnenberg was a collegiate and professional football player of some renown in the North-east, so he was a perfect fit for the hero role, despite his lack of wrestling background. What Sonnenberg didn't have in technique, he made up in flair, integrating a repertoire of football-style moves into the wrestling playbook—the flying tackle, most notably, which brought wrestling off the mat and into the air.[15] The crowds were dazzled by this new style and started coming to wrestling events in multitudes, despite its patent arti-ficiality. (In fact, the outlandishness of the new moves actually helped their credibility. "Obviously this type of wrestling could not be re-hearsed," as Grantland Rice put it, "since no opposing human body could stand such punishment oftener than once a month.") But the fans wanted action, not reality.

★ ★ ★

It took the fall of boxing in the second decade of the twentieth century for wrestling to regain its place as the country's chief pugilistic pastime. "The revival of a sport that was in the doldrums, and particularly its ac-ceptance by the select, is due chiefly to the decline of boxing," Morris Markey put it in *The New Yorker*. "Boxing has gone completely to pieces because the current crop of boxers is so extremely bad. . . . [W]hen it col-lapsed from within it left a great many people bereft of the sporting eve-ning, a ceremony to which they have become devoted." To wrestling they turned. The blue-collar fans—the immigrant populations of the North-east in particular—had never abandoned wrestling, but with the return of a more affluent fanbase, pro wrestling's influence began to escalate.

The newspapers still weren't treating it as a proper sport, nor should they have, but the distinction is striking in context. As *The New Yorker* pointed out in 1932, "The World Almanac for 1931, which faithfully re-corded the champions for the previous year in such sports as archery, handball, and the racing of sled dogs, found space for no word

---

**15** The credit for these innovations is sometimes given to another footballer turned wrestler, former Chicago Bears player Jim McMillen, but the historical timeline favors Sonnenberg in this regard.

on wrestling." (Oddly, it was largely left to the more highbrow national magazines, like *The New Yorker* and *Collier's*, to serve as the record of the sport.)

By the time that the Greek heartthrob Jim Londos—he had the "appeal of a Dempsey for the multitudes," said *The New Yorker*—was selling out shows in New York and Danno O'Mahoney—an Irishman imported by Bowser to entice the region's immigrant population—was reigning in Boston, the artifice was the art. Sure, many fans still took it to be "real," but there were just as many who didn't. The ambiguity mattered far less in those days than it may today. As Rice quoted a fan in '31: "As far as I know the shows are honest. But even if they're not I get a big kick out of them, for they are full of action and all the outward signs of hostile competition. It is either honest competition or fine acting and in either case I get a real show."

When Londos won the world championship from Dick Shikat in 1930, "no New York newspaper gave the event more than a few lines in its sports section the next day; for professional wrestling had already been exposed more times than Santa Claus." Within a year, Londos would be performing to sellout houses in Madison Square Garden, a feat that was unheard of even in the boxing world at its heights. But despite the attention from the highbrow magazines, the sports journalism establishment hardly cared. Perhaps they realized that pro wrestling made them expendable: The wrestling matches mythologized the athletes and wrote the stories themselves. The audiences need only watch the shows to see the symbolism. The promoters were putting on morality plays filtered through the lens of nationalism, with heroes constructed specifically to appeal to the ethnic origins of the fans. For years, Londos ruled in New York in repetitive fashion:

A Foreign Menace, in most cases a real wrestler, would be imported. He would meet all the challengers for the title whom Londos had defeated in any city larger than New Haven, and beat them. After that, he and Londos would wrestle for the world's championship in Madison Square Garden. The Foreign Menace would oppress Londos unmercifully for about forty minutes, and then Londos would pick him up for the airplane spin, which is like the climactic movement of an adagio dance or a hammer throw. Skeptics have pointed out that this movement requires cooperation from the adagio projectile.... Londos would whirl the current Menace around his head and dash him to the mat three times, no more and no less, and the match would end in time for suburbanites to get the trains they caught on theatre nights.

For O'Mahoney's part, he "said he'd heard a lot of talk about fixed matches but was sure wrestling was entirely on the level. 'I win every time out,' he said in justification of his faith, 'and I've never been asked to lay down.'" Of course he hadn't: Danno was a lousy grappler, but Bowser decided that he wouldn't lose until he took on Londos—some fifty matches into his career—and O'Mahoney won that one too. "Unforgettable was the 'winning' of the championship by Danno O'Mahoney," groaned *The New York Times* in 1952. "His ignorance of the sport was monumental enough to have filled the Irish Sea. But Danno meant packed houses in Boston where the sport was going big and so the Trust elected him the champion." (O'Mahoney eventually lost to Shikat, a perpetually aggrieved fighter who went off script and injured the underskilled O'Mahoney to prove a point.)

The fix was in, and the crowds were pouring in to see the wrestling cards nonetheless. In a world absent any viable alternative, the discussion turned not to ethics but to entertainment. Every year or two, some magazine would do a piece on the sport and slyly allude to its insincerity, but bizarrely a consensus never seemed to be reached on the subject. It's as if every journalist approached the industry as does a young child first exposed to wrestling's Technicolor morality plays: first to believe, unquestioning, and then, slowly, to doubt:

> "The veteran wrestling fans recall, with copious tears, how the hippodrome flourished in the land. It became a nice question for experts in entertainment to differentiate between a wrestling bout and the living statuary acts then in vogue."
>
> —John B. Kennedy, "Pillars of Sport," *Collier's*, September 19, 1931

"Not the least interesting of all the minor phenomena produced by the current fashion of wrestling is the universal discussion as to the honesty of the matches. And certainly the most interesting phase of this discussion is the unanimous agreement: 'Who cares if they're fixed or not—the show is good.'"

—Morris Markey, "Catch as Catch Can," *The New Yorker*, April 18, 1931

"If this be play-acting, then it is play-acting of the highest order and comes close to being the best entertainment in town. To cavil at it for being play-acting is to cavil at a Booth or a Barrymore for getting up off the floor and putting on his street clothes after the final curtain has been lowered on 'Hamlet.'"

—Joel Sayre, "The Pullman Theseus," *The New Yorker*, March 5, 1932

I quote these periodicals here at length for a reason. There's a general feeling that wrestling's artifice has only recently been exposed, that the facade began to crumble roughly around 1984, when John Stossel covered the sport on *20/20* and got smacked by "Dr. D" David Schultz. In this telling of wrestling's modern history, the jig was only fully up by the time reality shows in the early 2000s started acknowledging their production chicanery. That couldn't be further from the truth. Fans have been in on wrestling's ruse for a century—since the ruse began, more or less—and over the past eighty years there has been a steady procession of "exposés," each received with the same feigned surprise and then immediate-onset amnesia. But equivocations of the above sort have been repeated over the years almost verbatim. "Some of the fans know they are watching a show and feel certain of it when they witness the hokum and byplay between mat clowns," said sportswriter Joe Jares in his 1974 book *Whatever Happened to Gorgeous George?*, "but when the going is rough and exciting they are less doubtful."

It's precisely this equivocation that defines wrestling's fandom and disquiets its detractors. For non–wrestling fans, revelations about the sport's authenticity are compelling because they smugly assume the fans are dupes; for wrestling fans, each revelation is met with a relative yawn. Since the earliest days of pro wrestling, the sport's otherworldliness has been its calling card. And since the first moment that it was exposed to be a "fake" sport, the industry has adapted and thrived.

☆　☆　☆

It was a Polish impresario named Jack Pfefer who dragged professional wrestling, kicking and screaming, into the sunlight. Pfefer—a man of diverse interests with a deep love for opera, a comically malapropos usage of English, and the sublime nickname of the "Halitosis Kid"—had been a semimajor player in the backstage dealings of the wrestling biz in New York until a realignment of power left him unaffiliated and out of work. New York bigwig Jack Curley had a falling-out with top star Jim Londos, who decamped to Tom Packs's St. Louis domain, and Pfefer took Londos's side in the spat. When Curley and Londos made amends—as part of a new multiregional wrestling mafia that included Packs, Boston's Paul Bowser, Philly's Ray Fabiani, and others—Pfefer was left out. So Pfefer did what any scorned lover would do and dragged his former cohorts' names through the mud. He found encouragement from Dan Parker, the sports editor from the New York *Daily Mirror*, and set about announcing to the world in a series of articles from December 1933 through 1934 that the Curley-Londos regime had been fixing matches.[16]

Two qualifiers: (1) This was not exactly a revelation, and (2) insomuch as it was, it wasn't a full-throated one. People had known—or suspected—wrestling was largely fake for at least a decade. In 1931, Grantland Rice recounted how when he wrote a snippet about wrestling for his syndicated column *fifteen years prior*, a number of his editors around the country wrote back telling him that they had no interest in printing anything about such a nonsport. What's significant reading back through the *Daily Mirror* archives is precisely that willful neglect of the wrestling world, even as it filled up houses in the Big Apple. With the exception of a few very

---

**16** *The New York Times* once said that "the mischievous Dan Parker once drove the wrestling trust crazy by printing all the results of coming matches in advance. He had a secret pipeline to the inner councils." It's unclear when exactly this happened, or if they're just referencing the Pfefer incident obliquely.

brief asides about business-side trends like new venues or managerial re-alignments, Parker functionally ignored the wrestling game. When he was compelled to comment, he would address his target with snide precision, sarcastically throw in a "Now, I am the last person in the world to suspect that wrestling is not on the level," and then give his audience every reason to suspect just that. If he was confined by anything, it seemed to be his assumption that readers weren't as savvy to the shtick as he was.

Ever the gadfly to what he saw as an unbecoming spectacle, Parker was probably gleeful to give Pfefer his platform. Throughout his career, Pfefer always fell on the entertainment end of the "sports enter-tainment"[17] continuum—favoring midgets, giants, and lady wrestlers—and had little time for the pretenses of legitimacy. ("An honest man can sell a fake diamond if he says it is a fake diamond, ain't it?" he once said to A. J. Liebling.) But his admissions in the *Daily Mirror* were oddly trifling: They were accusations of match-fixing to get the marketable Londos to the title, not a full exposé of a dramaturgical enterprise. (Maybe Parker's sensitivity again played a hand in this slow reveal.)

Nevertheless, it's indisputable that, at the very least, the subject of wrestling's legitimacy was finally broached, and moving forward, journalists—and fans—could approach the sport with something ap-proaching ironic distance, no matter how invested they were in the pro-ceedings.

Traditionalists like Curley were peeved, insistent on protecting the realism of the sport above all else. And through the next fifty-five years or so—more or less until Vince McMahon began admitting to the WWF's il-legitimacy to get around state athletic commission fees in the late '80s—they were able to keep up the facade to some extent because the marks were always willing to accept the violence at face value, and the people who were clued in were happy to play along to further their enjoyment.

After Pfefer's revelation in 1933, maintaining the appearance of va-lidity was a losing quest, though Curley and the other promoters tried. The new New York State Athletic Commission intervened, insisting that

---

**17** Though this exact phrase wouldn't be coined until years later, I know.

pro wrestling label its bouts "exhibitions" rather than "matches"—a then-significant distinction that's often lost on the modern audience.[18] At the time, it should have been a big deal: It was a label announcing the wrestling product was counterfeit. To the fans, it didn't matter—the distinction was either insignificant or easy enough to ignore.

By 1938 Pfefer had reclaimed his career and he alone was ruling the wrestling world, largely by being the one who embraced the unreality of the sport. Though he had certainly been motivated by spite as much as anything, his accusations were sort of a beautiful gambit in retrospect: He got revenge on his erstwhile cohorts by accusing everyone of fixing matches, and then, once the hierarchy had been toppled, he assumed the throne by basically admitting that he was fixing matches. "It isn't a sport; it's show business. I'm not an athletic promoter; I'm a theatrical man," he told *Collier's* that year. "I don't tell people my wrestling shows are on the level; I guarantee them they're not. I've never seen an honest wrestling bout in my twenty years in the game. Maybe there was one, but I wasn't there. And I'd hate to see one; it'd be an awful thing!" As Liebling put it in '39: "The trouble, according to [Pfefer], is that the moneyed clientele has ceased to believe in wrestling as a sport and has not yet learned to appreciate it as a pure art form, like opera or classical dancing."

☆ ☆ ☆

A search for the moment at which wrestling became "fake" is a futile one; like many other such incidents of great significance through time, the moment does not exist so much as it is imagined back into history. To be sure, embedded in this quandary are two separate questions: (1) When did wrestlers start fixing matches for entertainment's sake? And (2) When did fans realize that the sport was counterfeit?

..............................................................................................

**18** Under the leadership of former wrestler William Muldoon (the Roman Gladiator himself), whose tenure ended a few years prior to Pfefer's revelations, the commission also remade the boxing game into its current shape, reducing matches in length dramatically. Muldoon, heart-healthy puritan that he was, also banned smoking during boxing and wrestling events in Madison Square Garden.

Both answers are more than a little ambiguous, but here goes: (1) From the very beginning, and (2) it doesn't matter.

Wrestling didn't *become* fake in any sort of active way. It could have diverged toward legitimacy like boxing did, but it did not, and it shouldn't ever be judged on those terms. It was once a purer sport, sure—a sport full of fixed matches and exploitative put-ons. But just as much as it was a sport, it was a sideshow—a carny act that eventually made it to Broadway.

So the next time you hear somebody say, "You know wrestling is fake, right?" you can tell him that yes, you know. That's exactly the point.

☆　☆　☆

A quick postscript to this long story. Frank Gotch, the "Peerless Champion," walked away from the sport in 1913 at the top of his game. He retired to his Iowa farm but eventually returned to the road, wrestling all comers for a traveling circus. While pondering a comeback in 1917, he fell ill, and the greatest wrestler America ever produced died at the age of thirty-nine of uremic poisoning.[19] Gotch would be a trailblazer not just in his life but also in his death. In the century that follows, wrestler after wrestler would die before his time.

In a way, it's fitting that this demigod of the mat world went before he got too old, when his legend was still vital. It makes it easier to forget his humanity.

---

**19** There were widespread rumors that he died of syphilis, but uremic poisoning was on the official coroner's report.

# HACKENSCHMIDT: THE FIRST HEEL TURN?

Though it's unclear when the trend started of turning friends against one another to create new villains (and, conversely, turning one villain against another to create a new hero), it was almost certainly a matter of Territorial Era expediency when faced with a small available cast and limited room at the top for long-term fan favorites. The biggest turns of the '80s were some of the most galling moments in wrestling history at the time: Larry Zbyszko turned on his legendary mentor Bruno Sammartino, icon of the WWWF, during a supposedly friendly exhibition match in 1980, smashing him over the head with a wooden chair and cutting him open—and making Zbyszko into the most hated man in the Northeast. In 1982, in Championship Wrestling from Florida, golden-boy tough guy Kevin Sullivan turned on his pal Barry Windham and embraced a bizarre, semisatanic gimmick (while carefully eluding the actual embrace of the Devil) that made him the most shocking and reviled heel in the region for years—a character he returned to multiple times in other areas in his career. In the Crockett territory in '85, Pez Whatley notoriously turned on Jimmy Valiant after the perceived slight of Valiant calling him "the best *black* athlete in professional wrestling."

In the early days of the twentieth century, though, before the roles of good and evil within the squared circle were defined, it probably came as something of a shock to George Hackenschmidt that he had been booked into a heel turn. After years on the vaudeville strongman circuit and some renown as one of the first famous bodybuilders, the Russian Lion was famous the world over, in all strata of society. (Teddy Roosevelt was once quoted as saying, "If I wasn't president of the United States, I would like to be George Hackenschmidt.") But after he won the world championship from Tom Jenkins and was positioned to take on Gotch, suddenly the international exemplar was cast contra the American hero Gotch as the bout's villain, whether he liked it or not.

Newspapers told the tales of Hack's insouciance: He arrived in Chicago for the match out of shape; he refused to engage in the public workouts that the promoter had arranged; he went on long, fugue-like walks around Lake Michigan. When he complained about Gotch's underhanded tactics in their match, Hack was accused of whining, of making excuses, and, in the end, of being a quitter. Sayeth the referee: "I say, that as the referee of that match, I thought that the 'Russian Lion' quit."

It was not a treatment befitting an idol of his esteem, but it laid the template for many wrestling villains that followed: the evildoer as weak, as deplorable know-it-all, as egotistical narcissist, as selfish coward. Most would agree that that wasn't who Hackenschmidt really was, but for American fans of 1905, it was the role he was born to play.

# THE
## ⭐ TERRITORIAL ⭐
# ERA

As wrestling's popularity grew in the first half of the twentieth century, there was sufficient stability in many larger regional markets to support their own local federations. Many of these started out as proxies for the Gold Dust Trio; at first it was a practical means of having a business-side infrastructure in place for Sandow and Lewis and Mondt when their troupe came through, but soon cities like St. Louis and Chicago were importing wrestlers from all over the country to fill up local houses on a regular basis. Before long, many of these regional promoters were industry power brokers unto themselves. They were putting on fully independent pro wrestling shows, developing local talent, and, above all, making good money.

With their newfound independence, many of the regions appointed their own "world champions," and while the appearance of finality was helpful in establishing independent legitimacy, eventually the credulity of the audience was strained. It was no secret to many a fan that the "world champion" in, say, Minneapolis wasn't recognized as such in Boston. The National Wrestling Association—note the last word there because it's important—was a national group, a spin-off of the National Boxing Association, that took it upon itself to anoint Lou Thesz as the national champ, but he rarely toured to the majority of wrestling towns, and in his absence, competing "world champions" proliferated.

And so on July 18, 1948 in Waterloo, Iowa, a meeting of the pro wrestling dons was called in which the first iteration of the National Wrestling *Alliance* was formed. Under the NWA banner, the major promoters from each region would cooperate, "share" a universally recognized world champion,[1]

---

1   The various regions would continue to have champions, but now they would be formally known only as regional titleholders, an acknowledgment of what was all but explicit before.

swap wrestling talent, and work together to keep upstart promotions from taking root.

That last part of the agreement was no small thing. The NWA was, from its start, functionally a cartel, and a lot of capable promoters were left out. Now, if any of them tried to run shows in an NWA fiefdom, the partners in other regions would send in their top stars to run a show on the same night and guarantee failure for the upstart.[2] The original six members of the NWA—Paul "Pinkie" George, Al Haft, Anton (Tony) Stecher, Harry Light, Orville Brown, and Sam Muchnick—were soon joined in their racket by other promotions from every reach of the United States, formally locking down the wrestling industry in the country.[3] There were fifteen major groups at the start; by 1956, as some of the larger territories fragmented and new areas opened up, there were thirty-eight NWA member groups, some operating through several contiguous states, while some states, like Texas, were split up into several parcels. The most influential promotions—Stecher's Minneapolis territory, Leroy McGuirk's NWA Tri-State Wrestling, Georgia Championship Wrestling, Jim Crockett Sr.'s Mid-Atlantic Wrestling, Bob Geigel's Central States Wrestling, Sam Muchnick's St. Louis office, Championship Wrestling of Florida, Pacific Northwest Wrestling, and the Central Wrestling Association out of Memphis, to name a few—were joined to the north by Stampede in Calgary and Maple Leaf Wrestling in Toronto, and of course promotions in Minneapolis, Dallas, and the Northeast would eventually make some noise on their own. The wrestlers themselves made out well in the deal because they could now venture from territory to territory to keep their acts—and their feuds—fresh, with considerably less risk. There would always be the hometown heroes who stayed in one city for much of their careers, but since no promotion had the wherewithal to employ a vast army of wrestlers, the rest of the roster was mutable. Now a villain could disappear from St. Louis and go to California,

---

2   There are widespread rumors that threats of violence were used as well. Throughout the history of the NWA, there was a common insinuation that organized crime was involved, which has never been substantiated to my knowledge.

3   And eventually Japan too.

a new villain would show up in St. Louis, and the cycle would begin anew. As long as you were working within the confines of the NWA, everybody was happy.

Founder Orville Brown was the first world champion, and the afore-mentioned Lou Thesz, who would define the NWA through much of its period of dominance, was the second. (When he claimed the mantle, the National Wrestling Association ceded control of the sport to the National Wrestling Alliance, and the former basically ceased to exist.) Thesz, who learned the grappling art of "hooking" from "Strangler" Lewis himself, would be the champion on and off for a combined period of ten years, and would be the man on whose back wrestling was made into a national enterprise, as he fought, sometimes off script, to ensure the unification of the various titles around the country.

The system worked well for all parties involved, and terribly for those not invited to the party. One man's gentleman's cooperative is another man's mafia, after all. The member groups fended off the competition, helped one another out financially when necessary, and together brought an air of positivity to the sport; if they weren't ushering in legitimacy, exactly, they were signaling a sort of organization that afforded them the sheen of propriety.

Perhaps unsurprisingly, this coalition of disparate businessmen was not without its internal politics. Their champion was chosen by a quorum in the owner meetings, but such democracy didn't leave everyone happy. This was especially so because, while the titleholder traveled regularly from territory to territory to defend the NWA crown, he would naturally be perceived as beholden to the promoter with whom he had made it big—not to mention that each regional manager was predisposed to feel neglected during the vast majority of the time when the champ wasn't there. And so with Thesz's ascendance in 1949, the power shifted toward his home turf, Muchnick's St. Louis Wrestling Club.

It was during Muchnick's NWA stewardship that the U.S. government actually intervened in the wrestling world, slapping the NWA with charges of monopoly and racketeering. Muchnick was ultimately able to negotiate down the charges into a "consent decree"—sort of a nolo contendere of the federal judicial world—which formally reduced the power of the NWA without mandating its dissolution. This was in 1956, and while it amounted to little more than a slap on the wrist (the NWA promotions were by then so entrenched that the threat of competition was minimal), the bottom began nonetheless to fall out.

By the mid-'50s, many of the promoters were ready to see Thesz dethroned, to spread the wealth to the top stars of other areas. But Thesz was entrenched, incredibly popular, and the contrarians within the NWA couldn't agree upon a successor. And so Thesz's reign persevered.

The NWA agreed upon a plan in which Thesz would lose the title to Canadian star Edouard Carpentier in disputed fashion, leading to dueling claims to the title and an eventual high-profile rematch. As is often the case in the bizarro world of pro wrestling, life would imitate art: The dispute not only played out behind the scenes, but it also opened the door to a convention of public title disputes that would characterize the NWA throughout the coming years.

Eddie Quinn ran Carpentier's home Montreal promotion and was a part-owner of the St. Louis club; he had a falling-out with Muchnick.[4] After the (deliberately) disputed first Thesz-Carpentier match, but before the storyline could come to fruition, Quinn ignored the NWA directive and started billing Carpentier as the champ, while Muchnick and most of the rest of the NWA groups stuck with Thesz and denied that the championship dispute had ever even occurred.

This led to an oddball series of semiofficial championship switches, as Quinn started leasing out Carpentier's services to have him lose his championship, repeatedly, to various regional headliners. Freddie Blassie[5] won the title from Carpentier in Los Angeles; Verne Gagne won

. . . . . . . . . . . . . . . . . . . . . . . . . . . . . . . . . . . . . . . . . . . . . . . . . . . . . . . . . . . . . . . . . . . . . . . . . . . . . .

**4** One major point of contention was Muchnick's association with Jack Pfefer, the same man who had outed pro wrestling in 1933. Though he was often on the outs with the power brokers in the wrestling world, Pfefer had carved out a niche as a purveyor of wrestling oddities and, indeed, was the top promoter in New York and to some extent the country, for a brief period in the late '30s. Muchnick was more willing to engage him than most other promoters, who were still peeved at his lack of respect for the tradition of kayfabe.

**5** Who would go on to be a legendary manager in the WWF.

it in Omaha; and Killer Kowalski won it in Boston. It was a reversion to the pre-NWA norm—multiple "world champions" proclaiming themselves king in their sundry fiefdoms.

As if that system weren't fraught enough, there suddenly emerged a new power player in the wrestling world—one bigger than any big-city promoter or world champion: television.

☆ ☆ ☆

The FCC gave the green light for national commercial television starting on July 1, 1941. The first two truly national TV networks were NBC—the two-decades-old radio company—and an upstart called the DuMont Network. DuMont—owned by DuMont Laboratories, a television manufacturer, in partnership with Paramount Pictures—went on the air in 1946. (CBS and ABC didn't go on the air until 1948.) Being much less entrenched than NBC, DuMont was at a serious disadvantage: It had less money than NBC, so it had to scrape for content, and the FCC broadcasting guidelines had been heavily influenced by NBC power player David Sarnoff in such a way so as to handicap any emergent competition. DuMont only lasted ten years, and it's largely forgotten today, but its impact on the television industry was significant. It was the on-screen pioneer of the sitcom and the soap opera, the original home of Jackie Gleason, and the creator of the multiple-advertiser model for TV commercial sales that persists to this day.

And it was the first network to broadcast wrestling.

Fred Kohler, kingpin of the Chicago wrestling world, had been broadcasting his cards locally on two stations (WBKB and WGN) before national TV took hold. He even had a brief show on the nascent ABC network. But it wasn't until DuMont came calling that he—and pro wrestling—took hold of the mainstream. Wrestling was a natural fit for DuMont; Kohler knew what he was doing, and the shows were cheap to produce—not to mention the fact that his central location and position of power within the NWA meant that he could import the top stars of the "squared circle" to the small screen.

By the early '50s, Thursday and Saturday night pro wrestling were two of the top shows on DuMont and a certified national phenomenon. The stars of DuMont—guys like despicable pretty boy Gorgeous George, northeastern sensation Antonino "Argentina" Rocca, Canadian big man Don Leo Jonathan, Italian superstar Bruno Sammartino, reviled showboat Freddie Blassie, African American trailblazers Bobo Brazil and Sweet Daddy Siki, and fighting ballerino Ricky Starr—were among the biggest sports stars in the nation. Kohler signed many of his wrestlers to exclusive contracts—a first in the sport[6]—because his local guys were becoming more famous than many of the NWA's entrenched headliners and Kohler wanted to keep a leash on them. He sent them to wrestle in other NWA regions and took a cut of everything they earned. Pro wrestling was more popular than ever, but the new fans wanted to see the TV stars. For the longtime fans, who had for years been taught to accept the primacy of their local product, this new national phenomenon must have been a rude awakening.

The national wrestling fad would not yet evolve into an institution. By the end of the decade, it had subsided somewhat and wrestling was largely absent from national network programming. DuMont shut down, and the other networks had enough other programming that they didn't feel compelled to sully themselves with "fake" sports.

Despite Kohler's success, it became conventional wisdom that television was bad business for wrestling because, the thinking went, fans wouldn't want to show up for the live shows if they could see events on television for free. (This tenet held in the larger sports world as well.) This despite the fact that Kohler's local broadcast, before his shows went national, doubled his gate receipts. Starting in the mid-'50s, though, a maverick DC-area wrestling promoter named Vincent J. McMahon started airing his Capitol Wrestling promotion on regional television stations and shocked the wrestling industry. Not only did his TV exposure not reduce his crowd numbers, it increased them, dramatically. Weeks after he started airing the Capitol Wrestling show in 1956, his

---

6　Previously, most wrestlers didn't have contracts at all other than handshake deals.

arena shows started selling out in advance, with fans driving in from Pennsylvania and Virginia to see the card. "It's television," McMahon told *The Washington Post and Times-Herald.* "If this is the way television kills promoters, I'm going to die a rich man." Through the TV shows he was able to build much more significance—and detail—into the feuds that were featured on his cards. Television functionally became a weekly commercial for the live events.

☆ ☆ ☆

After his brief era of television dominance, Kohler moved on to other matters. He had long been a proponent of Minneapolis champ Verne Gagne—who had by then acquired an ownership stake in the upper Midwest territory after Tony Stecher's death—but his vote wasn't enough to give Gagne the belt. In 1960, in a fit of frustration, Gagne seceded his promotion from the NWA with the blessing of Kohler and dubbed his new creation the American Wrestling Association, or AWA. With Kohler's Chicago territory and the partnership of several other neighboring groups, the establishment of the AWA severed much of the Midwest from the NWA oligarchy. For the appearance of legitimacy and continuity, they acknowledged then-NWA champ Pat O'Connor (whom Kohler detested, for whatever reason) as the AWA champ but demanded that he defend the title against Gagne, which they knew he wouldn't do, so after a grace period, Gagne was announced as de facto AWA champ, a reign that would continue for years.[7]

☆ ☆ ☆

"Nature Boy" Buddy Rogers beat Pat O'Connor at Comiskey Park on June 30, 1961, to become the NWA World Heavyweight Champion. It was billed as the "Match of the Century," and to the extent that it marked a

---

7 In 1961, the California federation that was home to Blassie left the NWA too, but with less fanfare. It returned to the cooperative in '68.

sea change in the business, that wasn't as hyperbolic as it might sound. Rogers was one of wrestling's transformative figures, one of the first nationally celebrated champions who was more form than substance— more "show" than "go," as a latter-day wrestler would put it. It was no coincidence that he entered the ring to the strains of "Pomp and Circumstance," after all. With his bleached-blond pompadour, sequined robes, and near-comical arrogance, he brokered in a new era of larger-than-life personality to the wrestling world. (But contra Gorgeous George, he wasn't an effete preener; he was a self-obsessed tough.) It was a presence perfectly suited to a maturing television generation. The difference between Thesz's old-school purity—also embodied by the earnest O'Connor—and Rogers's showmanship was night and day. Thesz was a fighter in the "Strangler" Lewis mold, a clean-cut, corn-fed traditional athlete; Rogers was the distillation of wrestling's newfound tomfoolery. Even though he didn't pin Thesz for the championship, Rogers's rise basically signaled the end of the classical era of wrestling that Thesz proudly represented.

Some of the NWA bookers were less than enthusiastic about this shift away from shooters, who had legitimacy even if the matches were rigged, and they were all upset at the Capitol Wrestling Corporation—Vincent J. McMahon's northeastern promotion that served as Rogers's home base— and its seeming reluctance to send champion Rogers out to their territories. Moreover, though, they were probably uneasy with McMahon's growing power, just as they had been with Kohler's. McMahon had gained control of the Northeast in a coup by technological proxy; he started airing his Capitol Wrestling TV program, filmed in DC, in New York in 1955 and was soon selling out venues in Manhattan better than the entrenched New York bookers. McMahon was partnered with Toots Mondt, who had been working with various promoters since the breakup of the Gold Dust Trio, including McMahon's father, Jess, a respected boxing promoter. Capitol Wrestling had only joined the NWA in 1953, but due to its television prominence and pivotal location, McMahon was practically running the NWA by the time that Rogers won the championship. One can only assume that the NWA was leery of McMahon's increasingly centralized power in the wrestling world, and that having his man be champion was, to some promoters, a bridge too far. And so, by decree of the NWA dons, Thesz defeated Rogers in Toronto in 1963 to put the title back around a more dependable waist.

In retaliation, Capitol Wrestling seceded from the NWA, much like Gagne had three years prior. McMahon's group refused to acknowledge the title change and proclaimed Rogers the first "national" Heavyweight Champion of the rechristened "World Wide Wrestling Federation." (The putative grievance was that the Thesz match was only one fall rather than the customary "best two out of three falls" championship match format.) With the power afforded McMahon by his dominance of the northeastern corridor of New York–Boston–DC, his separatist movement had a position of power and influence—and, in turn, an appearance of significance—from the start.[8]

☆ ☆ ☆

The NWA carried on after the defections, but the Territorial Era's death warrant had been signed. Though the NWA didn't immediately dissolve, the two factors that would spell out its end as a national power had already appeared: the secession of the WWWF and the advent of cable television.

The conceit that held up the territorial system was obvious but its implications were subtle: Even though the NWA was national, and everyone knew wrestling existed across the country, each territory was able to maintain the perception that what happened there was all that really mattered. The NWA champ coming to town wasn't so different from a monster heel who would appear in a region for a short run: It was a special attraction that buoyed everything else on the card. There's a common perception, fueled

........................................................................................................................

**8**   The WWWF actually rejoined the NWA in 1971 and seceded again in 1983. This fact is largely lost to history, and the reasons are unclear, though it's rumored that the WWWF needed financial support that only the NWA could provide. One of the lesser-known beefs by NWA members against the younger Vince McMahon's national expansion in the '80s is the professed fact that they had helped bail his father out at times when money was tight or competition was fierce.

by the fact that most modern wrestling fans only experienced territorial wrestling in its dying days, that the operations were self-evidently small-time. In fact, the territorial promotions gave every indication of being big-time—many regions had their own TV shows, and in some instances they were the highest-rated shows in the area—and their audiences mostly accepted them as such. If nothing else, they were fully insulated from any of the oddities of wrestling booking, like the incongruity of a wrestler who would play a good guy in Texas and a villain in San Francisco, or disputed title changes.

When Georgia Championship Wrestling—by then one of the most prominent regional promotions—started airing on a UHF station called WTCG in 1971, a die was cast that would forever alter the wrestling landscape. WTCG would soon be renamed WTBS[9] by its owner, Ted Turner, and become known nationwide as the "Superstation." The notion of a national cable network was a novelty at the time, but the impact of TBS and its counterpart, the USA Network, would be significant.

Just as had happened when national networks started in the '40s, these first national cable stations were low on content, so they turned to pro wrestling to fill a couple of hours of that void. TBS brought Georgia Championship Wrestling—and the NWA more broadly—back to a national audience. There were renewed complaints from rival NWA promoters about the confusion inherent in wrestlers playing different characters on GCW and in other territories—imagine the confusion if a local hero who paraded around on the regional show on Saturday morning appeared on the GCW show on TBS later that night as a bloodthirsty villain. But the complaints didn't end there: Many NWA members felt that GCW was stealing the spotlight and compromising their product by counterprogramming against their local television shows. GCW, of course, claimed that there was no conflict, that they were just running a local show that happened to be on a national network.[10]

........................................................................................
**9** Short for "Turner Broadcasting Station," naturally.

**10** There are rumors that GCW's plan was indeed to ditch the NWA and take its promotion national, but there's no definitive proof of this.

The USA Network, meanwhile, started airing wrestling on Sunday (later switched to Saturday) mornings in 1983, and later on Monday nights. Its product was an independent World Wrestling Federation, or WWF—which was a (slightly renamed) heir to the WWWF, now run by Vincent J. McMahon's son, Vincent K. McMahon, the man all wrestling fans know today as simply "Vince." After he took over from his father and bought out the ownership stakes McMahon Sr. had left to Mondt and wrestler-cum-announcer (and confidant) Gorilla Monsoon, he aimed to take his promotion national. He started hiring away the stars of other regions—cherry-picking the more outlandish ones—and signing them to long-term, exclusive contracts, something that many of the regional promotions had still never done, despite Kohler's precedent.

If the appearance of Georgia Championship Wrestling—a single NWA affiliate—on national TV was mind-blowing to the average wrestling fan, imagine the sudden appearance of the WWF. Here was a separate world, with different wrestlers and a wholly different concept of the wrestling enterprise. Where the NWA as a whole—and GCW in particular—had become increasingly gritty and realistic, the WWF was gaudy and cartoonish, a parade of outsize gimmickry. Where GCW was filled with angst, the WWF was all bombast. If GCW was a well-choreographed brawl in a bar parking lot, the WWF had the glittery sheen of a major boxing spectacle. They were in many ways similar, but to the Southern fan attuned to the traditional NWA sensibility, the WWF couldn't have been more alien.

Which is why, when Vince McMahon bought out GCW on July 14, 1984, the local fans and wrestling traditionalists called it "Black Saturday."[11] With WWF already airing on USA, McMahon thought that by buying the TBS show he could own the wrestling world; he was right insomuch as Turner was willing to give him the timeslot, but things quickly went awry. The fans of Georgia Championship Wrestling were unaccustomed to the bawdiness of the WWF product, and they revolted

---

11 McMahon got a majority of the company by buying out the stake of the Brisco brothers, Jerry and Jack, who went to work for McMahon thereafter.

via a mass-letter-writing campaign; meanwhile, WWF was treating the TBS show as a commercial for its USA production, airing old footage instead of original material. Turner himself stepped in and put real "rasslin'" back on the schedule: Bill Watts's Mid-South Wrestling (which ran Oklahoma, Mississippi, and Louisiana) on Sunday mornings, and the conspicuously familiar-named Championship Wrestling from Georgia on Saturday mornings.

With his audience diminished significantly by the new competition, McMahon eventually sold the Saturday night timeslot to North Carolina promoter Jim Crockett Jr.—son of longtime area matcher Jim Sr.—and retreated back to the USA Network. He had lost the proverbial battle, but in doing so he may have won the war. Crockett bought the TBS contract for a million dollars—money that, according to wrestling lore, McMahon used to fund his first WrestleMania card, setting the stage for his dominance of the industry for a decade.

To the bulk of wrestling fans, there wasn't a discernible difference between the Crockett show and the Georgia shows that had preceded it; they were all Southern, antebellum, roughneck shows, all NWA-affiliated, and much of the talent was shared. Soon Crockett would buy out his regional cohorts, and thus fully entrenched, Mid-Atlantic became the flagship of the NWA, and the other regional NWA affiliates served mostly as Triple-A outposts for the big-league Crockett show on TBS. Up to the '90s, the 6:05 Saturday night TBS show served as the counterbalance to the ever-expanding WWF empire.

The only promoters of any significance besides Crockett and the WWF were the AWA in Minnesota and WCCW in Texas and—to a lesser extent—Bill Watts's Georgia territory, which was rebranded as the UWF before it was sold to Crockett, and the Memphis territory run by Jerry Jarrett and Jerry "The King" Lawler.[12]

---

12 Jarrett and Lawler's CWA may have never reached the kind of scope that the others did, but its rabid local fans kept it going long after most of its contemporaries faded away—and Lawler's national renown stemming from his memorable angle with comedian Andy Kaufman briefly made it a certifiable national phenomenon.

Mid-Atlantic—eventually known simply as the NWA—expanded rapidly to Maryland in the north and Chicago in the west, occasionally running shows even farther away from home base. This Manifest Destiny would spell its demise. After being stonewalled out of the burgeoning pay-per-view market by McMahon, Crockett was absent a major revenue source as his expansion was overextending itself. Despite national popularity and sold-out venues, in 1988, Crockett's attorney told him that they were over a million dollars in debt. With no other choice, he sold his assets to Ted Turner, who had a vision of building a WWF-style wrestling monopoly of his own.

# GORGEOUS GEORGE

Perhaps the reason that many modern fans so frequently assume that pro wrestling wasn't a fraud during its early years is that, in the Golden Age of the enterprise, the wrestlers just seemed so legitimate, so earnest—even when the matches sometimes seemed less so. If one considers Gotch as the first star of the professional wrestling world and Lewis and Thesz as his heirs, and even if one took with them the Zbyszkos and Stechers and Sonnenbergs and lined them up, one immediately notices a uniformity of type. It's a murderer's row of clean-cut, white-bread athletes, something closer to an Ivy League fraternity than a league of professional fighters. And each of them is almost entirely alien compared with the outsize characters that we see on our televisions these days.

The transition from the old school to the modern model was not a steady evolution in style, as one might suspect. It was an overnight paradigm shift ushered in by an overnight sensation by the name of Gorgeous George. That he was born George Wagner in Butte, Nebraska, hardly matters, and neither does his upbringing in Arizona and Iowa and Texas, and frankly, neither do the first few semisuccessful years of his career. Before Wagner became "Gorgeous," he was someone else entirely: He was just another clean-cut nobody. The one thing that stands out at all is his training. He learned not at the knee of Farmer Burns or some other reputable trainer but at Houston's Sylvan Beach Park. At the time when Gotch was taking the sport to new heights of cultural significance and athletic legitimacy, distancing the enterprise from its sideshow roots, George Wagner was being broken into the biz by carnies.

Stories of the genesis of Gorgeous George vary, but it's the fact of the genesis that matters. When Wagner grew out his hair into Pollyanna-ish curls, bleached blond and held up with bobby pins; when he started coming to the ring in sequined robes with a purple spotlight trailing him, "Pomp and Circumstance" blaring on the loudspeakers; when his valet (Jefferies and Woodrow were two) sprayed perfume in the ring to accompany his arrival; when he posed in the ring, addressing the booing crowd with broad arrogance, infuriating them by the simple (if rather excessive) fact of his existence—*that* is precisely when wrestling entered its adolescence.

He called himself the "Toast of the Coast" and the "Sensation of the Nation" and the "Human Orchid," which seems almost inane to the modern ear, but it was—if you'll excuse the pun—deliberately florid. Just as with all the other parts of his shtick, the nickname was designed to repel. Just as George Hackenschmidt ushered into the American ring the era of the foreign foil—and more freakish baddies like the Terrible Turk and the French Angel signaled the advent of a more bestial, broader villainy, a sort of geopolitical commedia dell'arte, which led directly from the Iron Sheik and Nikolai Volkoff to the "Ugandan Giant" Kamala and Giant Gonzales and everyone in between—Gorgeous George invented the pompous heel. Within that archetype many subsets flourish: the scaredy-cat heel, the self-obsessed heel, and, of course, the faggot heel. To that end, a plurality of bad guys in the Modern Era owe the Human Orchid a tribute.

His innovations were manifold: His sequined robes were elaborate costumery; his bleached hair would become a signifier of the type; his manservant paved the way for irritant managers and valets aplenty. He is widely regarded as the first wrestler to use entrance music of any kind. He would hand out his golden hairpins to audience members and named them his "Georgie Pins"—he *named* them, for God's sake—which established the ur-marketplace for wrestling merchandise. As much as he revolutionized ring presence, he also reinvented the pro wrestling publicity machine. When George came into town, he would call the local sports desk and arrange an interview at an area hair salon, drolly belittling that evening's opponent while in curlers, sitting underneath the hooded dome of a hair dryer chair. More than anything, though, the very purpose of the wrestling enterprise shifted under his watch: No longer was the heel's defeat satisfaction enough for the fans. Now they demanded his humiliation.

☆ ☆ ☆

If the Gorgeous George persona was constructed to offend, it quickly became, with the advent of television, a persona built to enthrall. His debut on national TV on November 11, 1947, was determined by no less a modernity-blinkered publication than *Entertainment Weekly* to be one of the seminal moments of television history. "Who knew a bottle of peroxide and a trunk full of attitude would change pro wrestling—and TV—history? . . . Flamboyant George was like programming manna from heaven."

It perhaps goes without saying, but Gorgeous George was the first crossover superstar of pro wrestling, and a case can be made that he was the first true crossover superstar of any sport in America. He wasn't just a television wrestling phenomenon; he was a *television* phenomenon. If wrestling was always a Greek morality play writ via media hype and predetermined finishes onto the American sports landscape, Gorgeous

George was the first grappler to take that parallel to its logical conclusion: Through his distinct presence and his overwrought stylings, he was the first wrestler to metaphorically employ the oversized theater masks of the Greek fashion; he played to the fan in the back row, in other words. A tiny but unmistakable figure on a grainy black-and-white screen, he made wrestling comprehensible—he made it matter—to the home viewer. His fame is often said to have been on par with that of Milton Berle, Lucille Ball, and Bob Hope, who himself was a proud fan of the Gorgeous One—as were latter-day celebrities Bob Dylan, Muhammad Ali, James Brown, and John Waters. His ridiculous presence wasn't just a provocation; it was an invitation to be oneself loudly, or to be a very loud version of oneself.

His putative career highlight came when he won the American Wrestling Association (of Boston) "world" title in 1950, but that was secondary to the spectacle of his many losses, and none was more grand than his defeat later that year at the hands of Lou Thesz in Chicago on June 27. Thesz claimed the title and so unified the AWA and NWA championships, but the very presence of a fully modern celebrity competing against a stalwart of the old school was evidence of the sea change George's career had only to that point suggested. Thesz may have won the match, but just by climbing into the ring with the Human Orchid, he was admitting defeat.[1]

Gorgeous George's most famous match wasn't even a title match— but it was, of course, a losing effort. At Toronto's Maple Leaf Gardens in March 1959, he was felled by "Whipper" Billy Watson and, per stipulation, shaved bald in the center of the ring. The 20,000 fans there cheered in ecstasy, but their satisfaction was really secondary. There were millions of viewers watching at home on television sets, millions of people caring about professional wrestling, the country united in satisfaction at George's ceremonial humiliation.

Gorgeous George lived hard, both in and out of the ring. He was an alcoholic and a womanizer, purportedly a connoisseur of strippers and

---

1 And George was indubitably the financial victor. He was reported to have made $160,000 in the following year, 1951.

prostitutes and the father of illegitimate children the country over. By the time of the Watson match, George was already in his forties. When he was forced to retire a few years later—his liver pummeled by his drinking—he was a haggard shell of his old self, and even his blond curls couldn't hide that fact.

Less than two years after he retired back to his California chicken farm, he died of a heart attack. He was forty-eight years old. It's probably true that Americans didn't mourn his loss like they would mourn Lucille Ball. The fad of wrestling on national television had passed for the time being, and George himself had been removed from the wrestling spotlight by a younger generation of stars largely built in his image. He built the stage; he wrote the role; he made the character a star. And America changed the channel, and Gorgeous George was gone.

# THE FABULOUS MOOLAH

"For the money. I want to wrestle for the moolah." That's what a twenty-something Lillian Ellison told promoter Jack Pfefer[1] when he asked her why a small Southern girl like her was in the business. Pfefer, impresario of the wrestling backwater, probably laughed his oddball laugh and decided then and there that Moolah would be her new name.

Despite her moniker, though, Pfefer would make Ellison earn her check, and he started her out in servitude as "Slave Girl" Moolah, putting her in a risqué jungle dress and sending her out as a valet. Her name

1   Or a South African promoter when she was fifteen, or a newspaperman in South Carolina when she was sixteen—exact history is, as always, hazy.

was a portentous label for her career and the path that she would forge in the industry—she was half capitalism and half subservient eroticism. If male professional wrestling would be blood for bucks, its female counterpart was similarly fraught, a tangle of sex and money.

As a valet, Moolah worked first with the infamous "Nature Boy" Buddy Rogers—with whom, according to Moolah, she cut ties after Rogers began pushing her for a sexual relationship—and then for a wrestler known as Elephant Boy, who later said that he might have married Moolah if Pfefer hadn't been so protective. Elephant Boy was a dark-skinned, Afro-sporting prince of some uncertain province. Sometimes he was referred to as Indian; sometimes it was said his skin was darkened by the sun on his elephant-hunting safaris; always the crowd was to infer that he was a haughty emissary from a duskier race. (A fan, apparently offended by the miscegenation afoot, once tried to stab Moolah for the infraction of kissing Elephant Boy's cheek before the match, as she always did.) Moolah was his arm candy and his enforcer, riling the crowd by assaulting her master's opponents when the referee was distracted. As an Ohio paper reported in 1952, "Elephant Boy, with the help of Moolah, won the first fall from Carlos Mendoza in seven minutes. The bushy haired 'South African' used various choke holds to soften up his opponent and Moolah administered a few blows and held the Mexican on occasion while Elephant Boy pummeled him."

Ellison wasn't just in the game to be a valet, though, and getting illegal licks in on Elephant Boy's foes wasn't her goal. She'd been trained, after all, by Billy Wolfe, the biggest name in lady wrestling (this is a term of art) in the world. To say Wolfe had a sketchy reputation is an understatement. He had been a wrestler himself, but he married the statuesque lady wrestler Mildred Burke and became her manager, and eventually he entrenched himself as the official NWA promoter of lady wrestling. Whereas the other NWA promoters had territories, Wolfe managed a troupe of women nationwide and sent them out all over the country into all the NWA cities, to spice up shows—or, sometimes, to star in them. In the documentary *Lipstick and Dynamite*, Ella Waldek complains that they were demeaned by the promoters even as they were in high demand. Though they were usually brought in to be midcard special attractions, they would often end up in the main event slot when it became clear that most of the fans were there on account of the stars of the fairer sex.

Which is to say that Wolfe's borderless fiefdom was a boon to the NWA, and the job made Wolfe a rich man; he drove nice cars and wore extravagant jewelry even as his wrestlers grumbled about being underpaid. Although Burke lived a luxurious life during their marriage, Wolfe collected the bulk of the profits for himself and kept his wife in the dark on business matters; when they eventually divorced, his draconian management contract with her and the absence of a prenup left Burke in rough financial shape despite her being one of the era's biggest stars.

Ellison didn't last long under Wolfe's tutelage, though. Burke once said that Ellison couldn't make the cut because of her odd-shaped body (this sort of cattiness-as-factual-analysis is rampant in much of the history of the era), but Ellison insisted her time there ended after Wolfe tried to force her to sleep with him—which I hesitate to mention except for the fact that Wolfe was a truly legendary chauvinist. Some reports claim that it was merely the intimation of Wolfe's sexism that sent Moolah packing. Even if so, walking away was sensible; Wolfe ran a tight, egocentric ship and fined his lady wrestlers $50 if they were caught in the men's locker room. Regardless, Ellison soon struck out on her own and ended up in Pfefer's camp.

When she turned to wrestling full-time, she forsook "Slave Girl" in favor of "Fabulous"—a moniker befitting a champion, said Northeast promoter Vincent J. McMahon, who purportedly gave her the new name. And he was right: On September 18, 1956, Moolah defeated twelve other women in a battle royal to win the World Women's Championship. According to Ellison, McMahon said, " 'We're gonna keep the name Moolah, but I think that anybody who would win a thirteen-girl tournament in one night deserves to be called fabulous,' " to which she replied, "Whatever you say. Just write my checks and don't let 'em bounce."

Moolah wasn't initially recognized as the NWA champion, despite the fact that June Byers, who had supplanted Mildred Burke as champ after Burke and Wolfe divorced,[2] had retired that year. But because Moolah's old foe Billy Wolfe still held the reins of the women's division, he brought June Byers out of retirement to take Moolah on—and presumably to reclaim legitimacy for the NWA crown. When they met, Moolah beat her roughly. The historical accounts are vague on the script for that evening, but they all seem to emphasize Moolah's aggressiveness in a way that implies she was wrestling for real, in conflict with the script, and to be sure, it would have made little sense for Wolfe and Byers to agree to lose that match given their rivalry with Moolah. Nonetheless, there persisted enough enmity to keep the NWA title in "dispute."

By the time Wolfe died in 1963, his pull in the NWA had been negligible for five or six years. Byers finally re-retired in 1964, and Moolah—who had been defending her championship far and wide and was largely recognized as the sport's top female performer—was retroactively recognized as the NWA champ.

During her reign, Moolah set up her own wrestling school and started promoting matches—in opposition to Wolfe's outfit—along with her third husband, Buddy Lee.[3] It's around this time that rumors of Moolah's transgressions as a businesswoman start to surface; if the rumors are to be believed, she apparently had learned well from Wolfe's example in everything from underpaying talent to sexual indiscretion.[4] Just as with the shows she herself put on, sex and money were inextricably linked to the business. She ran a tight ship, just as Wolfe had: Her ladies were

--------

[2] Byers was, not incidentally, also his daughter-in-law. Wolfe always chose women over whom he could exercise control.

[3] After Moolah caught him in a compromising situation with another lady wrestler several years after she was officially knighted by the NWA, the two divorced, and Buddy Lee went on to backstage fame in a different industry, as the agent for country acts such as Hank Williams Jr. and Garth Brooks.

[4] She supposedly dallied with her students and sent them out on jobs where sex was expected of them, and although these rumors are nominally believable, they strike me as very, very unreliable.

expected to conduct themselves in ladylike fashion (surely a stretch for some of the brawlers she trained), to always appear in public with immaculate hair and makeup, and, of course, to not date the male wrestlers. Moolah and her girls toured the country, with Moolah playing the nefarious champion and one of her wards—usually a beautiful, curvy blonde like Judy Grable—playing the scrappy heroine.

As popular as the women were all through the Territorial Era, their road was a much rockier one than that of the men. The very notion of women engaging in a contact sport was widely considered distasteful, and any in-ring injury was seen in some conservative quarters as proof that women weren't cut out for the fighting game. Over the years, lady wrestling was banned in many markets, but the laws were eventually relaxed starting in the late '60s as wrestling was increasingly seen as more entertainment than sport and, in a broader sense, the country began unclutching its collective purse.

On March 16, 1969, lady wrestling returned to New Jersey after more than fifteen years.[5] *The New York Times*'s legendary sportswriter Robert Lipsyte was on the scene: "Twice Moolah had belted the referee, precipitating rollicking free-for-alls in which all four girl wrestlers ended up sitting on the poor man's head. . . . The sly, self-mocking humor of good burlesque was in the show, as well as a brisk and bouncy athleticism that was missing from most of the men's bouts." After their run in New Jersey, it was only a matter of time before the lady fights had their New York homecoming, despite the stingy sporting rules of Madison Square Garden and the state at large.[6] On July 1, 1972, lady wrestling returned to Madison Square Garden, and Moolah—at that point the recognized titleholder in the Northeast for sixteen years—was the

---

**5** Elizabeth, New Jersey, was chosen as the locale because it was a rather rough-and-tumble town where sensibilities were least likely to be offended; after the show went off without incident there, lady wrestling was allowed to migrate to the more upscale bastions of Trenton and Newark.

**6** From the time of William Muldoon's run as chairman of the New York State Athletic Commission, everything unbecoming, from wrestling masks on up, was subject to extreme regulation.

feature attraction. Moolah, already the sport's matriarch, was described lovingly by fans as looking like "a tough, middle-aged bird" and "a beaten-up old broad."

☆  ☆  ☆

In 1983, during the WWF's national expansion, when Vince McMahon set out to buy national legitimacy by hiring the superstars of other territories, as well as other promotions and their TV timeslots, he formally hired Moolah and absorbed her women's title into the WWF championship hierarchy. Moolah had been working at least part time for McMahon's father since he bequeathed her the "Fabulous" all those years before.[7] If it wasn't exactly a retirement plan—Moolah would wrestle for several more years, despite being sixty years old—it was a means of cementing her own legacy. Sure, the WWF had selected a new girl, Wendi Richter, to be the female face of the company, and with her modelesque build, neon spandex, teased hair, and trapezoidal sunglasses, she certainly looked the part of a Rock 'n' Wrestling heroine. Moolah would be her antagonist. It was a role Moolah knew well—Richter was a student of Moolah's, so their new act was really just the old territorial routine transplanted onto weekly television—and one she was more than willing to play for the sum McMahon was offering, even if the fans detested her: "They called me all kinds of names. I said: 'Call me anything you want. You don't write my check.'"

Upon her arrival, Moolah was announced as having held the title for twenty-eight years, and even though that wasn't exactly true, it seemed silly to take away those brief losses when Moolah herself had willingly let the title go. All of her losses were quid pro quo title trade-offs, the sorts of story turns that are scripted to build the excitement—and the potential gate—for the rematch, at which point the status quo would be reinstated. She dropped the belt to her sister-in-law, Bette Boucher, in 1966, only to

---

**7**  In *Lipstick and Dynamite*, Moolah says she's been with their organization for more than forty-six years.

regain it a few weeks later, and did a similar swap with Yukiko Tomoe on a Japanese tour two years later, and then again with Sue Green in 1976 and Evelyn Stevens in '78—at which point, it should be noted, Moolah owned the women's title (and all decision-making that went with it) outright.[8]

Moolah's feud with Richter was a proxy for a feud being waged in interviews between bad-guy manager Captain Lou Albano and mainstream crosser-over Cyndi Lauper. They had teamed up in Lauper's video for "Girls Just Want to Have Fun" but had since become at odds, as those in the wrestling world are wont to do, with Albano backing Moolah and Lauper in Richter's corner. The culmination of their rivalry was on July 23, 1984, at "The Brawl to End It All," a wrestling event broadcast to the masses on MTV. Richter vs. Moolah was the main event, which is an enormous anomaly in the spectrum of WWF/WWE history, but just as Waldek noted about the early days of lady wrestling, sometimes promoters just have to acknowledge that the women's match is going to be the biggest draw. Richter won the match, and a new era seemed to have commenced, with Richter as McMahon's female counterpart to Hulk Hogan and Moolah set to ride off into the sunset.

Of course, by that time Moolah knew her way around wrestling politics better than anyone, and once she saw her role being squeezed out, she reinserted herself. When McMahon was prepared to feature another Moolah student, Mad Maxine, as his top villainess, Moolah somehow took her out of the picture and claimed the post for herself.[9] And when Richter's relationship with the WWF began to fray during a contract dispute, Vince called upon Moolah to set the wrestling world right.

On November 17, 1985, Moolah regained the championship in one of modern wrestling's most overlooked controversies. Richter was set to defend her title against the masked Spider Lady, only to have Moolah

................................................................................
**8** Her onetime student Judy Grable claims to have beaten Moolah in matches now lost to official history, but Moolah denies that that could have happened: "I didn't teach her *every*thing I knew. I'm too smart for that."

**9** Maxine was supposed to be the evil female star of the *Hulk Hogan's Rock 'n' Wrestling* cartoon, a role that eventually went to Moolah.

come out in the Spider Lady's outfit. As she enters the ring, you can see Richter's real-life anger; she can tell who's under the mask and begins to realize something's afoot. When wrestling was at its most popular, its fakeness was most pronounced, or at least most widely presupposed. At this peak of pop-cultural relevance, wrestling was so widely known to be "fake" that that euphoric awareness clouded the fact that an actual double cross—and an actual shoot—was taking place. Moolah muscled Richter into submission, and the complicit referee counted a quick three. Richter yanked off the mask and exposed Moolah, but to little avail; Richter was never seen in the WWF again, and Moolah's malevolent star rose all the more for her deception.

☆ ☆ ☆

Moolah continued to wrestle, but without the tension she and Richter had together, the women's division in the WWF began to founder. Moolah finally relinquished the belt to Sherri Martel in 1987, ending her unprecedented decades-long reign atop the division.

In his review of that 1969 card, Lipsyte said that Moolah planned "to wrestle as long as the flesh is willing." And she did. She appeared in the WWF/WWE throughout the '90s and 2000s in various roles—as a comedic prop, as a living legend, as a heat-inducing punching bag. Well into her seventies, she was being hit with guitars and bodyslammed on television. And on October 17, 1999, at the age of seventy-six, Moolah defeated Ivory to regain the women's title—*her* women's title. And just as things went in the old days, she lost the title back to Ivory a week later.

Moolah retired to her South Carolina estate, where she then lived with fellow legend Mae Young and a former midget wrestler named Diamond Lil—both onetime students of Moolah's. It was a nice little kingdom for the queen of lady wrestling, a physical trophy of the success she'd had and the money she'd made: twenty-five acres, a ten-acre lake. As Moolah put it: "It cost a lot of pain to get that place. Every bit was worth it."

# THE GORGEOUS LADIES OF WRESTLING

While there have been any number of star female wrestlers over the decades, there has been perhaps no greater flashpoint in the women's wrestling world—on a cultural crossover level, anyway—than GLOW, short for Gorgeous Ladies of Wrestling, a syndicated psych ward of pro wrestling fairer-sex silliness.

GLOW was started by an impresario of the oddball sports world named David McLane—who would later go on to produce shows about sports you've never heard of, like roller hockey—who teamed up with Sly's mom, Jackie Stallone, to start an all-female wrestling company that was originally conceived as a spin-off of her gym, Barbarella's. As the concept evolved, GLOW became an entirely different animal. Launching in 1986, it called back to the wrestling studio shows of the dwindling Territorial Era while embracing—and amplifying—the outsize silliness of the emergent WWF. The initial roster of twelve girls was trained by Mando Guerrero (brother of

Eddie and Chavo Sr.) in the weeks leading up to the first TV shoot, and the characters they portrayed—Americana, Colonel Ninotchka, Matilda the Hun, Sally the Farmer's Daughter, Tina Ferrari, and of course the sisterly duo of Mt. Fiji and Little Fiji—were as broad and comical as their names suggested. But clowning aside, fight these ladies did, with glee and relative abandon. If the style was more slapstick than the pro wrestling mainstream, it hardly felt over the top within the confines of their Las Vegas Riviera Hotel arena, amid the freewheeling absurdity of the emerging direct-to-syndication television market, which was occupying odd hours on major stations with all variety of unusual content.

The confluence of GLOW's launch with the cultural relevance of pro wrestling as provided by the WWF's Rock 'n' Wrestling Era—and its concurrent push of female superstars like Wendi Richter—certainly helped GLOW's positioning, but their attraction didn't end there. With a "Super Bowl Shuffle"–style group-rap intro and an utter disregard for convention, GLOW became a minor national phenomenon, capturing the "serious" wrestling fans, a crowd of younger girls, and more general viewers who were taken in by what could only be perceived as a much lower level of self-regard than the wrestling they were used to. When it came to GLOW, there wasn't any question of whether it was real; one could be forgiven, though, if one wondered whether some of the wrestlers were actually as affected as they seemed. The organizing principle of GLOW, above all the craziness, was fun—a concept often lost in the broader world of wrestling.

Alas, something so countercultural couldn't last forever. As the novelty wore off and the mainstream had its fill of pro wrestling, GLOW closed up shop. McLane tried to replicate his success several times over the years, but it was never to be. That doesn't stop fans from remembering fondly those days when crazy women in spandex and sunglasses ran wild.

# THE VON ERICH FAMILY

Some kids dream about running off to join the circus, ditching their families, their friends, their boring lives, and setting out in search of something different, something new, something exotic. Jack Adkisson was kind of like those kids. But Adkisson didn't grow up to be a trapeze artist or a lion tamer. He became a Nazi impersonator. And when he came home, he brought the circus with him.

Adkisson grew up playing football in Texas, and he played sparingly in the offensive line that protected the legendary Doak Walker at Southern Methodist University, then briefly for the Dallas Texans before striking out for the Canadian Football League. In Canada he met another legend, Stu Hart, progenitor of the Hart family of wrestlers and owner of

Klondike Wrestling.[1] Adkisson had done some wrestling in Dallas for a brief spell before heading north—it sometimes seems like every football player did back then—and Stu looked at Jack's enormous frame and blond hair and decided he's make a good Aryan bully. He paired Adkisson up with a German immigrant's son named Walter Sieber and redubbed them Fritz and Waldo Von Erich, Prussian Nazis. This was the '50s, and just like in movies and comic books, Nazis (or, more broadly, evil nationalist Germans) were still a powerful foil. Neither Jack nor Walter was really a Nazi, but in the wrestling world, fact is rarely a disqualifier. The two toured the country, wrestling in many regional promotions that had grown up in the recent years, turning the still-palpable resentment toward the Axis powers into box office gold. Few heels in those days were as despised as the Von Erich brothers, but that animosity wasn't necessarily misplaced; by some accounts, the vitriol wasn't so much based in the fans' belief that the Von Erichs were Nazis but in anger that the wrestlers would seek to commercialize and monetize those fresh wounds—semiliterally, as any wrestling crowd in those days was sure to count a hearty contingent of veterans in its number.

The character suited Adkisson. He was known to be a brute in the ring and a bully outside of it. He roughhoused with his opponents and pushed around fans; he seemed to take delight in imposing his physical will on the world. It should be said that this is not an unusual character type in the wrestling world; Fritz, though, was notorious even in those brawny circles. As frequent opponent (and Mid-South wrestling mogul) "Cowboy" Bill Watts once put it, "The German gimmick was a natural. With that scowl of his, he was an easy guy to hate." Like so many other tropes in the wrestling world, the Nazism was a lie told to advance a greater truth about the existence of evil in the world and the need to overcome it with headlocks and such. It was a lie that Jack Adkisson embraced.

There's a crazy, apocryphal story about Fritz sitting in the dressing room in Chicago after a card. (Bear with me on this.) It was late. The rest

--------

1   The promotion would later come to be known as Stampede Wrestling.

of the wrestlers were busy taking down the ring. A small man appeared at Fritz's door and asked him about his service in the war. Fritz gruffly told the guy to go away. When the man persisted, Fritz told him it was an act—a gimmick—and the man wondered aloud if Fritz knew that *gimmick* was a Yiddish word. Fritz and the man went back and forth a few more times, with Fritz getting increasingly frustrated with the man's quiet insistence that Fritz realize the gravity of his offensiveness. Finally, Fritz threatened the man a last time, and the man rolled up his sleeve to expose the tattoo that proved him to be a survivor of the Holocaust. He told Fritz that he'd lost all seven of his sons in the death camps, and—here's where it gets good—he said ominously that he sincerely hoped that nothing like that would ever happen to Fritz. Adkisson went pale and tossed the man out of the locker room, running him into the door frame, cutting his arm, and tearing his coat, from which fell a scrap of cloth with a six-pointed star imprinted and a few drops of the man's fresh blood. By the time Fritz looked up, the man had vanished. A locker room attendant watched the scene from the shadows and recovered the patch from the trash can after Fritz left.

Of course, the wrestling world is a world of mythology, and even the "real life" side of it is filled with its own myths and legends and tall tales. But this story stands out not just for its allegory but also for its angle. Almost all of wrestling's fables are written by its historical victors. Rarely do you hear tales in which the player—Fritz in this case—isn't depicted in a good light, or doesn't have something to gain by its retelling. To be sure, this isn't a widespread story, but its very existence is telling: As hard as he would try over the rest of his life to script reality to suit his fantasy, Adkisson would never wholly succeed.

☆ ☆ ☆

In 1959, Adkisson's firstborn son, Jack Jr., died at the age of six after being electrocuted in the bathtub. Fritz and Waldo didn't strictly split up when Jack Jr. died, but Fritz stopped traveling as much, reluctant to go back to the East Coast. Both took their fearsome German characters with them—Fritz with his *Sieg Heil* and dreadful Iron Claw finisher, Waldo with his goose step and cartoon villainy.[2] Fritz moved on to St. Louis where he worked for Sam Muchnick, the NWA *macher* in the area. Muchnick was a central figure in the NWA power structure, and for years, as long as the power in the northeastern wrestling scene remained scattered, Muchnick was the closest thing they had to a pro wrestling godfather.

Fritz finally decided to go home to Texas, to get a real job and quit playing around with the fake fighting, but he couldn't quite let the fantasy go. He decided to work a match or two for Ed McLemore at the Dallas Sportatorium to make some cash, and ended up backing into an ownership stake in the promotion. Just as in any other consortium of that ilk, who you know is always as important as what you know: Jack's old boss Muchnick had the sway to give him the approval he needed, in that oddball underworld, to take the reins there. Von Erich partnered with McLemore, and they split off from Paul Boesch's south Texas office, and after McLemore died, Fritz took control. By the '80s, Fritz was a local legend—between his wrestling fame, his place in local football lore, his born-again Christianity, and his real estate dealings, Fritz was a proud member of Dallas's upper crust—and Fritz Von Erich went from Teutonic heel to Texas hero.

It took coming home for Fritz Von Erich to find himself. It's probably more accurate to say that Fritz Von Erich found himself by embracing his inner Jack Adkisson. After all, Jack was from Texas. Jack's dad was a constable, for Pete's sake. How's this for a subconscious act of rebellion: Jack Adkisson—good ol' Texas boy, son of a lawman, SMU footballer— went up to Canada and became a Nazi. He finally came home, but he never gave up the Von Erich name. He had chosen pro wrestling over family. But soon he would have a family of his own, a battling troupe of Von Erich boys built in his image, molded into Texas royalty by the expo-

---

**2** Waldo, left to his own devices, would go on to a fairly significant career, the highlight of which was probably feuding with fan favorite Bruno Sammartino in the WWWF—the ur-WWE.

sure afforded them in the World Class Championship Wrestling territory. That territory, it was going to be their whole world.

☆ ☆ ☆

Kevin Von Erich—the eldest son after Jackie died—started wrestling for his dad in 1976. David followed a year later, but beat Kevin to wrestling stardom because Kevin was busy playing college football. (David dropped out of school after he got the wrestling bug.) David was the superstar from the start, 6-foot-7, strong and agile, the complete package, a pre-steroid-era wrestling messiah. In a stride of individualism unusual for the Von Erich progeny, David defiantly left Texas for a few years early in his career and wrestled around the country, where he earned credibility among the big names of the era and, mostly by playing a bad guy, learned much of the ring psychology that his brothers never mastered. He followed in his father's footsteps, against his father's wishes, and only in doing so was he poised to surpass his father.

The other brothers followed their dad's decree and never left home. Kevin was barefooted and bowl-cut, the highflier of the family, a free spirit who would eventually become its emotional rock. After David came Kerry, the muscle-bound Prince Valiant with sleepy eyes and a powerful sort of charisma that emanated from his posture (and certainly not from his promos—Kerry was always halting on the mic). Then came Mike, and then Chris, the former the smallest of the bunch who frequently wrestled, the latter the smallest full stop. Chris was afflicted with medical issues that left him undersized and fragile; Mike, though healthy, wasn't the physical specimen that his older brothers were, and was transparently outmatched by most of his opponents in the ring. If the first lie of the Von Erich family tree was Fritz's Nazism, the second was Mike's legitimacy. It wasn't that he had no business being in the ring; it was that he had no business being successful in the ring, being booked as anything but an underdog, and the Von Erich brothers were largely put over as superheroes. Even to the believing eye and even during his brief physical peak, his tiny frame stacked with suspicious muscles, Mike wasn't the character he was portraying. He wasn't up to the standards of David or Kevin or Kerry, and certainly not the mythic spectre of Fritz. But the fans didn't object; they were too enthralled by the Von Erich clan to question.

☆ ☆ ☆

In the Territorial Era, in the world before international interconnectivity, the local wrestling stage was by and large *the* wrestling stage. After wrestling stopped airing on DuMont and before it came back on national cable networks, many of the regional promotions had TV shows that aired throughout their local territories. Even if fans in each area thought that they were watching the biggest wrestling show in the country, no territory was more rapturous about the local heroes than Dallas.

There wasn't any absence of charisma in pro wrestling in those days: Harley Race was around, Ric Flair was ascendant, and Dusty Rhodes was splitting his time between his Florida territory home, sellout houses all over the South, and Vince McMahon's New York City, where he battled against "Superstar" Billy Graham. But the heroes and villains up till then had been full-grown men, guys who had largely had careers in sports or the military before coming to wrestling, or at a minimum guys who had paid their dues wrestling through the territories, moving up from jobber to supporting act to tag team player before climbing up to the singles-champ tier.

But Fritz had control of Texas, and he had a different vision: If he was too old to be the star himself, he would push his boys as the stars. It was the standard modus operandi in the territories for the biggest star to be co-owner of the promotion. It was a vicious cycle: The bosses would give the wrestlers a stake so as not to risk them leaving, and then the owner-wrestlers would stay on top interminably because they were the only people they could trust not to leave. Fritz was only one of many who positioned their sons as heirs apparent to the throne for the same practical (and, one assumes, egotistical) reason. But he was by far the most successful at turning his sons into stars.

# A BRIEF HISTORY OF NEPOTISM IN WRESTLING

In the Territorial Era regional superstars owned (or co-owned) the promotions in which they competed. The rationale was simple: In a time when wrestlers regularly traveled from city to city, seeking better money or fame (or simply indulging the wanderlust inherent in the sort of person who seeks out that line of work), and in a period in which few if any wrestlers or promoters bothered with binding contracts, the only wrestler a promoter could trust to not leave him in the lurch was a wrestler with an ownership stake. Thus the earliest promoters started letting their stars buy into the business side, and in almost every instance, once the original owners started aging out, the star ended up being the sole—or at least operational—owner.

By the 1980s, once the previous generation of stars were too old to present themselves as realistic champions, many promoters turned to the only *other* wrestlers they could trust not to leave: their sons. Of course, the first generation of territorial stars who became owners built themselves into stars prior to becoming promoters—

which is to say, they earned their spots atop the card—but their children were not necessarily so compelling.

David, Kerry, and Kevin Von Erich are the exceptions that prove the rule, of course—they're the best example of a promoter successfully promoting his sons. But the contrasting examples—like their brothers Chris and Mike—are so much more plentiful. ("Macho Man" Randy Savage and "Leaping" Lanny Poffo—sons of renegade promoter Angelo Poffo—were exceptions as well, although their International Championship Wrestling promotion was less of an institution and more of a platform for the sons and a vehicle for the father to make money.)

Consider Greg Gagne (son of Verne) in the AWA. Greg was a scrawny, charisma-less guy with good acrobatic skills and a good head for the business. Nonetheless, he was pushed as a championship contender (after serving mostly as a tag team competitor for years) once AWA talent started defecting en masse to the WWF. Viewers were already bored by Verne Gagne's run as the top star into his sixties, and the ascendance of his middling son didn't do much for ratings. The lack of believable "heavyweight" contender size is a common thread through the nepotistic list. (Even passable performers like Mike Graham, son of Florida promoter Eddie Graham, were often too small to make it through to the main event.)

Tennessee was a particularly significant spot for wrestling nepotism. George Gulas was the son of Tennessee promoter Nick Gulas. Nick pushed his son as a top star despite the fact that he looked eerily similar to Andy Kaufman during his wrestling days, but without the taste to wear thermal underwear over his bird chest. When Gulas's allegiance to his son's success forced a split with his partner Jerry Jarrett, Jarrett partnered with wrestler Jerry "The King" Lawler, whose own son, Brian Christopher, would debut for his dad's promotion years later when it had morphed into the USWA. Despite his relatively small stature, he went on to a fairly successful WWF career as a white-guy hip-hopper (known as Grand Master Sexay)—but it's worth noting that, a few latter-day Memphis shoot interviews aside, he never traded off his father's name. Also notable was the bizarro career of Jamie Dundee, son of longtime Lawler frenemy

"Superstar" Bill Dundee. And the Poffo family was briefly a Tennessee institution as well.

Of course, your dad doesn't have to own the company for you to benefit from nepotism in pro wrestling. Second-generation stars aren't unusual in the wrestling world, but even the most pedigreed offspring usually still have to prove themselves worthy of a spot atop the card. Those examples that succeeded due to their father's fame alone are often groan-inducing memories in wrestling lore. Like, say, Erik Watts. Erik was a legitimate athlete, the quarterback for the University of Louisville football team, but more significantly, his dad was Bill Watts, former Mid-South Wrestling guru and mid-'90s booker for WCW. It was during his father's WCW tenure that he was signed by the company and allowed to repeatedly hammer on Arn Anderson, and when his dad left for the WWF a few years later, Erik went along there too, where he was outfitted in a silvery smock and put into a tag team called Tekno Team 2000.

Other notable examples include Ric Flair's son David, who was inexplicably a significant midcard player in the latter days of WCW, despite his lack of discernible training, charisma, or, for that matter, wrestling gear; Scott Putski, son of the "Polish Hammer" Ivan Putski; and Lacey Von Erich, daughter of Kerry. Garett Bischoff, son of Eric Bischoff, who was WCW's showrunner in its late-'90s heyday, is now seeing the spotlight in TNA Wrestling, where his father is presently in charge.

David and Kevin and Kerry toured around Texas together, causing Beatles-level crowd freak-outs at their every entrance. Fans of the old WCCW programming on ESPN might recall the fairly shocking sight of those Von Erich boys wading through the throngs of wrestling fans—not just guys, not just nerds, but real, everyday people—in Dallas's Sportatorium,[3] in Texas Stadium, wherever they could hold a frenzied mob, and being treated like conquering heroes. Women in the crowd grabbed them and kissed them—Kevin says he'd sometimes walk through the crowd with one hand over his mouth and one over his crotch—and handed them bouquets of yellow roses on the way to the ring. People like to call successful wrestlers "rock stars," and it's an overstatement despite being a metaphor. But these kids, they were rock stars. Even that slightly underestimates the reality of their stardom because Texas didn't have rock stars, really; they only had football. And for a few years in the '80s, the Von Erichs were bigger than the Dallas Cowboys. Sure, they were sheltered, but their shelter was a bodyslam paradise. That little enclave in Dallas, Texas, might have been the only world they knew, but they had that world on a proverbial string. Or, to put it another way, they ruled the Southwest with an Iron Claw.

The three eldest Von Erich boys—sometimes with Fritz at their side—were such straightforward good guys that goodness itself was their organizing attribute. "We were the only guys who didn't have gimmicks," says Kevin in the WWE's *Triumph and Tragedy of World Class Championship Wrestling* documentary. They never needed to play a character; they were beyond characters—they were Von Erichs, after all.

They feuded with all sorts of baddies that Fritz imagined up or imported from other territories. Their most memorable rivalry was with the Fabulous Freebirds, a trio of toughs who repped the state of Georgia in the same way that Fritz once did Germany. Michael "P.S." Hayes was the fancy-boy front man, Buddy "Jack" Roberts was the unstoppable

........................................................................................

**3** The Sportatorium was one of the legendary venues in pro wrestling history, but it was little more than a barn with a fancy name, a ramshackle setup with wobbly risers, exposed rafters, and no A/C. In its latter days you'd exit the highway and drive past a mile of nothing but liquor stores and bail bondsmen before you turned into a dirt parking lot to see a show there.

little asshole, and Terry "Bam Bam" Gordy was the permed, brutish man-child. Hayes came in first and won over the crowd with a variation on the bleached-blond, jive-talking white man act that had worked for both Dusty Rhodes and Billy Graham (among many others), but he soon imported his cronies Roberts and Gordy and turned against the Von Erich clan in a legendary match on Christmas night in 1982. The feud was epic, and the gritty irreverence of the Freebirds played perfectly off of the Von Erichs' institutional innocence. They played it as a Texas vs. Georgia issue, a matter of regional pride akin to a college football rivalry, but the subtext was Good vs. Evil. If, to the modern eye, the comparison to the Freebirds underscores the Von Erichs' robotic heroism, that was beside the point in 1982. This was still unequivocally the Territorial Era, the premodern wrestling world, a time of simple duality.

☆ ☆ ☆

Things weren't always simple for the Von Erichs, and the good guys sometimes got the worst of it. In early 1984 David—at just twenty-five years old—was without his brothers on the first night of a tour through Japan. The morning after he arrived, he was found dead in his hotel room. The first reports in the Dallas papers called it a stroke. Referee David Manning, who was on the trip, says that David ate so much the night before, he wouldn't be surprised if he had taken some painkillers and choked on his own vomit. The Japanese coroner eventually called it acute enteritis, a disease of the intestines, which may or may not have triggered a heart attack, depending on who you listen to. The widespread rumor was that the death was drug-related. Ric Flair's autobiography implies that Bruiser Brody—also on the trip, in Flair's telling—flushed David's stash before the police showed up. Reporting from a local show after David's death, the Dallas Times Herald keyed on the uncertainty promulgated by the unreal world that the wrestlers inhabited: "The rumor of death hung over the crowd like the cigarette smoke in the Sportatorium arena on Industrial Avenue Friday night. He was killed, one said. A drug overdose, said another. Many dismissed it all as a wild rumor or a publicity stunt."

The Von Erichs, ever intent on maintaining their act in public, even in the face of tragedy, said he'd gotten a "hard lick" in a match and that led to his death, but he hadn't even wrestled yet in Japan. That was their third lie.

With the huge success of the Dallas promotion and his sheer talent, David had been in line for a run with the NWA championship. After his death, both the Texas territory and the NWA overall were thrown into disarray. A supershow in Texas Stadium in May 1984 that had been meant to have David winning the NWA title from Flair[4] was rewritten to put Kerry in David's slot, and Fritz came out of retirement to team with Kevin and Mike against the Freebirds. The venue was packed, 50,000 people strong, come to pay tribute to the Von Erich family. Fritz and Co. beat the Freebirds, and Kerry won the belt in almost inexplicable fashion with the most unspectacular conceivable maneuver—not the Iron Claw but a simple backslide pin. It was an affecting match, but that ending was perhaps coincidentally somber. The crowd cheered his win, but it seemed even they could tell that it was a tribute to David and not a real victory for Kerry.

His title reign didn't last long (it was eighteen days, to be exact); on the national scene, he quickly earned a reputation for being "flaky," which in just about every retelling is a word laden with implications of drug use.

It should be said that, despite his innate charisma, Kerry didn't have the verbal prowess of his father or of David. He was the dumb jock of the family, slightly Neanderthal in both looks and spirit, and the villains in World Class weren't shy about pointing it out—pretty boy heel Gino Hernandez would call Kerry a "baboon brain," and Michael Hayes once said that "he's just as stupid as he looks. It takes him an hour and a half to watch 60 minutes." In the end, Kerry's win could do little to

---

4   In an on-screen promo that purported to extol David's talent but that alluded rather bold-facedly to backstage reality, Flair said, "I can tell you right now, he was close to being the world's heavyweight champion."

dampen the depression that was setting in with the Von Erich clan and its fans.

☆  ☆  ☆

Mike Von Erich was only ever conscripted into main-event duty because of David's death. The Von Erichs were a three-man unit, and purportedly, Fritz pressured Mike into the role, despite the fact that his only ambition in wrestling was to be a cameraman. In 1985, during a tour of Israel,[5] Mike hurt his shoulder and, after surgery, ended up with toxic shock syndrome. He survived a near-death scare, but he was left weakened and with brain damage. On their TV show, Fritz valiantly predicted an imminent return to the ring. Months later, Mike would appear, bone-thin and glassy-eyed, announcing his full recovery. He did return, but as a shadow of his former self.

His roster of sons depleted, needing to fill Mike's spot on the card, Fritz birthed a new kin. In late 1985, he unveiled Lance Von Erich to the world—a Von Erich cousin, he called him, Waldo's son. Everybody knew it was a put-on, not least because Kevin Vaughn was a local footballer who most fans recognized. But everybody knew that wrestling was fake. They just didn't want to be insulted. Fritz soon recanted, admitted on air that Vaughn was never a Von Erich, and promised never again to speak his name.

On June 4, 1986, Kerry wrecked his motorcycle, crushing his right leg. The doctors saved his mangled foot—and, in an unfortunate echo of Mike, Kerry videotaped a guarantee of full recovery that aired on WCCW television. After surgery, he reinjured his foot. The Von Erich family account is that, in the hospital, doped up, he tried to walk across the room; the conspiracy theorists insist that the foot was reinjured when he attempted a comeback ahead of schedule, shot up with painkillers to get him through the match. Regardless, his right foot was

---

5   WCCW was bizarrely popular there.

amputated. Nobody outside of the hospital staff and the Von Erich family could know. It didn't fit with the storyline.

After his own surgery, Mike had had several run-ins with the law for increasingly odd and unpredictable behavior—reckless driving, disorderly conduct, etc.—but in April 1987, he was pulled over and found to have a bottle full of nonprescription pills. The Von Erich family lawyer bailed him out. A few days later, on April 12, 1987, Mike deliberately overdosed on sleeping pills and ended his life. "PLEASE UNDERSTAND I'M A FUCK-UP! I'M SORRY," read his good-bye note to his brothers.

On Christmas night in 1987, at the annual WCCW Star Wars show, the Von Erichs were battling Freebirds Terry Gordy and Buddy Roberts and their associates "Iceman" King Parsons[6] and the Angel of Death. Fritz tried to help but was beaten down; upon exiting the ring he collapsed dramatically. He seemed to be faking a heart attack, but the Von Erichs claimed that it was a mere collapse from exhaustion and that nothing in such poor taste was implied.

When David died, the fans stuck with the Von Erichs. When Mike was hurt, then Kerry was hurt, and when Mike died, the Dallas fans were squarely in the Von Erich corner. But with Lance Von Erich and then Fritz's "heart attack," the Von Erichs had turned their backs on the unspoken agreement between the actors and the audience. They treated the fans as dupes instead of coconspirators. As World Class staggered onward, they were for the first time facing a wary audience. With the audience within the comfortable confines of the Sportatorium waning, the world outside seemed to turn on the Von Erichs too.

In 1990, Kerry was hired by the WWF and wrestled there to fleeting acclaim. He stuffed the bottom of his right boot and laced it tight, and the world was unaware that he was working on one foot. It was undoubtedly excruciating, and it's little surprise that this is when widespread rumors of Kerry's painkiller abuse began to surface, along with rumors of cocaine and other illegal drugs—but it's also probably no coincidence that these rumors were only allowed to surface once he was out from under

6    Then known as the "Blackbird," due to his partnership with Gordy and Roberts.

the protective umbrella of his father's Dallas kingdom. Kerry won the Intercontinental Championship from "Mr. Perfect" Curt Hennig and lost it back to him three months later.

On September 12, 1991, Chris Von Erich, the smallest of the family, shot himself in the head in a remote area of the family ranch. He had wanted to be a wrestler more than any of his brothers, probably, but—aside from a few feel-good tag team bouts, one of which left him severely injured—he couldn't do it, and that, presumably, wasn't good enough. And he had been closer to Mike than anyone. Kevin and their mother found him.

By 1992, Kerry had come back to Texas. He wrestled in the GWF, which had staked its claim on the foundering Dallas territory. Kerry too had run-ins with the police, and when he was arrested in February 1993, he knew that a lengthy jail term was on the horizon. He couldn't handle that, or handle the disappointment it would mean to his fans, or his family, or whatever. He went to his dad's house, told him he was going for a drive, and then shot himself in the chest under the tree that all the Von Erich brothers had played on in their youth. That was February 18, 1993. When they held his memorial service, his name was still on the marquee outside the venue where he was scheduled to wrestle that weekend. His opponent, in perfect wrestling tragicomic irony, was the Angel of Death.

Fritz died in 1997 of brain and lung cancer. When the family was inducted into the WWE Hall of Fame in 2009, Kevin accepted all six rings himself.

# THE LEGENDARY VENUES OF WRESTLING

**The Sportatorium (Dallas, Texas).** Castle of the Von Erich dominion, this tin-sided barn was, in its early going, home to the Big D Jamboree, Texas's answer to the Grand Ole Opry, but it soon was known foremost for its wrestling shows. Its prominence was such that, in May 1953, the building was set on fire, (supposedly) by a rival wrestling promoter. They rebuilt. When it caught fire again in 2001, the wrestling crowds had diminished to the point that it hardly seemed necessary. The building was formally demolished in 2003.

**Greensboro Coliseum (Greensboro, North Carolina).** Home to many of the biggest cards in the Crocketts' Mid-Atlantic territory in the '70s and '80s, and subsequently to the centralized NWA, the Greensboro Coliseum hosted the first four Starrcade cards. In the first, Ric Flair beat Harley Race to signal the changing of the guard atop the NWA.

**Madison Square Garden (New York, New York).** When pro wrestling made it to MSG, it was taken as a validation of the form. And wrestling has been a part of MSG's proud history, from the early days of the "Solid Man" William Muldoon, who wrestled there as early as 1880, to the days of Jim Londos and Antonino Rocca, whose fame stewarded a return of wrestling to the Garden in 1950 after a twelve-year hiatus, to WrestleMania I, and through to today.

**Kiel Auditorium (St. Louis, Missouri).** In the middle of the century, nowhere besides Madison Square Garden was a bigger draw than Kiel Auditorium, home twice a month to Sam Muchnick's NWA headquarters, the St. Louis Wrestling Club.

**ECW Arena (Philadelphia, Pennsylvania).** The onetime freight warehouse repurposed for low-rent sports shows, previously known as Viking Hall, was the site of much of Extreme Championship Wrestling's bloody history, including its first ever pay-per-view event, *Barely Legal.*

# TERRY GORDY,
# OF THE FABULOUS FREEBIRDS

In 1977, thirty-nine-year-old San Diego Chargers star turned wrestling bad guy Ernie Ladd squared off against a lanky, bleached-blond sixteen-year-old kid named Terry Mecca. It wasn't really a fair fight; that was the point. Unfair fights are great for getting bad guys over. The 6-foot-9, 307-pound Ladd was one of the most physically fearsome grapplers of his (or any) generation, and after watching him manhandle young Mecca, nobody in the building would have predicted that the teenager would go on to be one of the most intimidating brawlers of his own era. Of course, nobody's ever heard of Terry Mecca, but lots of people have heard of Terry Gordy, and they're the same guy. As far as he would go in the pro wrestling world, Gordy would always be the overgrown kid getting himself knocked around.

☆ ☆ ☆

The Von Erich clan ruled the Texas wrestling territory and, for stretches during the '80s, the late-night spot on ESPN. Compared to the more mainstream, over-the-top mode of the WWF, World Class Championship Wrestling seemed like documentary footage of a bar fight. Even set alongside the NWA, which was physical and gritty, the old-school television production of WCCW made matches feel as if they emanated from a separate reality—our reality. WCCW wrestlers may have moved around in the same ways that the fake WWF wrestlers did, but late at night on the channel reserved for real sports, the danger felt so much more severe.

In 1982, the Von Erichs introduced us to Michael Hayes. With his dark beard growing out from under his blond mane and his profligate pelt of chest hair, he was a virile epiphany in juxtaposition to the nearly sexless crew of Von Erich Adonises. An issue of *Inside Wrestling* magazine had Kerry Von Erich and Hayes posed together, Kerry holding a quart of milk and Hayes holding a bottle of Jack Daniel's. The Von Erichs were more Chippendales than chick magnet, with their cool demeanors and waxed (and waxen) bodies—and their healthy contingent of older-female-demographic admirers didn't help them seem any cooler. They seemed like automatons built for princely virtue.

So perhaps it should have been obvious that someone as contrary to the Von Erich aesthetic as Hayes would turn on the brothers Von Erich. When he did, he imported a couple of his buddies to even the odds against David, Kerry, and Kevin (and Chris and Mike and Daddy Fritz). Those buddies were Buddy "Jack" Roberts[1] and Terry "Bam Bam" Gordy.

---

[1] Contrary to any sense of necessity, Roberts's nickname originated from his love of Jack Daniel's whiskey.

(Hayes himself appended the nickname "P.S.," which was unnecessarily short for "Purely Sexy.") Together they were called the Freebirds, and they came to the ring to the strains of the Lynyrd Skynyrd classic—they were the first wrestlers to use *rock 'n' roll* music to mark their entrance.[2] Previously there had been some other music-accompanied entrances, most notably Gorgeous George's use of "Pomp and Circumstance," but still, the vast majority of wrestlers entered only to the cheers or boos of the audience, and the use of anything remotely contemporary was a revelation. In short order, the Von Erichs all had intro music—Kerry's was famously "Tom Sawyer" by Rush—and then the WWF caught on, and the rest is history.

Set opposed to the wholesome Von Erich boys, the Freebirds served as the closest thing to polar opposites that any promoter could muster in those days: They were proud Southerners of the arch variety (contrary to the assumptions of most Northerners, every person who has lived in the South or in Texas can attest to the fact that those are two totally separate regions), unapologetically brash and crass, and, above all, human—in all its flawed glory. Even though they debuted as friends of the Von Erichs, they were never cut from the same cloth.

The precise moment of the Freebirds' apostasy came on Christmas night in 1982. Kerry Von Erich was facing NWA champion Ric Flair in a steel cage match, and the fans had selected Hayes to be the special referee. Hayes in turn brought his cohort Gordy to ringside, apparently to further skew the odds in Kerry's favor. As the match progressed, Hayes— taking his job very seriously that night—got physical with both wrestlers. He finally punched Ric Flair in the face and begged Kerry to pin Flair, who lay prone on the mat. Kerry, good citizen that he was, refused, and when Gordy opened the cage door to let Hayes leave, Kerry went to close it, and Flair shoved Hayes into Kerry. Gordy brutally slammed the cage door on Kerry's head, allowing Flair to get the win. The staging here was immaculate: Hayes was disgusted with Kerry, but he was inclined to

......................................................................................................

**2** The Memphis-based CWA territory, primarily because of Jerry "The King" Lawler's obsession with the music biz (he had once been a DJ), had used rock music in video packages and the like.

walk away; it was Gordy who took it upon himself to sever the Von Erich–Freebird friendship with a singular act of violence.

The Freebirds were immediately the biggest villains Texas had ever known, their turn signaling that no one was safe from the temptations of the dark side.

☆ ☆ ☆

Before any fan knew what was happening, the Freebird trio set about whaling on the Von Erichs with a tenacity unusual even in World Class, where grudge matches were the norm. The feud would span years. Hayes was the outrageous talker of the trio, Roberts its incorrigible, angsty pest, and Gordy was the monster, the scariest guy in every bar you've ever walked into. At 6-foot-4 and 300 pounds, he was the unapproachable id to Hayes's ego and Roberts's superego, the mountain of instinctual violence that defined the Freebirds as not simply an irritant but a diabolical force. That he was only twenty-one years old wasn't just beside the point; it was unthinkable. Compared to the other guys in WCCW, he was a leviathan, and compared to some of the other monsters roaming the territories in those days who could scarcely punch or kick in a believable way, Gordy was a more natural, believable combatant than even A. J. Liebling could compose.

But the fact of his youth is central to his biography even if it was negligible when he was on stage. He started wrestling at fourteen years old—trained by Archie Gouldie, a.k.a. the Mongolian Stomper[3]—and partnered up with the charismatic Hayes a few years later. The two started making their name in George Culkin's Mississippi promotion,[4] which was a

---

**3** Gouldie was a Canadian who had reigned as a heel in Stu Hart's Stampede Wrestling, and who found a second home in Knoxville, Tennessee, near Gordy's hometown of Chattanooga. Bret Hart once called him the best wrestler ever to come out of Canada.

**4** Hayes tells a story about their first brush with fame while working there, when Nick Bockwinkel and Bobby Heenan came to Jackson and scouted them: "Terry and I were so excited, because we were hoping finally somebody, outside of where we were at the time, somebody big, somebody that had made it, could see us, and see that we were young, we were good, and maybe we could get out of 'jail' here."

territory that had been part of Bill Watts's Mid-South empire until a blow-up with Culkin, who had been his state organizer, led to Culkin striking out on his own. When Watts reestablished himself as a power player in the state, he brought the Freebirds onto his tour. Watts was famously serious about his wrestlers being legitimate brawlers,[5] and it was probably that tendency that led him to decide that Hayes was more of a mouthpiece than a wrestler, so he joined Hayes and Gordy up with Roberts and situated Hayes as their functional manager. Upon leaving Mid-South, Hayes would return to regular ring action but maintain his role as the group's barker. With this tag team now a three-man unit, what evolved was a revolution in pro wrestling rule-bending: the "Freebird Rule," whereby three-man units could defend tag team titles with whichever two members it saw fit on a given night. It was a mostly nonsensical rule, but—as with the Ladd match years before—unfair fights made for great bad guys. The Freebirds could pick their most advantageous combo or leave the decision up in the air until the last minute to addle their opponents—and, more important, the crowd. In such situations, each Freebird filled a defined role—Hayes was the rock star, and as such the prime target for eventual comeuppance; Roberts was the workhorse, the best mat man of the bunch, the guy expected to spend the bulk of the match getting beaten upon; and Gordy was the brawler, the force of nature. With his presence and his youthful exuberance, Gordy was rarely the odd man out under the Freebird Rule.

His nickname may seem arbitrary compared to the pointed jokes inherent in those of his compatriots—Hayes was the playboy, Roberts was a real-life drinker—but I like to think that Gordy's wasn't just a measure of his tendency toward fisticuffs. Just like the late-run *Flintstones* character, he was at his very core a cartoon roughneck, the troupe's baby with a big stick. He was the overgrown kid with the bad attitude and the perpetually skinned knees. Those skinned knees would come to play as big a part in his career as anything else. The best wrestlers are archetypes,

........................................................................................

**5**   He encouraged his employees to get into bar fights to impress upon the public their legitimacy, and would, for appearance's sake, fire anybody who lost such a fight.

and many of them are well worn; Hayes and Roberts, despite the cha- risma of their specific presentations, were characters the wrestling world has seen many times over. But Gordy was unique in how he was at once "other" in his ridiculous size and yet also familiar. Despite his phys- ical presence, he was always just an overgrown schoolyard punk. And what a punk: In the ring with Kevin or Kerry Von Erich, he was fully monstrous and fully human all at once, the sad, injured Cyclops. Unlike the other leviathans of his era, he wasn't a foreign terror or a caricature from Parts Unknown; he was simply a dissatisfied kid with bad inten- tions. And unlike his partners, whose presence in those gritty brawls served mostly to signify recompense, Gordy personified the sort of wrath that most of us are blessed not to encounter with any frequency.

☆ ☆ ☆

Despite their celebrity in Dallas—their on-again, off-again home for many years—the Freebirds would never be tied down. They were among the last of the itinerant generation of Territorial baddies, and they also played in the major promotions with as much success as anyone else. They had noteworthy stints in the AWA (Minneapolis), Georgia Champi- onship Wrestling, and Jim Crockett Promotions—and a cup of coffee in the WWF during the Rock 'n' Wrestling Era.[6] When they returned to Watts's regime, now called the Universal Wrestling Federation, or UWF—rechristened in an attempt at competing in the new national federation world pioneered by Vince McMahon—they had the run of the place. While Roberts won the Television Title, Gordy won the Heavy- weight Championship and only lost it due to injury. When a real-life car wreck left him in uncertain health, an angle was booked wherein Gordy's arm was "broken" during a melee by "Dr. Death" Steve

---

6  The rumor is that McMahon was only interested in Hayes, and once that became clear, Hayes walked with his brethren.

Williams, and Gordy was forced to forfeit the belt to the monstrous One Man Gang.

☆ ☆ ☆

As with many American giants of his day, Gordy would eventually find work in Japan, where he was esteemed for his size and his hard-knocks style. In All Japan Pro Wrestling, owned by Japanese wrestling legend Giant Baba, he teamed up with Dr. Death—putting aside their UWF history, apparently—to form a tag team that was immaculately dubbed the "Miracle Violence Connection" (God bless rough Japanese translations into English). The two shaggy goliaths ran roughshod over the Japanese competition before they returned stateside as a duo, coming to WCW in 1992 and feuding with the Steiner Brothers (Rick and Scott)—the other most significant team of gaijin in the Japanese game—until WCW went into a copromotional agreement with New Japan, All Japan's rival fed, and Gordy and Williams left WCW in solidarity with their old boss Baba.

Somewhere around this time, Gordy's substance abuse issues grew to the point where his coworkers couldn't use words like *recreational* with a straight face. People tried to intervene, but Gordy wouldn't listen; he was a kid, he was a monster, he was indestructible. In 1993, during a plane flight to Japan, Gordy overdosed on painkillers and fell into a coma; he was hospitalized and suffered permanent brain damage. For most people—for most wrestlers, even—this would have ended a career. But for Gordy it was just another scraped knee.

He was soon back in the UWF with the Freebirds, though by this point Roberts had been replaced with Jimmy "Jam" Garvin, which formalized the group's turn from redneck brawlers to glam rockers, and Gordy was a bad fit for this new troupe. He rebelled, veering further in the direction of masochism, headlining in Extreme Championship Wrestling and competing in the grueling deathmatch circuit in Japan.

In 1996, he turned up in the WWF as the Executioner, a new player in the Undertaker-Mankind feud. He wore a mask—which was just as well, considering that he was a shadow of his former self and the gimmick was laughable—and carried an obviously plastic ax to the ring. Terry Gordy should have been competition for the Undertaker, but this was not the Terry Gordy we had been so scared of ten years before—this was Terry Mecca with a gut. When the Undertaker beat him in their "Armageddon Rules" match at the WWF's December '96 pay-per-view, it wasn't the start of a larger story; it was an overdue period at the end of Gordy's sentence. It was the end of Gordy's career. That he kept wrestling in small independent shows thereafter doesn't amount to much more than a depressing ellipsis.

Gordy died on July 16, 2001, from a heart attack brought on by a blood clot. He was forty years old. He was survived by Hayes and Roberts—who died in 2012—and by his son, Ray Gordy, who, like an oddly high number of other second-generation wrestlers, competed briefly as a white rapper.

It's an ignominious ending for such a leviathan, but then, humanity was always Gordy's calling card. His physical presence amounted to the first violent and real threat the Von Erich family encountered. His legend in Japan—the land of borderline shoot fighting and deathmatch gore—was one of incomparable physicality. So it's hard to look too sadly upon his later years, when the weight of humanity overtook the man—or, rather, the boy. Despite his size and his might, Terry Gordy never grew up. So maybe it's fitting that he never grew old.

# BRUISER BRODY

Not long before Bruiser Brody was killed in 1988, he gave a no-holds-barred interview on the state of wrestling and what goes on behind the scenes. He talked at length about his days producing the WCCW telecast. After the interviewer asked if anybody outside of the business knew that he had done that, Brody paused, mild consternation creasing his grotesquely scarred forehead. "I don't think it's good that anybody knows that I produced that show," he said. And then, suddenly remembering that he had said his real name earlier in the conversation: "I don't think it's good that anybody knows I'm Frank Goodish."

In 2009, somebody uploaded this video to YouTube, and thus pro wrestling had its Dead Sea Scrolls of postmodernism: the first "shoot interview."

To many in-the-know wrestling fans, the shoot interview inhabits a place of great significance in the appreciation of the sport. It's that rarest thing in the unreal world of pro wrestling: realness, raw and divorced from any narrative manipulations. According to A&E's documentary *The Unreal Story of Pro Wrestling*, the word *shoot* comes from the old carny term *straight shooter*, which referred to rifles on the sideshow shooting range that were not tampered with to work against their operator. Hence, just like a straight shooter, a wrestling shoot was (and is) a rare moment of honesty in an otherwise thoroughly gimmicked game.

Sometimes these shoots occur during a wrestling event, though the general rule of thumb in the wrestling world is that if you see something on TV, you were intended to see that thing. More often than not, shoots—in the form of shoot interviews—are conducted away from the wrestling world, usually by enterprising wrestling websites, and always feature an unemployed wrestler of some former eminence giving the real stories behind the wrestling storylines. What goes unsaid is that all personal recollection is by its nature subjective, and particularly in the world of pro wrestling, where unreality is the status quo, even honest recollection often serves a greater purpose of buttressing an industry frequently uneasy with its own illegitimacy.

Which is all to say that Bruiser Brody was the first wrestler to go on camera and discuss the behind-the-scenes realities of the wrestling world. It was fitting that Brody would be the guy to do it: In the Territorial Era, no one straddled the line of vicious realism and outright fantasy more fully.

☆ ☆ ☆

Frank Goodish was a college football player at Iowa State and later at West Texas State, the latter of which churned out wrestlers in those days the way that gamma rays produced comic book superheroes: Tully Blanchard, Ted DiBiase, Manny Fernandez, Dory and Terry Funk, Stan

Hansen, Dusty Rhodes, Tito Santana, and Barry Windham were all alums. (Maurice Cheeks and Georgia O'Keeffe went there too, for the record.) Goodish had a cup of coffee with the Redskins and a brief tour in the CFL before he was discovered by Texas wrestling mogul (and fellow Texas college footballer) Fritz Von Erich. He had successful runs through a few of the regional territories until Vince McMahon Sr. brought him in and renamed him "Bruiser" Frank Brody. "Frank" soon went by the wayside. Bruiser Brody was a legend from the moment he came into existence. He was huge; he sported a feral black mane; he fought viciously. In the ring he seemed near lunatic, but in interviews he was shockingly coherent, his growl often bordering on eloquence. Which made him all the more frightening—like, wow, this guy has made a logical and empirically sound decision to dismember somebody.

The monster heel was a central figure in the Territorial Era. The top good guy in a region usually stayed at home as the promotion's mainstay, and certainly there were some baddies who stuck around as ongoing foils. But to compel audiences—to make them believe that their hero had a chance of losing—foes were imported from other regions and billed as top-notch competition. With the advent of television, the tone shifted from athletic competition toward the mythological epic. The imports went from storied grapplers to grotesque beasts more suited for a nightmare than a gymnasium. Brody was a transient leviathan of this latter sort. Before long, he was a scoundrel in high demand across the country. He epitomized the wanderlust—and economic model—of the period better than anyone (with the possible exception of his longtime rival Abdullah the Butcher), traveling from Central States Wrestling to Windy City Wrestling to San Juan's World Wrestling Council, hardly staying in any place long enough to get comfortable.

In a run back in Von Erich's WCCW, Brody split with his on-screen manager Gary Hart and took his first turn as a good guy, and from there the Bruiser Brody legend only grew. He kept touring, running the road just like he always had, but now he could split his time between the roles of monster villain and godlike babyface. He wasn't exactly a ring technician, but he was an imposing figure and one of the best in-ring storytellers of all time. He could get a near-epic match out of just about anybody he wrestled, and that list of opponents reads like the index in the *Iliad*: Sammartino, Flair, Bockwinkel, McDaniel, Dick the Bruiser, Jerry Blackwell. Whereas most monster wrestlers of that era were mythic beasts whose opponents were made legend by defeating him, Brody was both beast and poet: He wrote the epics in which he featured. He could turn any night at the wrestling show into a major event.

☆ ☆ ☆

The earliest grunts of the hardcore wrestling movement began at mid-century as the facade of the sport started cracking and promoters looked for new ways to establish the grimness, the realness of the fights. And so came gimmick matches—street fights, bullrope matches, steel cage matches—and more or less parallel with those came the earliest instances of intentional bleeding in matches. The first hardcore star of note was Bull Curry (né Fred Koury), a Lebanese American who started out as a toughman on the carnival circuit, started wrestling in the ring in Detroit in the late '30s, and took his act to Texas in the '50s. With his unibrow and lunatic expressions, Curry was as wild-looking as he was wild in the ring, where he commonly employed steel chairs, brass knuckles, and, at least once, a cinder block to fell his opponents. (Although he was a good wrestler, he wasn't as creative with his moveset as he was with his plunder; Wikipedia lists his finishing move as the "punch to the face.") He was roundly despised by the crowd and was famous for causing riots among the morally outraged audience. It was a quandary considered by Roland Barthes—whither the gall of the villain who places himself "outside the rules of society? Essentially someone unstable, who accepts the rules only when they are useful to him and transgresses the formal continuity of attitudes. He is unpredictable, therefore asocial. He takes refuge behind the law when he considers that it is in his favor, and breaks it when he finds it useful to do so." Curry left not just carnage in his wake but also the institution thereof: After he rose to fame in Detroit, the hardcore style was institutionalized by promoter-star Ed "The Sheik"

Farhat, and in Texas a Brass Knuckles Championship was created expressly for Curry. Many others there would hold the title over the years, establishing the brawling style as a Texas favorite for decades thereafter. Soon the rough-and-tumble style was being featured throughout the South and on the West Coast, and in Japan and Puerto Rico.

Once he (and his brutality) became established, Brody toured the no-holds-barred-loving regions of the country and the world, overlapping with a loose troupe of the early purveyors of the modern hardcore style like Abdullah, the (original, aforementioned) Sheik, and the Funk brothers. Brody, less horrifying and less an eyesore than most of these compatriots, found himself repeatedly used as the monster slayer, the fan favorite against a cadre of fellows like Kamala the Ugandan Giant, the One Man Gang, and, most famously, Abdullah. Once Brody and Abdullah started feuding, they could hardly be stopped, territorial separation and ring parameters be damned; one wonders if it was a matter of chemistry or simple physics—gravity bringing and holding the two great masses together. They battled across the country and world, their hatred seemingly unconfined by regional storylines and unmoored from traditional wrestling unreality. Wherever one of them went, the other was likely to follow, as was carnage.

They had one particularly memorable match in February 1987 in San Juan.[1] It was at Hiram Bithorn Stadium, a baseball park; the stands were filled, and the infield was a pulsing mass of fans moving organically to let the wrestlers into and out of the ring. For their part, Brody and Abdullah hardly acknowledged the ring at all.

When the only existing video of the fight picks up, they're already brawling in the crowd, hitting each other with the folding chairs set up as infield seating. Brody looks as if he's already bleeding. The crowd is cheering relentlessly, unremittingly, and yet they're giving Abdullah and Brody space, clearing away from a fake fight to let the two combatants perform. It's not a fear of either man so much as it is a fear

----

1 With its proximity to the United States, Puerto Rico has long imported American talent to amplify its bigger shows.

of becoming collateral damage. When the wrestlers are momentarily separated, the crowd uneasily orbits a bewildered-looking Abdullah, and a mob of zealous boys gathers around Brody as he clutches his bloodied eye, as if to will him back into battle.

Back in the ring, Brody removes his furry boot to use as a weapon, revealing underneath a simple striped tube sock: the Norse god in a simple act of violence becoming an average Joe—and, moreover, an admission of galling humanity. His violence is a choice, which is why it's a worthy spectacle. By the time he and Abdullah venture back into the crowd, they're both near blind with blood. The camerawork—which was shockingly competent through the first half of their melee—loses track of them almost instantly and doesn't fully find them again for three or four minutes. It's a blurry, grotesque, confusing mess, the two brawlers passing in and out of range and focus like so many legends before them: It's one part Bigfoot sighting and one part snuff film. Finally they collide in the middle of the crowd and are knocked in separate directions. One expects them to reengage, but they don't. The two behemoths stagger back inexplicably to whence they came—the depths of the sea, the fires of hell, the dressing room, a hotel in north San Juan. That's the whole fight. Or rather, that's the whole chapter. The story doesn't end because the story never ends. Theirs isn't a match; it's a mythology.

☆ ☆ ☆

Brody, ever looking to find use for his mind in a persistently physical world, went back to Texas to become the booker for WCCW. (He soon brought his nemesis Abdullah to join him.) That's when he gave the interview that has since been immortalized online. In broad terms, it was a plain violation of kayfabe, the law that ruled the wrestling world from its earliest carny days until the Modern Era, holding that the artifice of wrestling must be upheld at all costs, even in the face of audience skepticism: Good guys and bad guys couldn't be seen together in public, and the inner workings of the game were never divulged to the uninitiated. More particularly, Brody's interview was a direct affront to Fritz Von Erich and WCCW, but that was no surprise; Brody made a habit through his career of alienating the promoters he worked for. There were disputes over money and billing and over his usage, but all of the grievances likely stemmed from Brody feeling that he was smarter than the guys he was working for. He was probably right.

☆ ☆ ☆

During a brief tour back in Puerto Rico the next year (1988), he was repeatedly stabbed by fellow wrestler Jose Gonzalez (a.k.a. Invader I)—a close confidant of World Wrestling Council promoter and star Carlos Colon—while having a "business discussion" in the shower. They had been arguing over something—nobody knows what—and had moved the conversation to the showers for privacy. A wrestler named Dutch Mantel[2] who was there wrestling on the same card tells the story:

> We all heard a scream, and [through the frosted glass shower wall] saw someone's hand with a knife go into a bigger guy. Gonzalez ran out a secret hideaway in the back and we all ran in and I knew it was pretty bad. Brody's main chest wound had blood that was bubbling— so I figured his lung had been sliced open. He kept asking Tony [Atlas] to take care of his wife and kid. He knew he was dying, but could talk. It took well over an hour just to get an ambulance there, and it was a Mickey Mouse one at that. . . . I called Mrs. Goodish and told her she better come down a few hours before he died, that the rumors she heard were true. Abby met her at the airport as he was boarding a plane home for the U.S., and told her the news.

Brody had died in the hospital the day after his stabbing. The "Abby" in that story—the man tasked with delivering the news of Brody's death to his wife—is none other than Abdullah the Butcher, the man who in and out of the ring tried to kill Brody over and over again, in probably every major city in America.

Gonzalez was charged with murder, but the charges were reduced before trial, and neither Mantel nor Atlas nor any other American

---

2  Who's presently appearing in WWE as Zeb Colter.

wrestler on hand that night was brought back to San Juan to testify. (Mantel says his court summons wasn't mailed until after the trial had occurred.) Gonzalez claimed to have been acting in self-defense, and after Colon, a local hero without equal, testified in his defense, Gonzalez was acquitted.

☆　☆　☆

If you go back and watch the endless string of Brody-Abdullah matches, you can see that they were doing something magical, bringing together two forces in a brutal chemistry. Watch Brody against other people, and you start to see the real element of fear that he inspired. Brody could make you believe, if for a brief moment, that the danger was real. Partly it was his violence, his stiffness, his otherness, but mostly it was the look on the faces of his opponents, who, in their unguarded moments, so often seemed to be trying desperately to get away.

Wrestling's fake fighting has to look "real" in a really unreal way; a certain hamminess is required to meet an audience's expectations of what a fight should look like. It's a little like how Hollywood audiences became so accustomed to stylized movie fights that, after a while, the least-believable punches were the ones *without* all the editing and sound effects. In movie fights and in the wrestling ring, realism looks weird, a little off. But in an artist's hands, it can be terrifying.

Brody was a purveyor of an oddly specific sort of realism that wouldn't quite be suited for the modern wrestling world. He was a legend tethered to a fleeting era and a fleeting concept of violence—a violence so real that it ended up reality.

# THE CHIEFS: WAHOO McDANIEL AND JAY STRONGBOW

On the March 7, 1994, broadcast of *WWF Monday Night Raw*, an up-and-coming Native American wrestler named Tatanka was presented with the "Sacred Feathers" of a vague Native Americana by two legendary wrestlers of a bygone era: Chief Jay Strongbow and Chief Wahoo McDaniel.[1] It was a none-too-subtle passing of the torch from

---

1   McDaniel's name was misspelled as "McDaniels" in the on-screen Chyron, a perhaps deliberate pluralization that called back to the fact that his name was often misspelled during his career.

one generation's Native superstars to the next. But to the wrestling fans who knew McDaniel or Strongbow from their heyday, the comparison seemed almost an insult: Headdresses and war paint aside, these were two of the greatest stars of the Territorial Era, two men who overcame potentially cartoonish characters to achieve mainstream greatness; Tatanka, for all his success in the WWF, always seemed too preoccupied with living up to the caricature to overcome anything at all. Strongbow and McDaniel were certainly aware of this as they stood there, rumpled and complacent, halfheartedly engaged, like, well, two cigar store Indians. Their reward after years of legendary exploits was to be the cartoon characters that they had deconstructed during their careers.

☆ ☆ ☆

Note that I said "McDaniel *or* Strongbow" deliberately. Professional wrestling fans who grew up in the '70s generally come in one of two varieties: those who grew up with Big Chief Wahoo McDaniel and those who grew up with Chief Jay Strongbow. Their timelines don't exactly line up, but their territories were mostly distinct and their roles largely similar. You can count me among the former group—which isn't to say that I lack respect for Strongbow, né Joe Scarpa. He was a near giant in the Golden Age of New York wrestling, an icon of an evolving American identity. But his comparison to McDaniel is telling.

Ed McDaniel wasn't a full-blooded Native American ("My father was one-sixteenth Choctaw and one-sixteenth Chickasaw," he once said. "My mother was German. So you can do the math and determine what that makes me"), but his father identified as such; it was actually his dad who was called "Big Chief Wahoo" when Ed was growing up. After they moved from small-town Oklahoma to Texas, the Big Chief told his son tales about the mighty Native American Jim Thorpe, and Ed caught the sports bug. He was purportedly a standout decathlete himself until his ineptitude at the pole vault scuttled his Olympic dreams. He found a place for himself on the gridiron, though, and he would go on to play football for the Oklahoma Sooners, and the Oilers, Broncos, and Jets of the AFL—making him that most treasured sort of pro wrestler: the professional athlete convert. Moreover, he was a legit tough guy—stories abound, like the time he beat up two cops one drunken night, which got him traded to the Chargers.

The sports pages were likewise full of McDaniel mythmaking once he found a place on the New York Jets squad and got his first taste of fame. He was serenaded on several occasions by *Sports Illustrated*, the first time being in his Jets heyday, by Bud Shrake, who put it beautifully: "While the public address system was still booming his name, the chant began: 'Wahoo! Wahoo! Wahoo!' It was as if 50,000 people had sat on lighted cigarettes at the same instant." The fans adopted Wahoo as their favorite because of his energy and passion, and because of the catchy nickname that he had boldly had stitched on his shoulders in place of "McDaniel."[2] He enjoyed the fame, but the real upside, as Shrake notes, is that being famous meant he could charge more money for his off-season job: being a professional wrestler.

He started out in 1961—early in his pro football career—when a promoter[3] needed a Native American wrestler for a show in Indianapolis, and Wahoo took to the wrestling craft as surely as he had taken years earlier to decathlon and football. Training with Dory Funk, he developed such stereotypical moveset standards as the Indian Death Lock and the Tomahawk Chop. By 1966 he was making more money from wrestling than from playing pro football.

He was a huge draw throughout the Southern and Southwestern territories, claiming championship gold in Georgia, Texas, Florida, and, most notably, in Mid-Atlantic, where he would spark a feud with U.S. Champion Johnny Valentine. In 1975, Valentine was in an airplane crash

......................................................................

**2** The jersey name rules in the AFL were much looser than in the NFL.

**3** It was Jim Barnett, who was a part-owner of Georgia Championship Wrestling and a broker of the sale of the WWF's Saturday night TBS timeslot to the Crocketts, though history here is as hazy as ever; there's also records of him wrestling for Dory Funk in Amarillo a year before.

along with promoter David Crockett and wrestlers Tim "Mr. Wrestling" Woods, Bobby Bruggers, and a young upstart named Ric Flair, who had been teaming with Valentine. Valentine's career was over, and Flair broke his back in the crash and was told he'd never wrestle again. Wahoo was one of the first people to visit him in the hospital, and when Flair made a miraculous comeback the next year, Wahoo greeted him in the ring; the two had a brawl that spilled outside the ring, destroying a ringside table, and when Flair grabbed a broken table leg and swung it, Wahoo was left with a gash by his eye that took forty stitches to close.

From Shrake's piece: "'He has an Indian stoicism toward pain,' said Cowboy Trainer Clint Houy."

That sort of quote attended Wahoo throughout his career. As a kid, he had been uncomfortable with his heritage, but by adulthood, McDaniel had embraced the stereotype with subversive aplomb. His affect was almost comical, but the seriousness with which he approached his craft—and the brutality with which he dealt with his opponents—balanced the crass iconography with a grim pride. He wore the headdress—and fought in defense of its honor—but he stayed away from the halting movie-Indian speech that other Native wrestlers adopted. Wahoo might have been wearing leather fringe, but his roughness in the ring and outside of it was a challenge to any wrestler or any fan to see him as anything less than unique.

McDaniel took on top heels—and sometimes the top babyfaces—wherever he traveled: Harley Race in Florida, Tully Blanchard in Texas, Nick Bockwinkel in the AWA—even Roddy Piper when Wahoo returned to Mid-Atlantic, plus other luminaries from around the country like Sgt. Slaughter, Curt Hennig, Jerry Lawler, Rick Rude, Jimmy Garvin, and Larry Zbyszko. His matches were bloody affairs, the feuds often culminating in "Indian Strap Matches" wherein he and his rival would be tied together with a leather strap—another case of him taking a bit of cartoon prejudice and undermining it through sheer force of violence. While other Indians in pop culture were doing rain dances, McDaniel was drawing blood.

☆ ☆ ☆

At the same time that Wahoo was working his way through the territories in Texas, Mid-South, and the AWA, Chief Jay Strongbow was a headline attraction in Vince McMahon Sr.'s WWWF.[4] (McDaniel wrestled there too, but Strongbow was the regional mainstay.) In contrast to McDaniel's Native American heritage, Strongbow's ethnicity was largely a contrivance. He had started his career in the South under his real name, as "Joltin'" Joe Scarpa. He won some titles but made little lasting impact; it was only after being recruited to the Northeast and repackaged as a Native American that he became legend. It was an age of both racial stereotype and broad-stroke ethnic tribalism; guys like Pedro Morales and Bruno Sammartino and Spiros Arion were icons in New York's Hispanic and Italian and Greek communities, respectively, whereas foils like Mr. Fuji and the Iron Sheik were villains in straight Hollywood fashion. But suffice it to say that their ethnicity painted them as evildoers not so much because of geopolitics as economics; if there had been paying Japanese or Iranian fans clamoring for tickets, McMahon almost certainly would have painted their ethnic champions with more nuance. (Later, Vince McMahon *fils* would follow his father's rubric closely. Every star of the '80s WWF represented a stark ethnic or geographical group.)

Into this world of screwball diversity came Jay Strongbow, the Italian in chief's clothing. A few outlets indicate that Scarpa's mother was Cherokee, but I haven't seen that stated anywhere conclusively, and it sounds rather like the sort of story a wrestler would tell to embellish his backstory; regardless, it's significant that Scarpa's previous in-ring incarnation had no Cherokee affectation—or acknowledgment—at all. Scarpa was born in Philadelphia, but Strongbow would be from Pawhuska, Oklahoma (which, at least, is an actual place). Scarpa himself said fairly explicitly that the Indian persona was nothing more than a role: "A gimmick is what you make out of it. Saying you're a pilot doesn't mean you

---

**4** As far as I can tell, the two chiefs never crossed paths in New York, but McDaniel and Joe Scarpa were occasional partners years earlier in Florida.

can fly a plane. You have to learn to fly the plane as well. Same with the Indian gimmick." Or as somebody else put it, "All the world's a stage, and all the men and women merely players."

It's not likely that many fans recognized Strongbow from his previous wrestling existence, as the distance was too great for any real cross-pollination of pro wrestling fandom. And there was no reason for his ethnic legitimacy to be called into question. If he looked Indian enough to the average fan, consider that he was duskier than many of the men who played Natives in Hollywood at that time. And Scarpa was working at some distance from his audience; from the eighteenth row, anybody with headdress, black hair, and schnoz would pass muster. Scarpa fit the bill.

Unlike the other ethnic groups portrayed positively in the WWWF in those days, there wasn't exactly a Native American fanbase awaiting his arrival, but that wouldn't mean he would be painted as a heel. With a predominantly white audience whooping their "Indian war cries" in support, Strongbow was a fan favorite from the start. Of course this was storytelling, but it can also be seen as an emerging sociopolitical recalibration; the Indian-as-villain trend had finally met its match in pop culture with the ascendance of the Indian-as-American-hero iconographical meme, though it's debatable whether a positive stereotype is all that much better than a negative one. It was a pathos of uniquely American tribalism and burgeoning liberal apologia. Just as black performers like Junkyard Dog were becoming fan favorites seemingly in spite of their race, Strongbow was being embraced strictly because of his.

His feud with "Superstar" Billy Graham—the later vintage, evil-karate-enthusiast version—had echoes of Graham's earlier battles with Wahoo McDaniel in the AWA, but it's significant that Strongbow wasn't strictly a cartoon, not any more than was Graham or anyone else on the roster. Though so much of his presentation was based in caricature—and though the usually restrained commentator Gorilla Monsoon (who once teamed with Strongbow) couldn't resist saying things like "This is gonna be another great big feather in that bonnet that he wears if he can get a victory over 'Superstar' Billy Graham"—he was operating in a world of stereotype, of outsize mythic symbolism and representational politics. And Scarpa was a great performer.

In some quarters, Strongbow is purported (incorrectly) to have invented the sleeper hold, but he did nearly as much as McDaniel to popularize such stereotypical offensives as the Tomahawk Chop and the Indian Death Lock, a leg-lock in the figure-four family that was adopted by other mat technicians over time, such as Harley Race and Chris Benoit. His Tribal War Dance—the pain-shrugging preamble to the in-ring endgame—was the direct forebear of Hulk Hogan's "Hulking Up."

He epitomized the duality of the pro wrestling world as well as anybody of that time—outside of McDaniel: His feuds were cartoonish on the one hand and alarmingly violent on the other. He also was a notorious bleeder, being at various times busted open by villainous manager Captain Lou Albano (with a cast, with a trophy) and by any number of brass-knuckles-wielding baddies. When he eventually left WWWF for a time and traveled the territorial trail where McDaniel had gone before, he often worked a program wherein he would be attacked by the territory's top heel and respond with a particularly vicious version of his sleeper hold. In Georgia Championship Wrestling—which aired on TBS and was the precursor, more or less, to WCW—Strongbow debuted to much acclaim and was immediately thrust into a violent feud with "Big Cat" Ernie Ladd, with whom he had previously tangled in WWWF.

In his later days, Strongbow would invest more fully in the tag team scene, an arena even more prone to ethnic generalization than was the singles division. In the early days, his grandeur was such that he was set alongside such literally/metaphorically enormous protagonists as the aforementioned Monsoon and Andre the Giant. But now he would partner with Sonny King to take the tag team titles from "Baron" Mikel Scicluna and "King" Curtis Iaukea, before they lost the belts to dastardly Orientals Mr. Fuji and "Professor" Toru Tanaka. His second tag title win was with partner Billy White Wolf, another on-screen Indian who was actually an Iraqi wrestler who would go on to some renown as Arab menace Sheik Adnan Al-Kaissie and later, during the infamous anti-American turn of Sgt. Slaughter, as his ostensible spiritual adviser,

General Adnan. Strongbow later formed a more long-lasting duo with his "brother" Jules Strongbow to take on such foreign menaces as Mr. Fuji and Mr. Saito and, perhaps most poignantly, a new breed of untamed native being amalgamated into the American ethnic experiment: the Wild Samoans, Afa and Sika.

☆ ☆ ☆

It is probably to the benefit of Native American pop-cultural portrayal that the Polynesian populace emerged as a new witch-doctory substratum, and it's unfortunate for their replacements that thereupon the American expansion project more or less ended, and so the Samoan caricature is still to this day employed in pro wrestling circles as a race of unhinged prehistorics. (Their numbers, though, do include the success stories of those who escaped from the island's ghetto: Yokozuna, the fake Japanese sumo, was Samoan, as is the Rock, on his mother's side.)

This is the wrestling world in those days in a nutshell, though: If you were memorable at all, it was as either a transcendent star or an offensive caricature. It was the rare wrestler who could be retrofitted into a broad stereotype and be transcendent to boot. Wahoo McDaniel and Jay Strongbow were of this scarce breed.

In a sense, Strongbow's racial inexactitude and McDaniel's widespread success despite his overassociation with his ancestry were fitting; they were symbolic of an increasingly politically unsegregated America—a country where, despite continuing institutional racism toward African Americans (and segregationist policies toward Native Americans), the definition of "whiteness" was expanding rapidly to encompass the previously dispossessed Irishmen, Italians, and Eastern Europeans. If Native Americans weren't exactly part of this suffrage movement, their adoption as part of American iconography is perhaps symptomatic of an increasingly open-armed (or guilt-ridden) America.

Neither character was politically correct, but then neither was particularly political. The Native American throughout American pop culture was a sort of egocentric parody, a sagacious mascot meant to rewrite our nation's lineage through crass appropriation. To an extent, it worked. The types that Strongbow and McDaniel played weren't noble savages condescendingly celebrated, but they were both noble and savage, and widely adored in a real, concrete way. White kids looked up to them just like McDaniel had looked up to Jim Thorpe all those years earlier. But they weren't icons by virtue of their achievement; their achievement was dictated by their unequivocal iconography.

☆ ☆ ☆

Toward the end of his life, McDaniel was profiled lovingly (again in *Sports Illustrated*) by Mike Shropshire: "Wahoo McDaniel," the piece begins, "staggers as he attempts to negotiate the step up from the dining room into his kitchen."[5] It was a humanization of a lifelong demigod. Even his wrestling-world cohorts lived in awe of him—really, there's no other way to put it—both as an athlete and as a man. Even when he was alive, legends like Ric Flair and Dusty Rhodes would get nearly misty-eyed in simple recollection of Wahoo's sense of humor or galling physicality.

It may not be possible to recount the facts of McDaniel's life without hyperbole, but they're grounded in memory: that his Little League team was coached by future president George Herbert Walker Bush,[6] or the time he ran thirty-six miles in six hours on a hundred-dollar bet, or the time he ate a vat of jalapeño peppers, or the time he and Flair wrestled 180 times in one year.[7]

But Strongbow's life history is shrouded in uncertainty. Just as with the imprecision of his mother's ethnic origin, so much else about Strongbow is only vaguely recorded. Upon his death, mainstream outlets restated his life with heretical imprecision; *The New York Times*, of all places, says that he was "*at least* 6 feet tall" and "*about* 250 pounds" (italics mine) and either seventy-nine or eighty-three years old—a fact that

---

5   Shropshire later eulogized him when he died in 2002.

6   This is true, actually.

7   This could well be true too.

one would think could be established more or less definitively. That's fitting, though; for the man who lived the lie so fully, so much reality is subsumed by fantasy. And so it goes with the Native American tradition in America, swallowed up whole by the American mainstream, real history no match for the coarse simplicity of pop culture.

The only intercession of reality into the Chief Wahoo mythos was human mortality. In a telephone interview with *Slam! Sports* McDaniel grapples with the early deaths that had befallen so many of his wrestling colleagues. "I'm telling you, there's been so many of them gone and died. A lot of my buddies have died," McDaniel said. "It just seems like when all of them get over 55, between 55 and 60, it seems like 'boom!', they're gone. I don't know what it is." He died a few years later of liver failure.

☆ ☆ ☆

When Strongbow and McDaniel stood in the ring that night to anoint Tatanka, it was as if a rift in the pro wrestling space-time continuum had opened up, allowing these two mirror-image men to inhabit the same space at once. McDaniel looked ill at ease, but it's unclear whether that was due to his failing health or his discomfort with the sketch's tone, the sort he had bled so much to overcome in his career. Strongbow, though, was always at home in the WWF ring.

After he retired from active duty, he worked backstage as a WWF booker and was beloved by the next generation of wrestlers. He was a mentor to superstars including Hulk Hogan and Bret Hart. His most obvious protégé, of course, was Tatanka—real name: Chris Chavis—who was, it should be said, actually of the American Indian Lumbee tribe. Because, in the oddball world of pro wrestling, who better than a fake Native American to teach a real one how to act? As Scarpa said himself, one gimmick's not any different than any other.

# THE SPOILER:
## ANATOMY OF A CHARACTER ACTOR

The Territorial Era is filled not just with men in character but also men under literal masks: plain men who took to anonymity as a means of creating an aura of mystery or—more often than not—fear. The wrestling world has had its fair share of monsters, of ambiguously alien menaces, but nothing engenders in the audience such a direct response of loathing as the masked man. Perhaps it's because the crowd knows the cue, knows the trope, and so knows they're supposed to despise the disguised wrestler. Or perhaps it's because, contra to the foreign wrestler or the monster heel, the fans know that, underneath the mask, he's just a man, a human like you or me, and to see him act out such measures of villainy—that's what's really scary.

The first masked wrestler was likely a Frenchman named Theobaud Bauer who appeared, rather uncreatively, as the "Masked

Wrestler" on the European circus circuit as early as the 1860s. (Bauer was also one of the pioneers of the man vs. bear match.) The first time a masked man made waves in America was in 1915, when a multinight international wrestling tournament was disrupted by the appearance of the "Masked Marvel," a large hooded fellow who was sitting ominously in the audience and trumpeted by a manager who claimed he had been wrongly excluded from the card. The audience's interest was piqued, and soon the Marvel had joined the tournament. (It was all staged, of course, and he had been on the payroll all along.) It's a testament to the degree to which wrestling was taken seriously that at least two newspapers, *The New York World* and *The Day*, publicly identified the Marvel as Mort Henderson before the tournament was over. In the end, Gotch felled the Masked Marvel and won the tournament, but not before the enormous money-drawing potential of the mysterious masked villain was established.

Nobody embodied the masked nasty better than the Spoiler.

Don Jardine started his career in Canada as a straightforward babyface. Really—his ring name was "Babyface" Jardine. "Hey!" one imagines him shouting, desperate to get the fans' attention. "Likable vanilla good guy over here!" It's interesting that a guy like Jardine, who was big (6-foot-5 and nearly 300 pounds) and remarkably skilled in the ring, had to be packaged so artlessly. But while some might look at Jardine's first persona and see a failure of creativity, it was only the first in a long line of simplistic, classical character types that Jardine would excel with through his career.

Five years later he debuted in Los Angeles, sporting a heavy black beard, as Butcher Jardine. On a trip through Texas, promoter Fritz Von Erich would put him under a mask and dub him the Spoiler. And the crowd, presumably, went wild. Soon he was back in California, wrestling in San Francisco under a mask as the Masked Enforcer #2.

It turns out Jardine preferred the anonymity that the mask could provide: "At least I could go on the streets and not have idiot fans calling me nasty names." Under the mask, he played the Super

Destroyer in Mid-Atlantic in the early '70s and in the AWA in the latter part of the decade.

Along the way, Jardine would occasionally bring in tag team partners—among them were Ron Starr, Paul Vachon, Verne Siebert, Bobby Duncum, and Buddy Wolfe—who invariably wore identical masks and went by the name "Spoiler #2." (In such instances, Jardine likewise appended "#1" to his name.)

In the '80s, the Spoiler wrestled in Memphis's CWA and again in the AWA. But it wasn't Jardine—it was a journeyman named Frank Morrell. That's the peril of anonymity in pro wrestling: When the world's a fantasy and your face is under a mask, everybody knows you, but nobody knows who you are.

# THE
★ WRESTLEMANIA ★
# ERA

On December 27, 1983, at a taping in St. Louis, Missouri, a tubby middle-aged guy named Bill Dixon climbed into the ring. Dixon was a jobber[1] and fully looked the part, with his less-than-stylish goatee and moppy helmet of hair that stuck out so far from his head that it made him appear cartoonishly frightened to be there. That night, his fear could have been forgiven: His opponent was a statuesque, mahogany-tanned blond named Hulk Hogan.

This was the day that professional wrestling in its modern form began to take root.

☆ ☆ ☆

In 1982, Vincent K. McMahon—referred to hereafter as just "Vince"—took control of the WWF from his father. Since he had first met his father at the age of twelve (Vince *père* had left the family when his son was an infant), Vince had dreamed of being part of the wrestling business; after graduating from college, he formally joined the WWWF and climbed the ranks over the next decade, working as both an announcer—a job he would maintain in various forms until 1997—and a promoter, first starting off in a small-time Maine operation and working his way up to an influential role within the company's brain trust alongside old-time New York–area matchmaker Toots Mondt and monstrous wrestler turned avuncular announcer Gorilla Monsoon.

With Vince ensconced in the power structure, certain changes to the promotion's format started becoming evident: The name, for one, was shortened from the WWWF to the WWF, and there was a subtle shift

--------------------------------------------------

1   Industry parlance for guys whose entire job is to lose, night after night.

toward showbiz over substance in the in-ring product. The year 1975 saw the debut of "Superstar" Billy Graham, a performer so sui generis in his impact on today's stars that it's hard to comprehend how alien he would have seemed in the mid-'70s in a territory that had been dominated for almost a decade by Italian super-everyman Bruno Sammartino—the latest in a long line of ethnic stars in the immigrant-centric New York territory hierarchy—since he beat Buddy Rogers for the title soon after the WWWF seceded from the NWA. Graham was something entirely new: a jive-talking, tie-dye-wearing, bleached-blond bruiser whose wrestling prowess was minimal but whose physique was closer to his old workout buddy Arnold Schwarzenegger's than Lou Thesz's. When Graham won the heavyweight title from Sammartino on April 30, 1977, it was a triumph for the new breed of chemically enhanced grapplers; that he went on to hold the title for 296 days was a paradigm shift in the way the pro wrestling world told stories. It was at that point the longest reign ever by a bad guy in the WWF, and a larger anomaly in a sport where long reigns by heroes were the norm; villains were largely props used for the glorification of a babyface. Graham's reign institutionalized the role of the dominant heel in the New York region and, moreover, created the persona of the "cool" heel, the bad guy whom some fans loved to hate and whom others just loved, full stop. Before Graham, it had been assumed that guys who looked like him—steroidally muscled, flamboyantly dressed—could only be positioned as villains, while the heroes were mostly cast in the image of the common man. Graham eventually would lose the title in February 1978 to a corn-fed regular Joe named Bob Backlund, but the experiment had proved a success. It would inform the younger McMahon's wrestling vision over the rest of his career.

☆ ☆ ☆

In 1982, when Vince took over the WWF, he set about a plan of national domination, territorial system be damned. The popular version of the story is that Vince Sr.—who died in 1984—would have rolled over in his grave had he known about Vince's visions of Manifest Destiny; this is not really borne out by the timeline or the facts, and is likely a simultaneous effort to preserve Vince Sr.'s reputation and to create the legend of Vince Jr. the Visionary.

One thing Vince did do that went against his father's judgment, though, was to rehire Hulk Hogan. Hogan had worked in the WWWF in 1979 and '80, as a bad guy.[2] When Hogan got cast in *Rocky III*, he had a falling-out with Vince Sr., who supposedly felt that the role would call into question wrestling's legitimacy. So Hogan left for the AWA, where, capitalizing on his Hollywood celebrity, he worked as a hero, and where he struggled in vain for the championship, which was held (in storyline terms) by old-school baddie Nick Bockwinkel; in real-world terms, AWA owner Verne Gagne either didn't think Hogan was championship material or didn't think he needed to put the belt on him just yet, depending on who you listen to.

Either way, what's indisputable is that Hogan felt underappreciated despite incredible fan support, and when Vince Jr. came calling, Hogan was eager to be snatched away. His debut on that 1983 card in St. Louis against the forgotten Bill Dixon wasn't just a homecoming; it was the start of a new era.

The match was taped and aired a week later on local television as an episode of *Wrestling at the Chase*, the flagship television program of Sam Muchnick's midwestern wrestling empire. In fact, the twenty-four-year run of *Wrestling at the Chase* had ended four months prior, and this was the first installment of a new iteration, put on by McMahon's WWF. Much in the same way that Vince had tried to expand into the South by swallowing up Georgia Championship Wrestling's Saturday night TBS timeslot, Vince's earliest scheme for national expansion clearly was not so much a model of revolution as it was built on the idea of usurping existing wrestling institutions.

......................................................................................................

2   The "Hulk" moniker came from his days in the Memphis territory, when he appeared on a talk show with Lou Ferrigno and, as the host pointed out, dwarfed him; Vince Sr. gave him the Irish surname as part of his determination that every wrestler should have a discernible ethnic background.

Not only was it an affront to the ethos of the territorial system for the WWF to be running a show in St. Louis, but McMahon himself was announcing that card[3] alongside "Mean" Gene Okerlund, who would become famous as an interviewer in the WWF but who, like Hogan, had just been stolen away from the AWA. There was an industry-wide stigma against stealing talent from other promotions, and if the talent themselves decided to leave, they were expected to stick around long enough to finish out their storylines. More often then not, this entailed losing in humiliating fashion on the way out the door. Neither Hogan nor Okerlund finished out their schedules; in fact, according to Verne Gagne, they were paid extra by McMahon to do the opposite.

With the reacquisition of Hogan, McMahon showed that he wasn't averse to tearing down the status quo. And he was going to shake up the industry by shaking up the WWF itself. The night before Hogan's match in St. Louis, world champion Bob Backlund lost the title to the Iron Sheik, the very kind of transitional heel champion that Superstar Graham was not. The Sheik took the title solely to pass it to Hogan, and it's telling that the first half of the transition took place before Hogan even debuted.

On January 7, Hogan solidified his heroic bona fides by saving Backlund from a beatdown, and on January 23, he famously beat the Iron Sheik to claim the WWF title. His match with Dixon had actually been fairly technical, as Hogan showed off some of the chain wrestling skills he had learned in old-school AWA matches, but by the time he defeated the Sheik, Hogan had already perfected his new style of in-ring storytelling: an introductory offensive barrage, mostly consisting of punches, clotheslines, and an odd reliance on heelish illegal tactics, after which he would lose the upper hand, taking a severe beating from his opponent before finding his second wind, "Hulking Up,"[4] and disposing of his foil with an Irish Whip, big boot, and running leg drop.

......................................................................

**3** "You can practically hear Vince drooling on commentary," says Adam Nedeff in his invaluable review of this card on 411mania.com.

**4** The specifics of this technique, with head shaking and finger wagging, would come soon thereafter.

After Hogan disposed of the Iron Sheik, announcer Gorilla Monsoon swooned: "Hulkamania is here!"

☆  ☆  ☆

Hogan and Okerlund weren't the only names that McMahon poached. Within months, almost the entire top-tier roster was made up of wrestlers who got their starts elsewhere: Jesse "The Body" Ventura and manager Bobby "The Brain" Heenan also came from the AWA; the Junkyard Dog and King Kong Bundy were most recently from Mid-South; Ricky "The Dragon" Steamboat, Greg "The Hammer" Valentine, and "Rowdy" Roddy Piper all had been wrestling in the Crockett territory; Wendi Richter was fresh from Stampede Wrestling; and Mike Rotunda, Barry Windham, and Big John Studd were from Florida. Most of those guys had moved around fairly frequently through their careers, but the binge of signings was unusual for the era—and an affront to those other prominent promotions that were left suddenly shorthanded. McMahon's appeal to the wrestlers in question wasn't just his vision; it was the promise of big money and a guaranteed contract—and it was the absence of such contracts that allowed McMahon to nab most of those stars without any sort of legal repercussion. Other promoters were so entrenched in tradition—or so convinced of the disposability of individual wrestlers—that it hardly occurred to them to offer comparable contracts to their own talent. It's fair to say that in some ways McMahon didn't so much reinvent the wrestling world as he just brought it up to date.

McMahon would not be content to be a big-time wrestling promoter; he also wanted to be culturally relevant—something the wrestling world hadn't been in decades. A fortuitous meeting on an airplane between WWF (on-screen) manager Captain Lou Albano and pop star Cyndi Lauper—whose (real-life) manager and boyfriend Dave Wolff was a wrestling fan—led to Albano playing Lauper's father in her "Girls Just Want to Have Fun" video, and then to Lauper appearing on WWF television.

She feuded by proxy with Albano, who tried to take credit for her fame: They each chose a woman wrestler—Wendi Richter for Lauper and the Fabulous Moolah for Albano—to headline a card on MTV called "The Brawl to End It All."

The interaction between the rising tides of music videos and of pro wrestling introduced the pop culture mainstream to McMahon's new, Technicolor take on old-school rasslin', and introduced the existing wrestling audience to the Rock 'n' Wrestling Era, which led to further MTV bouts and a children's cartoon that saw Hulk Hogan and his merry band of multiethnic buddies ("Superfly" Jimmy Snuka, Junkyard Dog, Andre the Giant, et al.) in outlandish hijinks opposite "Rowdy" Roddy Piper and his crew of dimwit toughs (the Iron Sheik, Nikolai Volkoff, etc.). Suddenly the WWF, with Hogan as its figurehead, was everywhere, and pro wrestling as a whole was once again emerging as a cultural force. As *Sports Illustrated* put it in 1985:

> In the most recent Nielsen ratings, four of the nation's 10 top-rated cable-TV programs were wrestling shows. Two of them are produced by Vince McMahon Jr., commander in chief of the WWF; on the USA Network, McMahon's wrestling shows generate higher ratings than college basketball, tennis or hockey. The other two wrestling shows, which until last month were also McMahon productions, are on the WTBS superstation, where wrestling does better than college football. In Memphis,[5] a Saturday morning wrestling show is the third-highest-rated television program, trailing only *Dallas* and *Dynasty*.

☆ ☆ ☆

On March 31, 1985, McMahon put on an event called WrestleMania.[6] Jim Crockett Promotions, which had a national audience from its TBS show, had already started running its annual NWA Starrcade show on

---

5   Jerry Jarrett and Jerry Lawler's CWA promotion.

6   Ring announcer Howard Finkel takes credit for the coinage.

Thanksgiving 1983, distributing it throughout its southeastern fanbase via closed-circuit television.[7] But McMahon was determined to set a new standard, showing his WrestleMania card nationwide on closed-circuit and, perhaps more centrally, loading his show with mainstream celebrities—Mr. T, Muhammad Ali, Liberace—who would attract an ever-widening WWF audience. In the end, more than a million people watched the event. According to WWF lore, McMahon's investment in the event was such that, had it flopped, the WWF would have gone out of business.

Meanwhile, the other wrestling promotions were scrambling to make up some of the ground that McMahon had already claimed. The Crockett promotion joined up with Championship Wrestling from Georgia, the CWA from Memphis, and the AWA to form a confederacy called Pro Wrestling USA, but it collapsed under the weight of internecine squabbling.

The next year, WrestleMania 2—which featured Hogan squaring off against the blubbery King Kong Bundy—was broadcast on the new technology of pay-per-view television, which would prove to be a financial paradigm shift in the wrestling world. The main event of WrestleMania III featured Hogan going up against monolithic archrival Andre the Giant. That night, the WWF set an indoor attendance record at the Pontiac Silverdome.[8] In the years that followed, WrestleMania would become an annual tradition, and the WWF would add other annual events—soon simply called "pay-per-views"—that would serve as tentpoles around which the television product was structured.

The Survivor Series—a unique event format where teams of five battled, elimination-style, until one team was fully defeated—was launched on Thanksgiving night in 1987 as a bid to parlay the Hulk Hogan–Andre

........................................................................................

**7**  For the uninitiated, this was a system by which events were simulcast from the event site not to people's homes but to big screens in arenas and other large venues, so that large crowds could gather (and pay money) to watch the show in multiple cities at once. Coming from an era in which major wrestling shows weren't even broadcast on television, this was a really, really big deal.

**8**  This figure is widely considered suspect, as are most attendance records.

the Giant feud into a new, second pay-per-view and simultaneously steamroll the competition. The Crockett promotion by this point was expanding drastically, buying out NWA affiliates in Florida, Georgia, and Bill Watts's Mid-South territory, which had recently been rebranded as the UWF (for Universal Wrestling Federation) with an eye toward a national expansion of its own. In a show of national presence, Crockett decided to hold Starrcade 1987 in Chicago, far outside the promotion's normal stomping grounds (previous Starrcades had always been in Atlanta or Greensboro, North Carolina), and to air the event for the first time on pay-per-view. With the WWF's clout in the PPV arena already entrenched, McMahon saw an opening. He told cable providers that he was going to air his own show—the Survivor Series—that night, and if any of them showed Starrcade instead, he wouldn't let them show WrestleMania IV. (Some retellings say that McMahon threatened that they'd never do business with the WWF again at all.) The cable companies by and large assented to McMahon's power grab, and the NWA took a huge financial hit.

The following January, the NWA had scheduled a PPV featuring the Bunkhouse Stampede, a rough-and-tumble variation on the battle royal.[9] Again, McMahon went the route of cutthroat capitalism and put on his own battle royal–style event, the Royal Rumble, on free TV on the same night. (To see which wrestling promotion prevailed, check your cable package for NWA shows.) The difference between the two shows couldn't have been plainer. The Bunkhouse Stampede was gritty and real, as if the NWA was using the PPV format to push wrestling back in the direction of its earlier days, when the violence was closer to wrestling's surface. The Rumble, on the other hand, was shiny and contrived, a mainstream confection as only the WWF could produce. Again, the WWF succeeded. The NWA fought back by airing a Clash of the

---

9 A battle royal is a classic wrestling match style in which a number of men, usually twenty or more, are crammed into the ring, brawling in close quarters, until all but one has been tossed over the top rope.

Champions card on broadcast TBS television on the same night as WrestleMania IV; the WWF show's ratings were lower than expected, but the writing was already on the wall for the Crocketts. Facing bankruptcy due to overexpansion and profligate spending, they sold the company to Ted Turner in November 1988.

# S.D. JONES

There had been wrestling megacards before WrestleMania,
but they had been regional affairs, and even though they were in basketball and football stadiums, nobody would dare call them national
ventures.

That all changed when Vince McMahon the younger took the reins of
his father's company, and, within a few years, bought out his partners,
and wagered the whole operation on turning a New York–area wrestling
company into a modern juggernaut. That first WrestleMania show
wasn't the multi-main-event card of its latter-day incarnations, but it
was stocked nonetheless with epic battles: Junkyard Dog vs. Greg "The
Hammer" Valentine, Andre the Giant vs. Big John Studd, Hulk Hogan
and Mr. T vs. "Rowdy" Roddy Piper and Paul Orndorff. Earlier in the
night, shuffled in among the pageantry and bloodlust, was a match

between a titanic, hairless mountain of clay named King Kong Bundy and an unspectacular, upbeat WWF mainstay named S.D. (short for "Special Delivery") Jones—or, as announcer Lord Alfred Hayes referred to him, with palpable awkwardness, "that great star S.D. Jones."

Twenty-four seconds and the match was over: Jones charged Bundy; Bundy slammed him into the corner; Jones regained his footing; Bundy ran in and pancaked him; Jones fell to the mat; Bundy splashed his nearly 500 pounds down onto him. Before Bundy's flab even settled, the referee was halfway into his three count: It was a fait accompli in a world of fixed finishes. Jones was only ever there to get beat.

The man who would one day become S.D. Jones, Conrad Efraim, worked for the phone company until he decided to take up the wrestling trade. He was trained by Johnny Rodz (né John Rodriguez), legendary for his decades as a trainer at Gleason's Gym in Brooklyn if not so much for his unstellar career. Judging only on ignominy, he would be the perfect teacher for Efraim; as WWE.com puts it with characteristic earnestness, "While he may have lost more than he won, Rodz' unorthodox abilities and willingness to face any challenger earned him the respect of fans and Superstars alike."[1] After his training, Efraim found work in the Carolinas and was immediately inducted into African American wrestling semiroyalty as Roosevelt Jones, the "cousin" of area star Rufus R. Jones (real name: Carey "Buster" Lloyd) and the unfortunately monikered Burrhead Jones (real name: Melvin Nelson). The two had recently decided to decamp to Sam Muchnick's Missouri territory, but Rufus's stardom was sufficient to power another "relative" to relative stardom in battles against the nefarious Anderson "brothers," Gene and Ole.[2]

........................................................................................

1   Rodz's most famous students went on to be ECW standouts—Taz, Tommy Dreamer, and Bubba Ray and Devon Dudley—who, in the preceding era, also probably would have faced careers of S.D. Jones–level hierarchical immobility.

2   Gene Anderson's name was genuine, but much like Jones's "cousins," his siblings were false. Lars (Larry Heinemi), Ole (Alan Rogowski), and latter-day cousin Arn (Marty Lunde) were all Andersons in stage name only.

He had some success, winning the NWA (Los Angeles) Americas Tag Team titles with both Porkchop Cash and (presumed relative) Tom Jones, before finding what would be his life's calling: a middling role in the exploding world of the World Wrestling Federation. He sometimes won in preliminary bouts against other lesser lights like Rodz, but the chief role for Jones and Rodz and their other brethren in arms—forgettables over the years with names like Ron Shaw, Rene Goulet, Frank Marconi, Jose Luis Rivera, Bob Marcus, Gino Carabello, Brian Mackney, Steve Lombardi, "Iron" Mike Sharpe, Barry Horowitz, Rick McGraw, Mr. X, Bill and Randy Mulkey, and Jim Powers—was as reasonable but insufficient competition for the bigger stars. That's not to say that Jones didn't have some good days. He tag-teamed with Tony Atlas (known variously as "Black Superman" and "Mr. USA") and, later, Andre the Giant, to some success. The former duo won the WWF tag belts; the latter, though high-profile, was mostly a means of featuring Andre without overexposing him, and Jones's chief attribute in that tandem was his beatableness. He had to take the trumping to save Andre for the big finish, and moreover, he was singularly able to make a team with Andre on it seem conceivably destructible.

This was the beauty of what Jones and his ilk brought to those early WWF days. "Jobbers," or, more politely, "preliminary wrestlers" or "enhancement talent"—industry parlance for guys who exist solely to get beaten—weren't new to the wrestling world. But as with everything else in the WWF, they were new to a national stage. In the Territorial Era, the jobbers were often regulars, guys who the fans knew as well as the stars—the sort of guys who you could root for and, because of the structural and financial limitations of the territories, the sort of guys who fans had seen ascend the ladder of success before. The jobber in the WWF was something altogether different: Rather than a gatekeeper, a guy whom you could get legitimacy from beating, Jones was a space filler, an excuse to see a star wrestle without any real competitive risk at play. The elevation of S.D. Jones to the mainstream was an attempt at continuing the tradition of territorial jobbers, but it ended up being a meta acceptance of everything wrestling pretended it wasn't. Long forced to toil under the condescending title of "exhibitions" in New York—an unsubtle implication that the outcome wasn't in play as it was in other sporting events— wrestling now served up guys like S.D. Jones to showcase the biggest stars, and the endings were never in doubt: These were exhibition matches no matter what you called them.

In an industry where superstardom is the goal of all, the role player is the oddity. When everyone dreams of eating steak, the ham-and-egger is the exception. *Jobber* is an informative term, derived from the phrase "do the job"—that is, play your assigned role in a match, regardless of ignobility. But if for almost every wrestler the implicit career goal is the world title, S.D. Jones was notable because, for kids growing up watching him lose, it seemed like he probably just went home after the match and ate some dinner and watched TV the same way he would if he'd just gotten off work at the phone company. Like it was just his job.

Of course, on a stage that big, for a guy who had held big-time tag belts, who had won matches in Madison Square Garden, it was probably hard to reconcile to that role, even as he was defining it. When WrestleMania was first suggested, a guy with pedigree and loyalty like Jones probably thought he might at least get a win in an early match. So when McMahon approached him with the prospect of losing to Bundy in record time, Jones was taken aback.

He didn't want to do it at first, but McMahon convinced him that it was good for business—because they were building Bundy up as a monster who could go toe-to-toe with demigods like Hogan and Jones's old partner Andre. It was good business for Jones too since that spot on the WrestleMania card made him "a big, big, big, big payday."

Jones's struggle with his destiny is moving. The thing that defined jobbers in the years that followed, more than anything else, was their indefatigable spirit, the sense that, even though you knew they were going to lose, the wrestlers themselves didn't quite know it. That Jones himself was as confident in himself as his character evinces is testament to the vitality he and those that followed him offered the business. Before the match with Bundy, in a backstage interview, Jones said, "This is the moment I've been waiting for," with no hint of irony, because irony isn't part of the jobber's playbook. That irrational confidence was key to keeping the competition minimally believable.

*Believable* being the key word, since none of it is real. That twenty-four-second loss to Bundy at WrestleMania? Immediately after the match—and for the remainder of WWF/WWE history—it was called nine seconds. If the reality wrestlers occupy is malleable, then twenty-four can equal nine. Where anything is possible, nothing is real, and vice versa.

☆ ☆ ☆

In 2005, Jones told Canada's *Slam! Sports* that "after a while you just get comfortable where you are, and that's it. You're doing a job, you're making a living, and you just keep on going." Assumedly he wasn't using the phrase *do the job* ironically. The usage of *job* in wrestling lingo is a vernacular indication of the precise distance between wrestling and real sports. In football or baseball, your job is to try to win, but in wrestling, your job is to follow the script—and for some guys, a lot of the time the script says you lose. Even though all the outcomes are scripted, winning isn't described with such workmanlike euphemism. Despite the predetermination of the enterprise, winning a scripted match is every bit as glorious as winning a true competition. Losing, though, is seen as workaday obligation. "Doing the job" is just doing your job.

Years after Jones's heyday, such as it was, the Monday Night Wars reshaped the industry, and reshaped fan expectations so as to make them demand competitive matches between established superstars. But even with such even footing, the outcomes of those modern matches are seldom in any more doubt than were Jones's; they're just squash matches dressed up as main events. What Jones did was every bit as valuable as what 90 percent of modern wrestlers do; the fact that he's a functionary of a bygone era shouldn't diminish his value.

And yet, of course, it does. Jones's WWE.com obit reads more like a corporate press release about the retirement of an office worker than a stitch in the quilt of wrestling mythology: "Although Jones never attained elite Superstar status during his WWE tenure, no one could deny his unparalleled passion, dedication and efforts inside the squared circle."

After S.D. Jones quit the WWF, he went to work driving a truck for the *Daily News* and later moved back to Antigua, where he was born. He died there the next year, on October 26, 2008, at the age of sixty-three. By then he had largely faded from the memory of wrestling fans. The last time he was on the big stage was in 2005, when he inducted his old partner and longtime friend Tony Atlas into the WWE Hall of Fame. Jones isn't in the Hall, and he probably will never be, despite his tenure with the company; you can't put a loser into the Hall of Fame.[3] It's fitting, though, that Jones's last appearance was on the eve of WrestleMania XXV, putting over another, more significant wrestler. He was there to make Atlas look good, just like he was there to make Bundy look good at WrestleMania I. Jones got up, entertained the crowd, and got a round of applause. But the bigger cheers came for Atlas, even though his WWF tenure was much less profound than Jones's, no matter his winning percentage.

In subjugating himself, Jones made the product that much better, so of course he got his last moment in the spotlight for making somebody else look like a star.

---

3   Well, except Koko B. Ware.

# RACE IN WRESTLING

In the earliest days of the professional wrestling enterprise, race played the same role it did in boxing and geopolitics: The Foreigner was bad. George Hackenschmidt was a villain simply by virtue of being the European set across from our American hero. But when the Terrible Turk made his way to the States, the otherness took on a whole new dimension. He wasn't just on another team; he was from another planet. Crowds loathed him not just because he was Turkish but also because he was primitive, of indiscernible speech and unknowable intentions, and in possession of seemingly mystical techniques. In the decades that followed, the wrestling world has certainly seen its share of Hackenschmidts, generally respectable fighters who draw on their foreignness to draw boos from the crowd, but the legacy of the Turk is much more prominent.

In the Territorial Era, two trends emerged: the Ethnic Hero and the Evil Foreigner. In big coastal cities like New York, ethnicity became the calling card of otherwise unremarkable wrestlers who sought to harness the support of the various ethnic minorities that made up the bulk of the crowd. It wasn't unusual for the wrestlers' ethnic identities to be falsified; it wasn't even that rare for a guy to play an Irishman one night and a Greek the next. Not that there weren't authentics: Greek Jack Londos, Argentinean Antonino Rocca, and Italian Bruno Sammartino all ruled the New York scene at various times when their respective cultures held economic sway. But some promoters—most famously Jack Pfefer, who had spawned more from the sideshow than from the carnival—began to promote freaks from foreign lands to gin up public interest. The French Angel—a misshapen ogre of a man who was actually the model for the animated character Shrek—is a prime example. He was one of the nicest guys you'd ever meet backstage, but in the ring he was an unimaginable monster, the sort of creature that seemed more likely to tear his opponent's arms off than apply any sort of textbook wrestling hold. If he didn't directly draw on his Frenchness to terrorize the fans, there was a palpable implication that this sort of creature only emerged from the medieval dungeons of the European backwoods. Even in New York City, where tribalism reigned and ethnicity was a point of pride and means of popularity, certain more alien parts of the globe served as fictional spawning grounds for French Angel–esque wrestling monstrosities. From Asia came a cadre of mustachioed martial artists, underhanded Japs, and sharp-toothed Mongolian Neanderthals. Gorilla Monsoon (an Italian American who later became an articulate WWF announcer, always clad in sunglasses and a tuxedo) was a plus-sized Manchurian cannibal. The Middle East gave us nefarious cartoon Arabs like Sheik Adnan Al-Kaissie and, later, the Iron Sheik. (They were preceded in Detroit by the Sheik, and followed in Texas by devious manager Skandor Akbar.)

In the South and West, black wrestlers had begun to enter into the wrestling world by the '40s. There was a semiofficial "World Negro Heavyweight Champion" beginning in the '40s—the first on record was Ras Samara in Iowa—but the "title" was sometimes little more than a boast, disassociated from any sort of official championship lineage. Luther Lindsay claimed the title in the '50s and went on to be a close friend and sparring partner of Canadian wrestling paterfamilias Stu Hart. The "Ebony Giant" Dory Dixon of Jamaica wrestled against the "Nature Boy" Buddy Rogers in the main event at Madison Square Garden in 1962, a match that ended in a double pin. (The two had wrestled a ninety-minute time limit draw the month before in Texas.) African Americans in the wrestling ring started out as the sideshow's sideshow, but soon cards were being integrated, and matches were integrated soon thereafter.

The transition didn't get off without complaint. Boxing had already begun to integrate by then, and wrestling—though it had evolved quite a distance from its Greco-Roman origins and even its early Iowa-centrism—was considered the "white man's sport," in comparison to its pugilistic parallel. Eventually, some audiences saw black wrestlers compete on otherwise-white cards, but always against other African Americans—black-on-white violence could have caused a riot—and some all-black wrestling shows were held for exclusively black audiences.

Such shows proved profitable, and soon economics made proper integration inevitable. With black customers willing to pay to see wrestling shows—even situated, as they often were, in crow's nest balconies or other segregated sections of the audience—white promoters were willing to take their money.

☆ ☆ ☆

Sputnik Monroe was a white wrestler who headlined Memphis in the '60s. Sputnik (the name comes from an old woman who, upon seeing him with his arm around a black man, used the term as an insult, a sort of blend between "Hippie" and "Commie") hung out on Beale Street in a period when it was entirely black and was arrested by the (white) police for vagrancy several times to discourage him from such audacious acts. His most defiant act, though, was forcing the integration of Ellis Auditorium, where the big wrestling shows went on. To that point, blacks had been segregated in a small balcony area, even though, largely because of Monroe's popularity, there were often hundreds or thousands more African Americans waiting outside. Sputnik bribed the doorman to let more in than would fit in the balcony and eventually told the promoter that if he didn't let his black friends sit where they pleased, he wouldn't perform. This was at a time when most other public events in Memphis were segregated. Monroe was wrestling as a villain, but he made more money for the Memphis promotion than any other performer, and a younger generation of fans venerated him for his liberalism.

Often finding themselves in a position of being early adherents to public integration, promoters were in a sensitive spot when it came to crowd reactions. In "legitimate" sports, an athlete's skill was measured by his performance, but in wrestling, even in those early days, the athlete's promotability was a key factor. And "promotability," such as it was, was hard to discern. Owners worried that white audiences wouldn't cheer African American wrestlers, but they worried even more that black bad guys, provoking the crowd as part of their shtick, would cause uprisings. A few notable black wrestlers helped change the perception that they couldn't be fan favorites and charted the course for African American wrestlers for years to follow.

☆ ☆ ☆

Bobo Brazil (real name: Houston Harris) is considered the Jackie Robinson of professional wrestling. He started wrestling in Detroit in 1951 as "Bubu Brasil," the South American Giant; one has to assume that the Latin American Other was more acceptable an employee in those days than a 6-foot-6 black guy from Little Rock. Soon Brazil became a national star, traveling widely and frequently in places where he was banned from many restaurants and hotels. Brazil spent the early part of his career wrestling other blacks in regions where race was sensitive, but his greatest fame came when rivalries weren't restricted by segregation; he became so popular every-where he went that race hardly seemed an issue in his feuds. He was the first person to beat the Sheik for the title in Detroit's Big Time Wrestling—his home territory and site of his greatest fame—and he fought Andre the Giant to a draw. He went toe-to-toe with the greats of the Territorial Era: Ric Flair, Dick the Bruiser, Rikidozan. (He also institutionalized the uncomfortable myth that African Americans have unusually thick heads with his popular headbutt finisher—the Coco Butt—that many black wrestlers still employ to this day.)

On October 18, 1962, Brazil beat "Nature Boy" Buddy Rogers to become the first African American NWA World Heavyweight Cham-pion. It was a decision made by the local Newark promoter to gin up support for a return match: Brazil won after Rogers pulled a muscle in the match, and afterward Brazil refused to accept a tainted vic-tory. The two had their rematch on October 30, and Rogers re-claimed the title. As the switch was made without the approval of the NWA governors—and because Brazil never formally "accepted" victory—Brazil's reign isn't recognized in NWA history. To be fair, this sort of unauthorized, storyline-tainted title change happened with frequency in those early days of the sport (Bruno Sammartino had a very similar win against Rogers), and since there was no na-tional reporting of most verdicts, the wins could be kept off the record books. But Brazil is notable above all other crypto-champs in that he was the first black man to achieve even a tainted champion-ship win.

The ascendance of Brazil and the black wrestlers who followed in his footsteps to headliner status in the territorial wrestling world served as a proxy of racial utopia: Rather than booing them because they were black, white audiences who may have been less liberal in their daily lives embraced the opportunity to root on the worthy black man in isolation. Promoters soon steered storylines in this di-rection, having white villains act as subtly (or occasionally overtly) racist bullies, making insensitive comments at which the crowd would universally boo. (One can only assume that some crowd members snickered first and then booed appropriately.)

When black wrestlers finally emerged as top-tier villains in the '60s, emotional and metaphorical integration neared completion. "Big Cat" Ernie Ladd, a San Diego Chargers player who moonlighted as a wrestler in the off-season, was perhaps uniquely situated to explore these tensions: He was a legitimate professional athlete, so his acceptableness to white crowds was already somewhat established, and moreover, the very fact that he had a day job underscored the semi-self-evident put-on of the whole endeavor. Regardless of whether or not wrestling was fake, to most fans it was now unequivocally show business, and you could hardly fault a black man for playing the role. Despite his trailblazing—or perhaps because of it— Ladd was as much a racial provocateur as anyone in those days. In reference to foe Chief Jay Strongbow, he said that "the drunken Indian was out here again and I know he was full of whiskey. . . . He belongs back on the reservation in a tepee. . . . Brotha, I'm gonna pluck them feathers." He separately referred to Wahoo McDaniel as a "drug store Indian with a cigar stuck in his mouth." He called fan favorite Rocky Johnson (father of the Rock) "Uncle Tom Johnson."

Eventually, the evil immigrants of the pro wrestling world came to include those from Africa, inaugurating a new era of racial insensitivity that relegitimized antiblack racism in a seriocomical guise. On one side were heathens like Abdullah the Butcher, the Sudanese sadist, and Kamala, the Ugandan Giant, who came to the ring with an animal-print loincloth, tribal painting on his face and chest, and, sometimes, a tribal mask and a spear. He was so "wild" that he needed a handler, so he was often accompanied by a masked fellow in a pith helmet who was called Kim Chee. On the other side were the earlier imports, the black superstars who played on America's history of slavery as their own proud heritage, none of whom was more popular than the Junkyard Dog, the dog-collar-and-chains-wearing, jive-talking brawler who became the most popular wrestler in the Deep South prior to his famous WWF tenure.

JYD's rise to regional celebrity was abetted by promoter Bill Watts, who, despite being a certifiable good ol' boy, did more to advance the cause of equal opportunity in wrestling than just about anybody. He was running things in WCW in 1992, when Ron Simmons—a former All-American nose guard for Florida State—became the first recognized African American world champion upon winning the WCW World Heavyweight Championship from Big Van Vader. The fact that his number-one contendership was decided by raffle might have diminished the victory, but all that was lost in the celebration of the milestone. Simmons held on to the belt for five months.

☆ ☆ ☆

Despite WWF's late-'80s diversity, its vocabulary wasn't exactly progressive. Though his English was faltering, Mr. Fuji threw around terms like *yard ape* and *lawn jockey* and *honky* in his prime. His protégé Don Muraco called Pedro Morales "a dirty Mexican pepperbelly," and when it was suggested to him that Morales was actually Puerto Rican, he said, "Who cares? They're all the same." (He later attempted a more accurate bit of racism when he called Morales "a Puerto Rican hubcap thief.") He was one of a few wrestlers for whom "Mexican wetback" was a throwaway descriptor of Tito Santana.

If the acts weren't always bald-facedly racist, their matches were often peppered with the patently offensive bad-guy shtick of legendary color commentator Jesse "The Body" Ventura. At various times Ventura reacted to a Junkyard Dog interview by saying JYD had "a mouth full of grits," calling his rope-a-dope in-ring routine "a lot of shuckin' and jivin'." He commonly referred to fan favorite Tito Santana as "Chico," dubbed his finishing move the "flying burrito" finisher, and, when Santana was getting pummeled at WrestleMania IV, Ventura said, "I betcha Chico wishes he was back selling tacos in Tijuana right now!" He similarly referred to black wrestler "Birdman" Koko B. Ware as "Buckwheat" until eventually Vince McMahon himself put a stop to it.

"Rowdy" Roddy Piper, a Canadian who was billed to be from Glasgow, Scotland, was a one-stop shop for racial insensitivity. He became a top-tier villain in California early in his career by insulting the region's Latino community. He once insisted on making amends by playing the Mexican national anthem on his bagpipes, but he played "La Cucaracha" instead. In the WWF, Piper exhibited a similar false apology when he invited Jimmy Snuka onto his "Piper's Pit" interview segment to apologize for Snuka not getting a chance to speak on his previous appearance. Piper decorated the set with pineapples and coconuts and eventually smashed a coconut over Snuka's head. (Piper's indiscretion didn't end there; he once talked soul food with Tony Atlas, said that Mr. T's lips looked "like a catcher's mitt," called T's fans monkeys, mock-fed bananas to a poster of Mr. T, and told him that he would "whip him like a slave." At WrestleMania VII, he was wrestling Bad News Brown, who was presented as a black street thug but who was actually half black; Piper—who, it should be said, was the good guy in this feud—came to the ring with his body painted half black, down the middle.)

Piper's racist grunts may have been part of a larger heel character, but it's likewise a part of a broader history of villains gleefully playing up racist tropes to get easy boos from the crowd. There were virulent racist personas like Colonel DeBeers, the AWA heel known for his pro-apartheid politics, and John Bradshaw Layfield, the conservative Texan in the WWE who briefly railed against illegal Mexican immigrants. Michael "P.S." Hayes, ringleader of the Fabulous Freebirds, often resorted to race-baiting to intensify feuds: The Freebirds' feud with Junkyard Dog turned on Hayes calling JYD "boy," and the Freebirds once came to the ring in a major match against the Road Warriors at Comiskey Park with the rebel flag painted on their faces. In 2008, Hayes was suspended from his backstage duties with WWE for supposedly telling African American wrestler Mark Henry, "I'm more of a nigger than you are." He was said to have used the N-word casually over the years without causing a stir. He is also credited with the notion that black wrestlers don't need gimmicks because being black *is* their gimmick.

When you consider the recent history of African American wrestlers in pro wrestling, to simplify a performer's character to his race isn't as offensive as what's come when promoters try to give black wrestlers personas with more, shall we say, idiosyncrasy. In 1987, a small-time wrestler once known as "Soul Train" Jones in Memphis was introduced to the world as the "Million Dollar Man" Ted DiBiase's bodyguard-cum-manservant, Virgil. Over the years, DiBiase bought the services and the souls of numerous wrestlers, but Virgil wasn't just a sellout; he was a slave, almost unabashedly. His name, purportedly coined by Bobby "The Brain" Heenan, was a subtle jab at NWA showrunner and star Dusty Rhodes, born Virgil Runnels, who was known for "acting black" in speech and mannerism.

Similarly, in 1988, a famous villain named the One Man Gang, who sported a mohawk and denim vest and generally looked and acted like a monstrous Hells Angel, was repackaged with minimal explanation as Akeem the African Dream, a white man of African descent who dressed in a dashiki and spoke in jive while sluicing his forearms through the air like a '70s-movie pimp. This character too was supposed to be a joke aimed at Rhodes, who counts semiforgotten African American Sweet Daddy Siki among his greatest influences (Siki's bleached-blond hair, "Siki strut," and verbal style are direct precursors of Rhodes's affect). Rhodes was raised in poverty in Texas and pegged his accent more on socioeconomics than race, but he was nonetheless the subject of racially charged ribbing, though, as with Virgil, targeting Rhodes was more a general shot across the bow at the Crockett promotion than anything. (That said, Rhodes once borrowed from the Junkyard Dog's playbook by returning under a mask after he'd lost a Loser Leaves Town match.) Anyway, Akeem (whose real name was George Gray) suddenly was announced as being from "Deepest, Darkest Africa" (also Kamala's land of origin) and was speaking in a parody of a parody of a "black accent." Managed by Slick—who was known alternately as the "Jive Soul Bro" and the "Doctor of Style," dressed in polyester suits and pageboy hats, and later became, in real life and exploited on-screen, a Reverend—the duo seemed to embody every sketchy African American stereotype in one middling act.

If one perhaps thought that the introduction of a white African nationalist signaled some sort of postracial era of racial insensitivity, one would be wrong. When late–Territorial Era megastar "Black Superman" Tony Atlas came to the WWF in 1991, he was recast as tribal headhunter Saba Simba. (Atlas credited the Saba Simba character for rescuing him from poverty and saving his life, for whatever that's worth.) The year 1992 saw the WWF debut of Papa Shango (real name: Charles Wright), a voodoo witch doctor who cast diabolical black-magic spells on his opponents. (Wright would later become even more famous as the Godfather, a wrestling pimp who came to the ring with a bevy of hookers and who implored everyone to take a ride on the "hoe train.")

When the famous WCW tag team Harlem Heat (made up of brothers Booker T and Stevie Ray), who had previously gone by the moniker the "Ebony Experience" in the GWF, came to WCW in 1993, they were originally presented as a pair of convicts who had been *won* in a card game by Col. Robert Parker, a Mark Twain villain of a wrestling manager, who came to the ring as if straight off the plantation, in off-white three-piece suits and a cowboy hat, chomping a cigar and demeaning his foes in a syrupy drawl. They tried out the gimmick at a couple of house shows, with Booker and Stevie in jumpsuits and leg shackles, before it was determined that this might be slightly offensive. In the end, Harlem Heat was presented sans Parker and sans chains, and the team became incredibly popular. Booker T went on to be a world champion in both WCW and WWE, which is a long way from cartoon slavery. Nonetheless, in 2003, while feuding with Booker T, Triple H called out Booker's (legitimate) criminal past, referenced his "nappy" hair, and said that "people like [him]" couldn't win championships in WWE and that they were just there to "dance" and "entertain" people.

Even in the modern WWE, where the Rock's numerous championship reigns were seen as evidence of a postracial wrestling world, there have been plentiful steps backward for every step forward. First black champ Ron Simmons was repackaged as a bad-guy black nationalist. Black gangsta and rapper personalities persist, from

R-Truth to the tag team Cryme Tyme. When black wrestlers weren't broad stereotypes, they were subtle ones, playing ominous thugs with hip-hop entrance music or slam poets with hip-hop entrance music or comic relief with hip-hop entrance music—or, in the case of Mark Henry at various points, all of the above.

☆  ☆  ☆

All of this does a disservice to the Latino wrestling experience. Stemming mostly from Mexico's masked luchador history, Mexican wrestlers were introduced into the American wrestling mainstream as conquering heroes (or villains). Mil Máscaras—"the man of a thousand masks"—was a huge star in Mexico and parlayed that into a similar status in the American territories. But for many others, the Mexican style—lucha libre is what it's called—didn't translate. Luchadores couldn't find opponents who could work well with them, and the traditional luchador masks were the stuff of villainy in the United States—and, moreover, crutches used by dull characters. That Mexican wrestlers have often come north without much of a grasp on English hasn't helped their acceptance into the monologue-heavy American mainstream. The unadorned luchador was the Hispanic Noble Savage from Máscaras, on through the luchador bouts of those early days of *WCW Monday Nitro*. They were simple, but their portrayal was only offensive in its oddity. In a sense, this was a simpler time, and political correctness was buoyed by it. Once the dam opened, though, offensiveness poured out. As the wrestling promotions tried to integrate their Latino hires more fully by giving them characters—and, often, by removing their masks—they followed the rest of the history of racial identity in the wrestling world down the rabbit hole of straightforward racial stereotype. Before long, Konnan, a superstar in his home country, traded in his colorful tights for Dickies, a wifebeater, sunglasses, and a bandanna: the superhero devolving into a common street thug. It was a caricature we were unfortunately comfortable with. And that became the norm: A team of unmasked luchadores called the Mexicools were ferried to ringside on a riding lawnmower. Los Guerreros, two scions of a proud wrestling family, garnered their greatest fame by "lying, cheating, and stealing" and riding around in hydraulics-boosted cars.

The Asian contingent followed a similar trajectory. They started off as simplistic devilish warriors and evolved over the years into concise stereotypes. The line between ethnic slur and Hollywood stereotype became increasingly indecipherable: Mr. Fuji's bow tie and bowler begat a million deadly karate chops and judo kicks. In the late '90s, a stable of established Japanese wrestlers called Kai En Tai, led by a flashy caricature named Yamaguchi-San, were embroiled in a feud with a wrestling porn star named Val Venis; their beef culminated in a scene where Yamaguchi attempted a castration via samurai sword while shouting "I choppy-choppy your pee-pee!" If the treatment of Latinos in modern pro wrestling has been driven by the perceptions of fearmongering news reports, the depiction of Asians has followed an out-of-date Hollywood template. It says a lot when you can look at such storylines and say, "At least the black wrestlers aren't suffering this sort of indignity."

# THE JUNKYARD DOG
# (SYLVESTER RITTER)

WrestleMania I: the culmination of the feud between the
Junkyard Dog and loathsome Intercontinental Champion Greg "The
Hammer" Valentine. The ending of the match goes something like this:
Valentine first wins by (illegally) propping his feet on the ropes to lever-
age JYD into a pin; imperturbable third-tier good guy Tito Santana
comes to the ring to alert the referee to Valentine's maleficence; the ref
restarts the match; Valentine, seething, refuses to reenter; Valentine is

counted out; JYD wins the match but, per the rules, doesn't win the title belt. The crowd applauds JYD's victory, tainted though it was, and JYD does his best to show his gratitude. So it would go for JYD—he was popular, very frequently victorious, but was never granted entrance to the promised land.

This, for better or worse, is the way we remember the Junkyard Dog, a.k.a. Sylvester Ritter: operating successfully but basically ignobly, unable (or disallowed) to reach the highest level of the game. In retrospect, it's too easy to dismiss the Junkyard Dog, either as a minstrel-style sideshow (the dancing, the ghetto affectation, the chains around his neck) or as a plain midcarder, a popular but unspectacular sidebar with no upward mobility. But his shtick and his persona made him as popular in the early days of the WWF as anyone save Hulk Hogan, and that's without the merciless publicity machine that went into the Hulkster's ascendance. And, if history is any indicator, JYD had already established himself as championship material.

☆ ☆ ☆

Sylvester Ritter played football at Fayetteville State, and it's often said he was drafted by the Packers, though there's no record of it. After injuries ended his gridiron career, he turned to wrestling. Usually known as "Big Daddy Ritter," he did stints in Jerry Jarrett's Tennessee territory and in Stu Hart's Stampede Wrestling before settling in at Mid-South Wrestling, where promoter Bill Watts gave him the persona that would make him famous. Running the show in a territory comprising Oklahoma, Arkansas, Louisiana, and Mississippi, Watts would never be mistaken for a civil rights activist, but he was a businessman, and he knew that an African American wrestler could be a huge moneymaker. Borrowing a line from Jim Croce's "Bad, Bad Leroy Brown," Watts dubbed Ritter the Junkyard Dog—and, ever the literalist, gave him a dog collar and junk cart. The *Sanford and Son* reference was flagrant—Watts was borrowing clumsily from a limited knowledge of black culture—and the collar with (ahem) chain leash was borderline obscene. (That Ritter made such a racially charged accoutrement a staple of his later color-blind celebrity is evidence of his magnetism.)

Prior to the 1960s, black wrestling—insofar as it existed—was almost entirely separate from the wrestling mainstream. Starting in its earlier days of legitimacy and continuing to the '60s, wrestling was seen in some quarters as a white man's sport, after boxing had been taken over by black fighters. But by the '60s, so many sports were integrating that black wrestlers were inevitable, and what's more, black audiences were beginning to come to wrestling shows in force.[1] The first major black stars were Bearcat Johnson and Bobo Brazil, and they were soon followed by the likes of Rocky Johnson[2] and Ernie Ladd, the San Diego Charger who moonlighted as a diabolical heel. It's noteworthy that until the 1960s black wrestlers were almost always cast as good guys because the promoters worried that black villains would incite white fans to riot.

From this inelegant tradition sprang the Junkyard Dog. Entering the ring to the thudding bass line of Queen's "Another One Bites the Dust," JYD was soon the top babyface in the region, and his feuds with (mostly white) baddies quickly became the stuff of (local) legend. Unsurprisingly, the race issue was immediately at the forefront.

JYD's long grudge with Michael "P.S." Hayes and the Fabulous Freebirds—who notoriously "blinded" JYD in the ring with (ahem) hair cream—culminated in a blindfold-and-dog-collar match (wherein both participants were blindfolded and bound together by a length of chain between two collars). Hayes didn't hesitate to call JYD "boy" to solidify his wicked credentials.

........................................................................................

1  The documentary *Memphis Heat* discusses at some length the segregated seating in the old Tennessee territory, and the locker room animus between the wrestlers who didn't care for black audiences and those—notably Sputnik Monroe, who was a borderline civil rights pioneer—who were more open-minded.

2  Father of the Rock.

When Hayes pushed racial buttons, the audience read his racism mostly as an indicator of vileness and booed accordingly—his racism didn't make him bad so much as he made the racism bad.[3] And, of course, JYD reacted justifiably. Even with the chains, what Junkyard Dog was doing was a sort of inversion of the racial stereotype act—and, moreover, a kind of artful integration-by-transposition in the world of pro wrestling. By playing up the antipathy inherent in racist sentiment, a wrestling storyline got the Southern audience to cheer for JYD *because* he was black.

The Junkyard Dog's rivalry with his former protégé Ted DiBiase would come to a head in a 1982 Loser Leaves Town match that JYD improbably lost. After all, it was much more common in those days for the bad guy to lose this sort of match as an explanation for his real-life decampment for another territory. When JYD lost, the fans were crushed, but their anguish was short-lived.

There soon after appeared a masked man who was tall, thickset, black, and went by the name of Stagger Lee. Obviously, it was Ritter in disguise, and as would be expected, the crowd was thrilled, DiBiase was incensed, and the referees were oblivious.[4] The choice of the moniker "Stagger Lee" was particularly inspired, carrying with it deep mythic resonances. From Greil Marcus's book *Mystery Train*:

> Somewhere, sometime, a murder took place: a man called Stack-a-lee—or Stacker Lee, Stagolee, or Staggerlee—shot a man called Billy Lyons—or Billy the Lion, or Billy the Liar. It is a story that black America has never tired of hearing and never stopped living out, like whites with their Westerns. Locked in the images of a

---

3  For a master class in this act, see Colonel DeBeers, wrestling apartheid advocate of AWA fame.

4  If this storyline sounds familiar to non-Mid-South fans, it should: Neighboring territories during this era often passed storylines from one to another in the way that old football teams stole plays or hoboes borrowed stories. Running the same program, Tommy Rich masqueraded as "Mr. R" and Dusty Rhodes as "the Midnight Rider" in different regions, to similar acclaim, and decades later, Hulk Hogan took on the mantle of "Mr. America" after he was "fired" by nemesis Vince McMahon.

thousand versions of the tale is an archetype that speaks to fantasies of casual violence and violent sex, lust and hatred, ease and mastery, a fantasy of style and steppin' high. At a deeper level it is a fantasy of no-limits for a people who live within a labyrinth of limits every day of their lives, and who can transgress them only among themselves. It is both a portrait of that tough and vital character that everyone would like to be, and just another pointless, tawdry dance of death.

Billy died for a five-dollar Stetson hat; because he beat Staggerlee in a card game, or a crap game; because Stack was cheating and Billy was fool enough to call him on it. It happened in Memphis around the turn of the century, in New Orleans in the twenties, in St. Louis in the 1880s. The style of the killing matters, though: Staggerlee shot Billy, in the words of a Johnny Cash song, just to watch him die.

Over the years and by benefit of a widely recorded song,[5] Staggerlee became a symbol of a black man sticking it to the white establishment. Even to the mostly white crowds of Mid-South, this storyline played to great success. The black-white implications were melded with David vs. Goliath and Good vs. Evil symbolism. "Stagger Lee" was a signifier of a man fighting against all odds—and anyone can sympathize with that. In this way, a vision of black empowerment, smuggled under the guise of universal empowerment, became fashionable to a predominantly white audience.[6]

Stagger Lee pestered his foes until the stipulated ninety-day banishment ended, whereupon JYD returned. He feuded with another former ally, Butch Reed, in a series of brutal grudge matches. But being that Reed was also black, the traditional matches were heavily freighted with

---

**5** Lloyd Price had the first big hit in 1958 followed in the next decade by Wilson Pickett, James Brown, and Tommy Roe. Other renditions were subsequently performed by Woody Guthrie, Elvis Presley, Fats Domino, Bob Dylan, Neil Diamond, Nick Cave, and Beck.

**6** This is particularly potent when one considers Marcus's theory that Stagger Lee was actually white and his victim black, and that African American legend usurped and reversed the story.

racial implications: the dog-collar match again, but also the tar-and-feather match and the "ghetto street fight."

☆ ☆ ☆

In 1984 JYD was hired away by the WWF, which was then making itself into the first national wrestling promotion and was poaching the top stars from around the country to build its stable and its audience. They were also rather blatantly assembling a roster that traded on national and ethnic stereotypes to differentiate each wrestler in the broadest strokes possible. JYD was, in no uncertain terms, the Black Guy—just as Tito Santana was the Mexican Guy, Mr. Fuji was the (ambiguously) Asian Guy, the Iron Sheik was the Middle Eastern Guy, Nikolai Volkoff was the Russian Guy, Jimmy Snuka was the Pacific Island Guy, Andre the Giant and Big John Studd were the Big Guys (though Andre was also demonstrably French), and Wendi Richter and the Fabulous Moolah were the Women. "Rowdy" Roddy Piper and Hulk Hogan were, as their names suggest, originally set up as Scottish and Irish Guys, respectively, though their celebrity grew (particularly in Hogan's case) to demolish those parameters. (Bob Backlund, the long-reigning good guy champ shortly before Hogan's ascendance, was unquestionably the White Guy.) The Junkyard Dog hardly stood out in this motley crowd of caricatures—except, of course, for his great popularity. JYD was a wrecking ball in the ring. Never the most technically proficient wrestler, JYD's WWF-era routine was reduced to a crowd-pleasing blur of punches, headbutts, and powerslams.[7] The chains and white boots from his Mid-South days came along as well—as did "Another One Bites the Dust" until several years later, when it was replaced with a new original theme song (which JYD sang) called "Grab Them Cakes." The more literal part of his "junkyard" persona was largely abandoned, except in the *Hulk Hogan's Rock 'n' Wrestling* cartoon show, in which JYD not only owned and lived in a

----

7 "Thump," the unspectacular name of his powerslam finisher, was imprinted on the back of his tights.

junkyard but also spoke lines like "That junkyard rat's been jivin' with my junk again."

JYD became an idol particularly to the younger audience, and he famously invited kids into the ring to dance with him after matches. So, yes, the trope of the dancing black man. No one would deny that JYD was a panderer, but he was a panderer in an almost visionary way. His crowd interaction, signature moves, theme music, and outsize character presaged later stars like Rick Rude, the Rock, and "Funkasaurus" Brodus Clay.

JYD feuded notably with Terry Funk, Jake "The Snake" Roberts, "Adorable" Adrian Adonis, and the aforementioned Greg Valentine, who, perhaps borrowing from Hayes, race-baited JYD in some memorable interviews.

JYD emerged from that feud with only a moral victory. Despite his fame, and despite the WWF's multiethnic roster, it's fair to say that in his WWF period, JYD was hamstrung by race. Whether or not the world was ready for a black champion, the WWF title scene was dominated by white men—particularly one white man named Hulk Hogan, whose preeminence made it nearly impossible for other good guys, white or black, to ascend to the top for most of a decade. But being a black icon for a company trying to expand its audience nationwide certainly didn't help.

His last feud of note, and probably his most popular, saw him battling "King" Harley Race[8] over the crown that Race had won in a King of the Ring tournament—but even this honorific would escape JYD's grasp. Their big match at WrestleMania III stipulated that if JYD lost, he would have to bow to his opponent. And although he did lose (cleanly), he bowed mockingly and then stole the crown, robe, and scepter and strutted across the ring, atoning for his loss: Stagger Lee, terrorizing the white world once more. The crowd cheered wildly—a response that hinted none too subtly at a missed opportunity. It was a poignant moment. (And yes, it's equally poignant that JYD's most famous feud in the WWF was against Race.)

......................................................................................................

**8** The legendary former NWA champion—from whom Ric Flair had won the belt—was at this point in his mid-forties and approaching his in-ring dotage.

☆ ☆ ☆

That match was the highest JYD would climb in the WWF. He left the promotion soon thereafter. He reemerged in 1989 in the NWA, which had recently rechristened itself WCW. They too were going national, but they were somewhat late to the game and so were eager to import identifiable WWF talent like JYD. Ritter's WCW run was unmemorable, though, except for his being part of a mostly ridiculous stable that feuded with the venerable Four Horsemen. Helmed by Sting, they called themselves "Dudes with Attitudes." Ritter left WCW soon after and "retired" in the way that old wrestlers often do, which is to say that he took a couple of months off and then started wrestling at occasional indie shows.

In 1998, Ritter was driving near Forest, Mississippi, on his way home from his daughter's high school graduation. He apparently fell asleep at the wheel, and his car flipped three times, killing him. He was forty-five years old.

So what to make of JYD's career now? It's worth noting that many wrestling fans and commentators place JYD, in hindsight, on the crasser side of black wrestling history. Ladd, Rocky Johnson, Tony Atlas, and Ron Simmons (prior to his role in the Black Panther–esque Nation of Domination, one assumes) portrayed more straightforward wrestlers-who-happened-to-be-black. Certainly no one can ever overestimate the racial insensitivity of the wrestling promotional machine.

But whether you view JYD as a shirtless Stepin Fetchit or more of a muscle-bound Bert Williams is beside the point (although it's significant that both are being granted subversive cachet through the revisionist lens). In pro wrestling, everyone is a stereotype of one kind or another. The sport may have been capitalizing on JYD's Scary Negro juju, but it also made his foes so cartoonishly bigoted that even the most benighted sectors of wrestling's audience could feel virtuous for hating them. Wrestling made it easy for its fans to be broad-minded. It's cheap sentiment, maybe, but it's sentiment all the same, and certainly not something one associates with minstrelsy. The Junkyard Dog was just jivin' with our junk all along.

# A BRIEF HISTORY OF ROYALTY IN WRESTLING

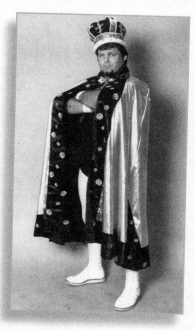

On July 27, 1974, a young wrestler named Jerry Lawler defeated his mentor Jackie Fargo to claim the NWA Southern Junior Heavyweight Championship, which, presumably to increase the belt's prestige, was then renamed the NWA Southern Heavyweight Championship (Memphis version)—not to be confused with the NWA Southern Heavyweight Championship that was the top belt in the Florida territory. (The title would again change its name in 1978 to the AWA Southern Heavyweight Championship.) But even though the title—which Lawler would hold on and off until it was merged with the AWA Championship in 1987—was the prize in that match, it wouldn't prove to be as significant as the honorific attached to the win. By beating Fargo, the regional legend, Lawler could claim to be the "king" of wrestling in the area. And he did, with gusto. There were other "kings" in the Territorial Era—King Curtis Iaukea, the

"King" Ernie Ladd—but Lawler's reign was unquestionably the longest and most storied.

As the years went on, Lawler—never much for subtlety—would wear a kingly goatee, carry a crown, sometimes with a scepter and fur-trimmed robe, and decorate his tights with regal insignias. Lawler took his kingship seriously, going so far as to sue—in real life—the WWF over its use of the "King" moniker in 1987. (The lawsuit basically boiled down to an injunction against WWF using "The King" in promoting Memphis-area events. Lawler actually referenced the lawsuit in storylines but treated the specifics of the suit only vaguely, alleging that his court victory proved that he was the true king of wrestling, whatever that meant.)

The WWF king in question was one Harley Race, former NWA champion and longtime headliner of the NWA's St. Louis outpost. When he came to the WWF in 1986, the promotion searched for some way to establish his pedigree with fans without acknowledging his NWA legacy. (As a rule, the WWF never mentioned its competitors on air until the Modern Era.) The WWF settled on having him win the second annual King of the Ring tournament and embrace the mantle wholeheartedly, dressing in full royal regalia and entering the ring to the strains of Mussorgsky's "The Great Gate of Kiev."

When Race was forced out of action after getting a hernia by colliding unfortunately with the announcers' table during a match with Hulk Hogan, his manager, Bobby Heenan, was determined to anoint a new king, and he selected Haku, a Samoan ruffian. Haku, elevated by the crown and instilled with a newfound shamanic regality, eventually lost the crown to pro-American tough guy "Hacksaw" Jim Duggan, who understandably treated the royal vestments as comedy props rather than affectations, before he himself lost the WWF kingship to "Macho Man" Randy Savage, who took the role more seriously, if not more literally; he modified his nickname to "Macho King" and paired a streamlined crown with his ever-present sunglasses for an iconic look of insane posturing. Savage took the mantle into (his first) retirement after WrestleMania VII.

Thereafter the WWF kingship was an incidental titular, used irregularly by King of the Ring winners in Harley Race fashion when it suited their (necessarily villainous) characters. Owen Hart became the maniacal "King of Harts." Mabel—whose character up to that point was basically that of a threatening, electric-color-clothing-wearing, fat black man—became "King Mabel," who was basically the same guy as before but with a crown. (His old partner Mo became "Sir Mo.") Edge called himself "King Edge the Awesome," Booker T did a mind-bendingly incredible turn as "King Booker," and Sheamus shoehorned medieval-looking royal gear into his Irish character.

When Bret Hart won the 1993 King of the Ring, he didn't take on any kingly affectations, but his kingship was challenged by a new WWF announcer—named Jerry "The King" Lawler. It's good to be king, after all, so you might as well fight for it.

# ANDRE THE GIANT

When Hulk Hogan and Andre the Giant met in what is still considered the biggest wrestling match of all time, exaggeration was in the air. According to various contemporary reports, there were 95,000 people on hand at WrestleMania III to see the 7-foot-5, 525-pound Andre square off against Hulk Hogan, who stood 6-foot-8 and weighed 320 pounds and whose biceps measured twenty-four inches around. Probably the only number in that last sentence that's unimpeachable is the III.

Pro wrestling is abundant with such embellishments (and misdirections, fabrications, and lies of omission), even within the sport's Big Lie. But when Andre was involved, the mythologizing always hit fever pitch. It's a testament to his outsize greatness that reality—as impressive as it was—couldn't do him justice.

It should be said up front that every detail of Andre's life is subject to fantastical reinterpretation and, failing that, normal human error. For every stated fact that follows, there is a contradictory fact somewhere out there.[1] "Truth" hereafter should be graded on a curve.

Born André René Roussimoff in 1946 at the foot of the French Alps, in a town called Grenoble, Andre was normal-sized at birth, but with adolescence came an incredible growth spurt. Details are hazy, of course, but various stories put him at 6 feet at the age of twelve, 6-foot-7 at the age of seventeen, and 7-foot-4 by nineteen. (There is much dispute over whether he ever actually reached 7-foot-4.) He had an affliction called acromegaly, a syndrome wherein the pituitary gland overproduces growth hormone.[2] One legend: When he made the long walk to school as a child, he would sometimes hitch a ride from his neighbor, Samuel Beckett. In his teen years, Andre worked on a farm, in a factory, and as a woodworker before he was discovered in his late teens (not by Lord Alfred Hayes, as one legend suggests, though Hayes did meet him early in his career) and introduced to the world of wrestling. He traveled widely almost from the start—throughout Europe, where he was known as "Monster Eiffel Tower"; into Japan, where he was dubbed "Monster Roussimoff"; and at home in France, where he was called the "Butcher" or simply "Giant Roussimoff." Soon, though, he took on a new moniker: "Jean Ferré," a play on the name of Géant Ferré, sort of a French Paul Bunyan. At a time when a wrestler's name had to sell tickets, it was obvious almost from the start that mythology was the only means of adequate articulation of Andre's presence.

Soon he was in Montreal, where he had been recruited by Canadian legend (and onetime disputed NWA champ) Edouard Carpentier, and where, under the tutelage of wrestler-promoter Frank Valois, he was

---

1  I am nonetheless indebted to Michael Krugman's *André the Giant: A Legendary Life* for its "official" timeline of Andre's early life.

2  There are stories that his grandfather in Bulgaria had the same affliction and grew to a height of 7-foot-8.

first exposed to the rabid wrestling audiences of North America. Fans all over the continent began to hear whispers about this new monster, this "Eighth Wonder of the World." This was, of course, after the heyday of P. T. Barnum's sideshow exhibitions and before the modern era of the YouTube phenomenon. Likewise, Andre's career peaked before the cable television era, before the world at large could keep tabs of his every match and movement. Andre's first major feud (and first in a long, long line of giant vs. giant programs) was against Don Leo Jonathan, who supposedly stood 6-foot-9. Their feud electrified Canadian audiences. Even so, it would take a deliberate hand to ensure that crowds didn't tire of Andre; the unbeatable monster is fun once, maybe twice, but it soon loses its luster. So Valois delivered Andre's career to the only promoter he thought could manage such a legend in the making: Vincent J. McMahon, father of Vincent K. McMahon and paterfamilias of the WWF empire.

Vince Sr. took the reins of Andre's career in 1973, and his first matter of business was to change "Jean Ferré" into something more straightforward but nevertheless something duly mesmerizing: Andre the Giant. Although McMahon's territory encompassed only the Northeast, he knew that keeping Andre on the move was the only way to keep him fresh. For the next ten years, Andre stayed on the road, lumbering from territory to territory, as McMahon rented him out as a special attraction to promoters across the United States and the world. Andre would almost always play the good guy, coming to the rescue of the area's top hero when the heels began to outnumber and overpower him. This young Andre, before age and size starting wearing him down, was an incredible athlete and a pure spectacle in the ring. He was billed as being undefeated, which was presumably untrue but functionally valid; he may have never lost a straight singles match to pinfall or submission during this period. He didn't need to, though—he would elevate his opponents in the audience's eyes just by letting them get in a few good minutes against the Giant.

As Jerry "The King" Lawler, one of the many local heroes to get the rub from Andre, put it to Krugman: "He'd let you do anything you wanted in a match. Other than beat him. . . . But if he didn't like you, he'd make you look like crap, and there wasn't anything anyone could do about it." This became a pattern in Andre's career, the willingness to make his opponent look good, unless he personally disliked the guy. The explanations for this are assorted—that Andre was protective of his place on top of the food chain, that Andre respected the tradition of wrestling and detested anyone who didn't—but Andre's temperament reminds one of the old tales of the angry and unpredictable Greek gods. And if you were one of the unlucky few whom Andre decided to smite, well, God help you.

By this time, Andre was undeniably a megastar. In 1974, *The Guinness Book of World Records* named him the highest paid professional wrestler, with a one-year take of $400,000. The Washington Redskins considered offering him a tryout—which, even viewed as a publicity stunt, shows the degree of Andre's celebrity. He appeared (in costume) on *The Six Million Dollar Man*, playing a dastardly Sasquatch. In 1976, on the night that Muhammad Ali fought Japanese pro wrestler Antonio Inoki in a terribly ill-conceived interdisciplinary match, Andre fought ham-and-egger Chuck Wepner (the inspiration for the Rocky movies) in Shea Stadium. The match was unscripted, which was less a novelty with Andre than it would have been with any other wrestler. This was Andre's whole mythos, after all; every match is scripted only because Andre deigns to follow the script, only competitive by the Giant's godly grace.

In the pro wrestling world, he was feuding notably against another big man, footballer-slash-wrestler the "Big Cat" Ernie Ladd, and he won the NWA tri-state tag team titles with Dusty Rhodes as his partner. For a star of his wattage, Andre held very few titles over the course of his career. Partly this was because he moved through territories so frequently (in fact, he vacated two tag team title reigns simply by never being there to defend the championship), and partly it was because he was a "division killer"—once he won a belt, he had no credible opponents. But the truth of the matter is at once more subtle and more obvious: As famed WWF ring announcer Howard Finkel succinctly put it, "André didn't need a title." In pro wrestling, wearing the title belt is sometimes less an indicator of your popularity than it is an instrument to earn you as much popularity as possible. Andre was such an attraction that there was nothing a championship belt could add to that. If anything, wrapping that gigantic waist in a belt would bring him down to the plane of mortals.

In 1980, Andre first faced an up-and-comer named Hulk Hogan. This was Hogan's first WWF run, and he was then playing a villain—he came to the ring flexing in a metallic cape and headband accompanied by his manager "Classy" Freddie Blassie—but he already had visions of superstardom. Andre looked at Hogan and saw a presumptive bodybuilder more interested in fame than in wrestling, and in their first matches, he took it out on Hogan in the ring. But after the two men toured Japan together and Hogan had shown sufficient deference to the Giant, acting as his personal barback and even offering up a case of fine French wine in fealty to Andre on his birthday, the men reached a sort of détente. And in mid-1980, when the two did battle at the Philly Spectrum and later at Shea, Andre won both matches but gave Hogan the gift of a disqualification ending in the former bout and a postmatch bloodying in the latter. The degree to which this established Hogan's career can't be easily quantified, but the effect was profound. When Andre broke his ankle getting out of bed the next year—it was sold to wrestling fans as the result of a diabolical attack by Killer Khan—a newly ascendant Vince McMahon re-hired Hogan and elevated him to the role of top star in the new world of the WWF.

Vince had Andre under contract, and he let him continue to wrestle in Japan but not for any other American promoter. Andre agreed to this deal out of respect for his history with Vince Sr. and acknowledgment of Vince Jr.'s vision, but he wasn't entirely happy about it. Andre loved touring the United States, loved being hailed as the conquering hero in each successive town, loved overindulging with his cohorts at the bars around the country. The WWF would make him a bigger star, but would one stage be big enough for an icon the size of the Giant?

The question would be put to the test in short order. In his first WWF storyline, Andre took on Big John Studd in a series of bodyslam challenge matches. Studd—a goliath in his own right at 6-foot-10 (or, in real-world terms, 6-foot-6) and 360 pounds—managed first by Blassie and later by Bobby "The Brain" Heenan, offered $10,000 to anyone in the WWF who could slam him, but when Andre took him up on the offer, Studd's arrogance quickly turned to cowardice. The feud, which started in early 1983 and continued improbably until WrestleMania I in 1985, ended in one of the early WWF's seminal moments, when Andre slammed Studd, took claim of the bag containing the prize money (now a whopping $15,000), and proceeded to toss handfuls of cash into the crowd.

If one were to posit that Andre was the first sports star to "make it rain," one would probably be correct. If one were to use the meteorological reference to draw another parallel to the Greek gods, one would probably be stretching the metaphor too far. Nonetheless, 1984 had seen Andre actually play the role of another ancient god: Dagoth, the horned fiend in *Conan the Destroyer*. (The part was uncredited.) As in *The Six Million Dollar Man*, Andre was heavily costumed, but his immensity was irreplaceable. Before CGI, there was only Andre.

In WrestleMania 2, Andre competed in a twenty-man battle royal that included, among others, William "The Refrigerator" Perry. (Perry got into a scuffle with Big John Studd in the match.) But soon Andre's health was in a state of serious decline, and he was written off WWF television under the guise of a suspension nefariously engineered by Bobby Heenan. During his off-time, Andre returned to work in Japan, and then repaired again to Hollywood, where he appeared (finally without makeup) as Fezzik, the roguish but lovable ogre in *The Princess Bride*.

Andre was notoriously proud of the movie and insisted on watching it over and over again with his fellow wrestlers in the years that followed. Andre also found fame with a younger generation around this time in the Saturday morning cartoon *Hulk Hogan's Rock 'n' Wrestling* as an oafish, sport-coat-wearing animated sidekick, and as a comic prop in the live-action bumper segments.

Andre's fame was, almost inconceivably, growing. And the WWF's star continued to rise as well. As WrestleMania III approached, Vince was determined to have the biggest story in wrestling history at the center of the card. He approached Andre about playing the bad guy— which he had done with some frequency in Japan but never in

America—in a main event program against his on-screen buddy Hulk Hogan. Andre was intrigued, but he was in too much pain after years of the torment of acromegaly, the hard hits in the wrestling ring, the steady torture of undersized beds and cars, and his famously self-destructive lifestyle.

The legend of Andre the Giant's drinking almost overshadows his wrestling triumphs. There are numerous stories of his drinking feats: 119 beers in one sitting, 156 beers in one sitting, a case of wine on a four-hour bus ride, a $40,000 bar tab while filming *The Princess Bride*, an average of 7,000 calories of alcohol intake a day. (A cursory Google search will show you that the Internet is more interested in incidences of Andre's drinking prowess than in details about his career.)

When Andre told Vince that he was in no condition to wrestle, Vince offered to pay for whatever surgery he needed and to help him rehabilitate in the McMahon family home. Andre accepted. Legend has it that the anesthesiologist responsible for putting him under for back surgery had never before had a giant for a patient and was forced to use his alcoholic consumption as a guide for his dosage. ("It usually takes two liters of vodka just to make me feel warm inside," Andre purportedly quipped at the time.) The formula created for Andre is (supposedly) still used today.

☆ ☆ ☆

In 1987, Andre returned to WWF television on a "Piper's Pit" segment in which Hogan and Andre both received trophies for their accomplishments—Hogan for his three years as champion and Andre for his career-long undefeated streak. Andre felt that Hogan upstaged him— he did, actually—and the seeds were sown for Andre to turn on his erstwhile friend.

Andre brought on Heenan as his new manager—the ultimate signal of his turn to the dark side—and in a moment of shocking realism, he tore off Hogan's shirt and ripped the gold crucifix from around his neck, incidentally scratching Hogan's chest and drawing blood. Clearly, Andre was neither subject to the "demandments" of Hulkamania nor the mores of common Christianity. After all, what does one god have to offer another?

When Hogan and Andre finally climbed into the same ring at Wrestle-Mania III, the crowd had been teased into a certifiable lather. Jesse "The Body" Ventura said from the commentary table that it was "the biggest match in the history of professional wrestling," and there was no room to argue with him. This was Hercules vs. Zeus, with immortality on the line. When Hogan bodyslammed Andre, it wasn't (in truth) the first time that Andre had been slammed.[3] And when Hogan pinned Andre for the victory, it wasn't (in truth) the first time that Andre had been defeated. But that's how it was billed, and that's what the crowd believed.

Hogan stood victorious, but the spectre of Andre still loomed. Heenan "sold" the Giant's services to the "Million Dollar Man" Ted DiBiase, a newly emergent top-level heel. Hogan and Andre met again almost a year later, on February 5, 1988, in NBC's *Main Event* (a renamed version of *Saturday Night's Main Event*). Thirty-three million viewers tuned in to see Andre get his revenge. As it turned out, the Million Dollar Man's money had bought not just Andre's services but also the betrayal of referee Earl Hebner (who had "gotten plastic surgery" to pass for his brother Dave Hebner, the match's referee of record), and Hogan was pinned even though he'd clearly gotten his shoulder up after a count of two.

Every young wrestling fan learned about injustice on this day. For many of us, this was perhaps the most infuriating, gut-wrenching moment in television history. We could halfway understand Andre as the bad guy, a foreign giant with foreign motives, but we couldn't comprehend his need to cheat to win. After the match, Andre relinquished the belt to DiBiase, and we were apoplectic. He was not just a villain, not just a cheater, but now he was a sellout. He was no better than any other WWF bad guy.

The storylines that followed backed up that sentiment. His feud with Hogan over, Andre was relegated to the midcard, where he feuded with Jake "The Snake" Roberts (storyline: Andre was deathly afraid of snakes).

---

**3** Harley Race, Stan Hansen, and the Masked Superstar had all supposedly done it before.

a returning Big John Studd (storyline: it's the same feud as before, only now Studd is good and Andre's bad), and the Ultimate Warrior (storyline: Warrior can beat up Andre). In most of these feuds, his still-failing physical state was hidden in multipartner tag matches. Andre teamed with Haku to form the Colossal Connection, and the duo (managed by Heenan) won the tag team titles. But soon permanent retirement was beckoning. The Colossal Connection lost the belts to Demolition, and when a livid Heenan came into the ring to reprimand Andre for the loss, Andre attacked his manager.[4] Andre had seen the light, and he was finally once again in the good graces of the WWF audience.

☆ ☆ ☆

Andre appeared only sporadically thereafter. His last U.S. television appearance, on 1992's WCW Clash of the Champions XX special, was depressing for a number of reasons: Andre's crutches, WCW's shoddy production values, the impertinence of the whole thing. He wrestled his final match in December '92 in Japan, but it was a sorry spectacle even for the entertainment-style legends match that it was. He needed help getting to the ring, moved around in obvious discomfort, and at one point danced with one of his opponents to the ironic delight of the crowd. Perhaps most depressing of all, he couldn't even climb over the top rope to get into the ring anymore.

Three months later, Andre died. In terrible physical pain, he had traveled from his North Carolina ranch to France to attend his father's funeral; one night, in the Paris hotel room that he stayed in (presumably because it fit him better than his family home would), he died in his sleep. There was no autopsy, but the cause of death was ruled a heart attack due to various complications from acromegaly.

He had had a magnificent career, and his in-ring work was by that point almost certainly over. But there was a pervading sense in his

---

4 Or tried to. After an obviously missed slap, commentator Gorilla Monsoon yelled, "Andre just paintbrushed him!"

obituaries that he had lived up only to the cusp of something, that pro wrestling was about to become bigger than ever, that Andre was a sort of Moses, unable to get to the promised land. It's certainly the case that he didn't live to see the full explosion of the Modern Era of wrestling, but that's just as well. He was an icon of a different era, the last in a long line of real men—William Wallace, Vlad the Impaler, Davy Crockett, etc.—who became gods in the retelling of their tales. In the Modern Era, with television and later the Internet, there is no folklore, no mythmaking outside of the sort of postmortem spit-shining that's been done to the legacies of those like Ronald Reagan. Andre's death, heartbreaking as it was, elevated him into the pantheon, into the world of memory and legend, which is where he always belonged anyway.

In his forty-six years, everything that Andre touched turned not into gold but hyperbole: He was the biggest athlete of all time; the Wrestle-Mania III bout was the biggest wrestling match of all time; his 1981 *Sports Illustrated* profile was the biggest *SI* profile of all time. One would think that, at his size, the superlatives would be sort of redundant.

Ric Flair tells the story that when he started out in wrestling, some of the old-timers told him that Andre the Giant—who was passing through the territory at the time—had multiple rows of teeth, like a shark. Whenever Ric got close enough, at the right angle, he snuck looks into Andre's mouth to see if the legend was true.

Andre the Giant was as much a man of myth as a man of reality. He was a god who couldn't be contained by the outsize world of professional wrestling, but moreover, he was a god in the classical-historical sense: His existence was sustained by his legend, and his legend evinced his existence.

# CAPTAIN LOU ALBANO

One could forgive a child of 1991 if he were to look at a photo of Captain Lou Albano and say, "That's Super Mario," or a teenager from 1986 if he were to say, "That's Cyndi Lauper's dad." And one could forgive a late-'80s wrestling fan if he saw Albano only as a buffoonish torch-bearer for the good guy wrestlers, or an older wrestling fan if he knew him only as a loudmouth heel hypeman.

The popular image of Captain Lou Albano is probably a crude amal-gamation of the first three; the lattermost is certainly the most accurate if longevity—or the opinion of wrestling diehards—is the measure of a reputation. But if Albano can't be defined without some acquiescence to all of these disparate parts—if he's as much none of them as he is all of them—the confusion was largely of his own creation. And in that way, he kicked open the doors for wrestling's erratic Modern Era, his dissociative personality spreading to his sport at large. In retrospect, it's paradoxical that a performer footed in the Golden Age of wrestling would incite its unraveling.

☆ ☆ ☆

After a lackluster go in the '50s as a singles wrestler—sometimes known as "Leaping Lou"—Albano teamed up with Tony Altomare to form the "Sicilians," two stereotypical Italian mob goons who were securely situated on the repugnant side of the Territorial Era spectrum. It was also of a more naive era: Not only were Albano and Altomare hated by the fans, but their shtick was also convincing enough that, during a run in the Midwest, they elicited threats from actual organized crime in Chicago. Despite the fact that they were holding the Midwest tag titles, the threat of reality won out, and afraid for their well-being, the duo hightailed it back to the Northeast without even dropping the belts.

Albano and Altomare also appeared on a 1963 episode of *Jackie Gleason and His American Scene Magazine* (a.k.a. *The Jackie Gleason Show*), as professional wrestler Sandpaper Sam Staccato and referee Harry Hornet respectively. Gleason, in bringing the wrestling world in all its oddity to mainstream culture, chose a young Lou Albano as his shepherd. And Albano straightforwardly and eagerly affected a new character—he became someone else—for mainstream exposure. This basic equation would repeat itself throughout Albano's career.

The Sicilians had a good run—they even briefly held the United States tag titles in Vince McMahon Sr.'s WWWF—but by 1969 they had dissolved their union. Never the most talented ring technician to begin with, Albano was nonetheless indisputably good at provoking the fans.

On the advice of the iconic Bruno Sammartino, Albano made the first significant shift of his career, ending his days as a grappler and refashioning himself into a diabolical manager,[1] determined to dethrone Sammartino and end his years-long championship reign. He dubbed himself "Captain Lou"—a direct (albeit imprecise) reference to Albano's pre-wrestling military career. His persona was more Italian thug than the broader character he took on in the '80s; he wore silk shirts and fur coats and big watches. The manager shtick was a convenient storyline for pro wrestling's Territorial Era: Sammartino was a WWWF mainstay, but his villainous opponents were often imported on short-term contracts to feud and, once dispatched, to disappear into a different territory. This kept the card fresh, but it limited the long-term storytelling potential. In his new role, Albano bridged the gap. He became Sammartino's principle foil, despite the fact that he hardly set foot in the ring; Albano sent fearsome heels at Sammartino like an ornery god lobbing thunderbolts at antiquity's heroes.

Under Albano's tutelage, Ivan Koloff, a Russian monster,[2] defeated Sammartino for the heavyweight title—though he quickly dropped it to fan favorite Pedro Morales. (This is the quintessential example of the "transitional champion"; it was imperative that the good guys not be required to face off directly; in wrestling's Golden Age, a face-to-face rivalry would have been unthinkable.) His goal had been accomplished, but Albano's diabolical coterie didn't fare quite as well in the following years. Never again did Albano manage a wrestler to the heavyweight title, though Greg "The Hammer" Valentine and Don Muraco each won the intercontinental belt with Albano as his mouthpiece. Albano would

---

1  The concept of a manager in wrestling is a sort of catchall description of a paternal adviser, equal parts corner man, mouthpiece (especially for the charismatically challenged wrestler), and, most important, instigator. Note that the manager is almost always a noncombatant male; the female counterpart is a valet, though valets are usually ineffectual eye candy, and a formidable male in a similar role is usually called an enforcer or bodyguard.

2  Who was actually a Canadian named Jim Parras.

find his real niche managing tag teams; over the remainder of his career, he led seemingly innumerable duos to championship gold.

☆ ☆ ☆

The tag team manager displays the manager's role in its most distilled state. The world of tag teams is the land of the also-ran—the wrestler incapable of working out the psychology of a full-length solo match, too small to act as a believable adversary, or unable to summon the voice or charisma needed to convey the element of threat. This last type was the bread and butter for Albano and other managers of his ilk.

Even as a heel—some would say especially as a heel—Albano was a ragtag supernova of charisma: long, frazzled mane; Hawaiian shirts unbuttoned to the navel; rubber bands tying off his unkempt goatee and dangling from safety pins piercing his face. He was in some ways the same streetwise bully he had portrayed in his earlier wrestling days, challenging his rivals' manhood and hurling decidedly un-PC epithets at the gathered crowds. He was a jerk, but above all he was a weasel, a guy willing to talk big but unwilling to compete, and in the arena of theatrical fisticuffs, that made him truly detestable. There were other managers who can be said to have worked the routine as well as Albano,[3] but Albano's act was an inversion of the usual loudmouthed, string bean manager type: He looked like your tough uncle, like he could actually throw his weight around, and yet he remained safely situated behind his various protégés. His cowardice seemed inexplicable, so it was all the more infuriating.

Albano did make one notable return to the ring in this era as the payoff to a feud against "Superfly" Jimmy Snuka. Snuka had been in a rivalry with Albano disciple Ray "The Crippler" Stevens, but since feuds against Albano's stable members were always de facto feuds against Captain Lou himself, Snuka eventually got Albano into a steel cage at Madison Square Garden. Years removed from the ring at that point, Albano

--------

**3** The Grand Wizard and "Classy" Freddie Blassie were the other two greats of that period, and they, along with Albano, are referred to as the "Holy Trinity" of heel managers.

nonetheless put on a satisfying show, recoiling comically from Snuka's blows and (ostentatiously) razor-blading his forehead to bloody himself—or, in wrestling reality, to be "bloodied at Snuka's hands."

☆ ☆ ☆

Albano's career continued along this crowd-(dis)pleasing midcard path until an odd confluence of events landed him in an unlikely cultural spotlight. In 1983, Captain Lou Albano met pop star Cyndi Lauper on a flight to Puerto Rico. Perhaps seeing in Albano a kindred spirit—or maybe because her manager-cum-boyfriend Dave Wolff was a longtime wrestling fan—Lauper asked Albano to play her father in the video for "Girls Just Want to Have Fun." As legendary rock writer Richard Meltzer puts it in his devastating WrestleMania I treatise "The Last Wrestling Piece": "Granted you might not've had an actual concrete rock-wrestling Connection—so-called—at least not the *official* horror the thing is currently saddled with, had not Lou Albano made a guest appearance in one of Lauper's videos (and History proceeded from there)." It's unarguable that the video instigated a wildly commercially propitious period for wrestling—the first "mania," if you will, that the sport had seen in decades. Due to both his notoriety from the Lauper video and his electric, eccentric personality—to say nothing of his shaggy, bloated accessibility—Captain Lou would serve as the mascot and ambassador of pro wrestling to the world at large.

Albano's appearance in the video was an incredibly high-profile cameo for a pro wrestling personality; wrestlers were often ghettoized by their unconventional enterprise. Moreover, though, the Lauper video offered a distillation of the burgeoning mainstream Captain Lou persona. "Girls" is often viewed as the antic counterpart to the more self-serious "Papa Don't Preach," and Albano stood out in stark contrast to the distractingly earnest Danny Aiello, who played the father in the Madonna video. Where Aiello was sober and cinematically gauzy, Albano's Papa was an overacted neon epiphany, wagging his finger and throwing up his arms in dismay—all the camp that served him so well as a blowhard antagonist playing to the wrestling world's cheap seats now made newly potent under the lights of MTV hyperactivity.

It must be said that Albano was playing only a very minor variation of the "Captain Lou" character—he was uncostumed, or rather costumed simply as Captain Lou Albano. Setting the stage for much of the rest of his Hollywood career, Albano portrayed his WWF character with minimal affectation rather than delving fully into any new character. It's stunning—galling even—how seamlessly he adapted to his new role. For years, the pro wrestling world had protected its secrets under the veil of kayfabe, keeping "wrestling reality" from being disrupted in any public setting. But Albano's appearance on MTV was bizarre simply for the fact that he took his persona from the (putatively nonfictional) wrestling world and transposed it wholesale into the (obviously fictional) music video enterprise. As such, it was the moment modernity at last entered the petrified WWF. And rather than evict Albano for crossing the line, the younger McMahon, who recently had taken over the company from his father, embraced the crossover appeal it provided. It would prove to be a savvy business decision, but it would also bring to wrestling what modernity brings to every precinct it touches: a culture that values histrionics over history, a culture in which everything is disposable, a culture of . . . whatever.

☆  ☆  ☆

The Albano-Lauper relationship segued into WWF television, where Lauper made a surprise appearance on "Piper's Pit." Albano—still a bad guy to the WWF audience—interrupted and cruelly tried to take credit for Lauper's celebrity.[4] Once suitably provoked, Lauper assaulted Albano with her purse—he sold the attack with all the gusto that he summoned for Snuka's headbutts years earlier—and challenged him to a proxy

---

**4**  Such an assault on Lauper by the predominant heel manager of the era was actually a masterstroke in lending her pro wrestling credentials. Wrestling fans are notoriously touchy about outsiders invading their turf, but Albano's factually absurd anti-Lauper rant cemented her as a comprehensible presence on the wrestling stage.

match between female wrestlers of their choosing: a setup for the legendary Fabulous Moolah–Wendi Richter match on July 23, 1984, on MTV—an event solemnly titled "The Brawl to End It All."

It was odd that they would choose the near-invisible realm of women's wrestling as the site of their duel, but this was the dawning of a new era, so . . . whatever. The WWF touted the twenty-eight years that Moolah had held the women's strap, so her defeat at Richter's hands was made epic despite the notable lack of women's wrestling intrigue in the preceding decade.

Richter's win earned her the title, but more importantly, it signaled the victory of the incipient Rock 'n' Wrestling movement.[5] The younger McMahon, who was eager to expand the promotion nationally, thrilled at the potential for such exposure. He wedded Hulk Hogan, newly reacquired from Minnesota's AWA, to the Rock 'n' Wrestling phenomenon, and Albano, newly chastened by Moolah's loss (and brimming with crossover popularity), converted and joined forces with Lauper and Hogan.

It was a logical business decision—and a positive career move for Albano—but it was another slap to wrestling's purist history. As Meltzer snarls:

> While roleplay flexibility, including the option of 180° reversals on a dime, has always been a vital part of the trip, bad-to-good transitions have become an all-too-prevalent fact of life, as witnessed by the surrender-of-self of far too many Significant Malevolents in the last couple annums: Hulk Hogan, Sgt. Slaughter, Superfly Snuka and—saddest of all—Lou Albano. (Reagan Era culture death at its most chilling.)

For all his enthusiasm, Albano was basically neutered by being a fan favorite. Before long, he was marching the other Rock 'n' Wrestlers to the

---

5  Interestingly, Richter herself proved disposable; she never became as significant a wrestler as she was here a symbol—a vessel for Lauper-style feminine strength and coolness. Her WWF run was interrupted due to a contractual dispute, and her later employers were unable to muster the hype that attended her WWF run. Yet in retrospect, the fact that the legendary Moolah was jobbed out to such a one-hit wonder hardly seems significant; legacy has become disposable too.

ring as little more than a glorified corner man. These were good guys who, if decades of wrestling strictures had taught us anything, didn't need a manager. If it wasn't culture death writ large, it was still an awkward shift. Nevertheless, this new interdisciplinary endeavor pushed wrestling—as now defined by Vince Jr.'s WWF—to new heights of cultural "legitimacy."

The year 1984 saw the debut of the aforementioned cartoon *Hulk Hogan's Rock 'n' Wrestling*, which featured Hogan and his band of fan favorites—including Captain Lou—in an orgy of semicomical, multicultural animated horseplay opposite "Rowdy" Roddy Piper's team of bad guy all-stars. Sold to children on Saturday mornings, wrestlers were fully in the mainstream, albeit in animated form. And it must be said that their portrayals were borderline parodic and oddly inauthentic— the wrestlers didn't even voice their own on-screen avatars.[6] This was followed in short order by wrestlers on talk shows, on awards shows, seemingly everywhere. Here was the ultimate victory for the Rock 'n' Wrestling movement: Wrestling had been there all along, lurking in the shadows, but suddenly it was inescapable.

And there in the middle of it all was Captain Lou, the nominal patron saint of the whole WWF. Now commonly appearing in too-tight T-shirts emblazoned with his own visage, he was wrestling's ambassador. Hogan—the champion, the figurehead—appeared on MTV and in commercials, but Albano was the era's true crossover star, amplifying his wrestling career with appearances in Lauper videos, on TV shows *Miami Vice* and *227*, and in the movies *Body Slam* and *Wise Guys*.

Of these, only *Body Slam* merits special mention. It's a straightforward, comedic rendition of the WWF universe, a story about a hapless music manager who finds fame and fortune bringing wrestling to the masses. With a game Dirk Benedict roughly portraying Vince McMahon and Roddy Piper repackaged and polished into a clean-cut babyface, the film was either easily digestible rasslin'-lite for the nonfan or a mind-bending circus-mirror caricature of the sport for the zealous viewer. If

----

6   The actor Brad Garrett, of *Everybody Loves Raymond* fame, portrayed cartoon Hogan.

Albano's turn in "Girls Just Want to Have Fun" imperiled kayfabe, this mockumentary treatment did more to dismantle the barrier than anything in wrestling until the late '90s, when a postmodern wave discarded the whole concept altogether for the sake of the pseudoreality of in-jokes and obscenity. In *Body Slam*, Albano, as was his standard, more or less played himself. Technically, his character went by "Captain Lou Murano," but he wasn't trying to be anything other than Captain Lou Albano—in some ways he was a sort of bastion of wrestling "reality," a concrete connection to the "real" fiction of the ring beyond the "fake" fiction of the film. But more than that, the resemblance of Murano to Albano actually underscored the gap—or lack thereof—between pro wrestling's unreality and Hollywood's plain falsehood.

And again, there was something off-putting about the ease with which he moved between worlds. His familiar presence made the movie seem palatable, but it raised deeper questions: If pro wrestlers weren't going to keep up the facade, then why should viewers continue to act like they believe, or care? When Albano appeared on Gleason's show under a new identity, the television market was new and its ramifications for kayfabe were indiscernible. With *Body Slam*, though, the same couldn't be said. Albano and Piper either didn't know what they were doing, or they didn't care.

☆ ☆ ☆

Albano did finally put on another costume, but only in deference to a cultural icon even greater than himself: He portrayed the live-action Mario in *The Super Mario Bros. Super Show!* (He also voiced the cartoon Mario.) Albano once said that he almost turned down the show out of reluctance to shave his famous goatee, but that too proved to be disposable.

Despite a paltry number of unique episodes, the series has achieved remarkable cultural currency. It functioned not just as a touchstone but also as a larger culmination: the union of the new (video games) with the old (children's programming). The cartoon sequences were mundane, no more remarkable than those of *Hulk Hogan's Rock 'n' Wrestling*, basically fantasy adventures based on the video game lore. But the live-action segments—featuring the two Mario brothers running a plumbing outfit from a basement in Brooklyn—were often bizarre and Beckett-esque nonlinear quandaries; somehow grounding the fantasy in live-action reality made the enterprise even more bizarre. There were frequent celebrity cameos, and Albano and Danny Wells (as Luigi) sometimes played other characters, including female versions of themselves. One of the most bizarre sequences has Lauper appear in pursuit of a missing Captain Lou, whereupon "Mario" professes to be a big Albano fan. This can certainly be viewed as a great victory, if not for wrestling at large than certainly for Albano: His fame was suddenly on equal footing with Mario's, the role to which he subjugated himself.

After his Mario chapter ended, Lou made a return to WWF television, managing the Headshrinkers. (Lou had a history handling Samoan wrestlers—he managed the Wild Samoans in the early 1980s, and Fatu played Tonga Tom, Piper's tag team partner in *Body Slam*.) In his return to ringside, Lou continued to play the good guy, but he otherwise reverted back to the elements of his early managerial heyday: Blustery and grating, he steered the Headshrinkers almost instantly to the tag team championship. He had reappeared in the WWF almost incidentally and disappeared without the booming farewell one might have thought he deserved. It has to be said that Lou's absence was hardly noticeable—but again, this was his own doing; he had turned his back on wrestling when he donned Mario's red coveralls. Nostalgia was disposable now too.

☆ ☆ ☆

In 2008, on his seventy-fifth birthday at a restaurant in Queens, the Sandman, a mainstay of the ECW promotion, gave a drunken toast to his longtime friend Albano, then got into a brawl with the restaurant's owner. The melee made the New York papers and was heckled widely on the Internet, Albano once again shepherding his sport and all its silly excess into the mainstream.

Much of the story of wrestling is the story of its slow liberation from its old moorings—from the territories, from the traditions, from the physical event itself—so that what actually transpires in the ring now is almost incidental to the sport. To become a part of the cultural wallpaper today, pro wrestling had to absolve itself of its distinctiveness. Above all, it sacrificed a great deal of its wonderfully peculiar internal logic for the logic of television, where there is little room for history or tradition, where there is no such place as "Parts Unknown," where the culture of disposability will always hold the belt. Albano's role in this can't be overstated. He led pop culture into pro wrestling and led pro wrestling into pop culture; he was an ambassador for the crossover success that redefined the wrestling trade, a manager on a grand scale.

The older wrestling fans might see this change as a travesty, and to the late-'80s wrestling fan it might seem wholly insignificant. Pro wrestling is in everyone's life now to some degree, and Captain Lou was the trailblazer, for better and for worse.

# "MACHO MAN" RANDY SAVAGE

June 25, 1984: We're in Memphis, and the hugely popular
Rock 'n' Roll Express is brawling with the dastardly Poffo clan—Randy
(né Poffo) Savage, Lanny Poffo, and their ever-present father, old-school
great Angelo Poffo. The melee spills outside the ring and immediately
turns frenzied. Event security swarms the wrestlers with postures that
suggest they're not quite as in on the staging of this match as you might
expect. There are cameramen and announcers adding to the tangle of
bodies, and audience members stand only inches away, visibly nervous.
The three villains get the better of Rock 'n' Roller Ricky Morton, whose

legacy is that of opponents getting the better of him. Morton is thrown on top of the nearby announcers' table, whereupon Savage picks him up and piledrives him *through* the table and onto the floor.

The crowd on hand is aghast. People throw up their arms in exasperation and dismay. A woman positioned immediately beside the table recoils and covers her mouth with both hands. But then, in the lower right of the screen, ten or fifteen feet from ground zero, three men begin high-fiving each other. A babyface star has been driven headfirst through a table by a maniacal loon who has been antagonizing the Memphis fans for months, and these men are inexplicably cheering. This isn't the way we are supposed to react.

Even among young wrestling fans, there were some who defied convention and fell under Savage's spell—likely the same sort who never much caught on to the Rock 'n' Roll Express fad. There was something strangely magnetic about Savage, the wild-eyed brawler who had been stealing airtime (and stealing the show) from Jerry Lawler and his average-Joe cohort over the preceding months. But actually *cheering* for him was out of the question. It just wasn't done.

This is not to say that wrestling fans of that era were rubes, but rather that they played their traditional role in the pro wrestling show construct with little deviation: You cheered for the heroes and booed at the villains and whooped at the pretty ladies. Somehow, that night, Randy Savage had turned this convention on its head and, you might say, dropped it through a table. He was engaging even at his most reprehensible, which had everything to do with the unexpected note of pathos in his character, an oddly relatable paranoid streak: We the viewers were suspicious too. Just like Savage, we looked slit-eyed at all the activity in and around the ring, wondering what the angle was.

☆ ☆ ☆

Savage and the Poffos had been hopscotching around the country ever since Angelo closed down his own territory in Tennessee to get his sons—Randy in particular—more national exposure. When they briefly settled in Memphis, the clan was immediately a major player; Savage called out Lawler, the area's biggest star, in his first on-screen appearance. (In his mod leather jacket and fedora, he was dressed more as a '70s-movie villain than a pro wrestling badass.) After the family's feud with the Rock 'n' Roll Express cooled off, Savage found himself in Lawler's good graces, and the pair went up against the monstrous duo of King Kong Bundy and "Ravishing" Rick Rude. The Savage that emerged during this period was a minor revelation as he maintained the derangement of his heel persona while embracing a sort of glam eccentricity: the first real indication of the superstar we would come to know.

As such things go in the world of wrestling, Savage soon reembraced the dark side and reignited his rivalry with Lawler. The feud became violent and heated, but Lawler's supremacy in the region was never really in doubt, and after Savage lost a rugged steel cage match between the two that was conducted under Loser Leaves Town rules, Savage was sent packing.

☆ ☆ ☆

Savage soon reemerged on WWF television, presented as the top free agent in wrestling. All of the name managers of the day courted Savage—the "Macho Man," as he was now commonly known—to offer their services. Savage eventually gathered the cadre of baddie mentors into the ring and sincerely—and hilariously—thanked them one by one "for their consideration" and for the knowledge they had imparted during the selection process ("Mr. Fu-ji, the devious *ways* that you put in my *mind* will come to *use*") before rebuffing them all in favor of Miss Elizabeth, Savage's real-life partner and a newcomer to the WWF universe.

The couple's act was an inversion of the usual wrestler-manager relationship. Rather than leading the charge to the ring and cunningly helping him in his matches, Elizabeth was a fully passive bystander, occasionally clapping and sincerely wincing in reaction to pain inflicted upon Savage. And rather than letting Elizabeth do his talking for him in interviews, Savage issued mind-bending soliloquies with Elizabeth more often than not offscreen, until he deemed her presence necessary and he dragged her into view, bullying her into confirming his greatness.

Savage had been an incredible orator from his earliest days in the business—first as a warbling ecstatic and later as a frenzied, bloodthirsty psycho—but his move to the WWF truly allowed his style to flourish. For the audience, the consummation during this period of the Savage interview style was shocking. Chaotic in flavor and punctuated liberally with his signature *"Oooh, yeah,"* his interviews sometimes involved more digression than substance as he held forth in metaphor-heavy diatribes on matters of violence, current events, and tough guy hierarchy—much to the dismayed bewilderment of ever-present straight man interviewer "Mean" Gene Okerlund—with only a passing regard for the specific rivalry at hand. It was the wrestling promo as scripted by David Foster Wallace—main text in a high-volume snarl, footnotes in a lupine, maniacal whisper. His oratorical style was a mesmerizing experiment in free associative thought.

Savage's first noteworthy feud was with Intercontinental Champion Tito Santana, and he finally wrested the belt from Santana at the Boston Garden on February 8, 1986, with the aid of an illegal loaded punch. He soon thereafter became embroiled in an oddball love triangle with burly dimwit George "The Animal" Steele, who had developed a crush on Elizabeth, who seemed too kindhearted to reject him outright. Though the storyline was farcical, Savage's exorbitant jealousy was at least in some part a reference to reality; Savage's real-life paranoia and protectiveness, especially in regard to Elizabeth, was well documented. Hulk Hogan has said that Savage would make Elizabeth keep her gaze fixed on the ground backstage at wrestling events so she wouldn't make eye contact with any of the other guys, and it's frequently reported that he locked their home—from the outside—when he left, sometimes shutting her inside for days at a time.

Odd (and abusive) as this may be, it's important to note that there was minimal distinction between Randy Savage the wrestling personality and Randy Poffo the real guy. To the extent that other wrestlers knew him personally, Savage was said to be the same person outside the ring as inside, sometimes to a fault.[1] But in terms of his on-screen persona, his personal eccentricity was rendered as maniacal psychopathy, and it found a suitable venue in the WWF ring, which was even more an "arena for angry minds" (in historian Richard Hofstadter's phrase) than the political realm. The "heated exaggeration, suspiciousness, and conspiratorial fantasy" of the average Savage interview functionally defined the Paranoid Style in American pro wrestling. He was McCarthy in spandex.

After a WrestleMania III loss for which he blamed WWF president Jack Tunney, he started an interview with nihilism and went straight into conspiracy theory:

"Nothing means nothing! . . . I'm justifiably in a position in that I'd rather not be in, but the cream will rise to the top. Macho Madness's got more to offer than President Jack Tunney thinks that I got. And let me tell you something right now, cards stacked against the Macho Man Randy Savage in WrestleMania III . . . let me say it out loud, and let me point to the president of the World Wrestling Federation, that Macho Man is not happy with your decision. I am the cream in the World Wrestling Federation."

"Wait," interjected interviewer "Mean" Gene Okerlund, "do you really blame Tunney?"

"Yeah, I do. Outside interference in my moment of glory! And now I'm living in a nightmare. . . . And now not only the Intercontinental Heavyweight Championship belt must fall, but the World Heavyweight Championship belt! . . . And there is no one that does it better than the Macho Man Randy Savage. On balance, off balance, doesn't matter. I'm better than you are. And I'm talking to everyone in the World Wrestling Federation, and I'm even talking to Jack Tunney: I'm on my way, and nothing is going to stop me! . . . I've been maligned from the top to the bottom 'cause they can't handle the Macho Man Randy Savage. The cream of the crop. Nobody does it better!"

Amid all of those implications of collusion, he was holding an individual-serving-size plastic cup of coffee creamer, which he would

---

1 Dutch Mantel said that he trained his "real" voice to be the Macho Man voice—there was no put-on there either.

present to the camera every time he pointed out that he was the "cream of the crop."

Macho Man's emotional imbalance was paralleled in his punishing in-ring style. While not exactly a physical beast, Savage was convincingly destructive in the ring, the most famous example of which probably comes from his 1987 conflict with Ricky "The Dragon" Steamboat. Savage notoriously jumped Steamboat, cruelly shoving his neck down onto the ringside railing and then jumping off the top rope with the ring bell and driving it onto Steamboat's throat, purportedly crushing his larynx. After a period of recuperation—where Steamboat had to relearn how to speak, to the guffaws of the WWF home viewer—the two men met at WrestleMania III in a match that defined both careers. Any discussion of the legacy of the Macho Man would be incomplete without this match. The show was headlined by the epic clash between Hulk Hogan and Andre the Giant, but the fifteen-minute brawl for the intercontinental title stole the show.

Between his in-ring performance and his manic, oddly beguiling personality, it was probably inevitable that Savage would be tapped for what's known in the parlance as a face turn—a bad guy going good. He got into a dispute with then–Intercontinental Champ the Honky Tonk Man,[2] and when Honky's stablemates the Hart Foundation aided him in beating Savage down after a match, Elizabeth procured help in the form of Hulk Hogan. The two men did away with their foes and momentously shook hands. The Macho Man's transformation into a good guy was complete.

The chief signifier in Savage's transition to the side of right was that he started treating Elizabeth more politely. It should be said that pro wrestling is not a world opposed to misogyny; degradation and abuse of female characters, both mental and physical, is common enough. But wrestling is also a world that leans heavily on more timeless tropes, and

--------

2  For the uninitiated, imagine Honky Tonk Man as a wrestling Elvis crossed with, um, a wrestling Elvis.

"Big Bully Degrading His Girlfriend" was chief among these: We booed him chiefly because we were supposed to. We knew our cues.

But even if Savage's actions were detestable, wrestling fans were drawn to the character at the core of the Macho Man, just as some women are drawn into unhealthy relationships with bad boys. Part of it was that we could sympathize with Savage's, well, savagery, with its thoroughly human mix of paranoia and chauvinism that distended cartoonishly enough to let us maintain some ironic distance. And certainly, we were looking for a hint of the man he would become as a good guy.

His association with Hogan established—the pair would come to be known as the Mega Powers, a nod to the wattage the two commanded—Savage began a yearlong period as Hogan's running buddy, and so began a decade of living securely in Hogan's shadow. Even at WrestleMania IV, when Savage won a fourteen-man tournament for the vacant WWF Championship—a moment that could have signaled a new era for a federation that had long relied too heavily on Hogan's singular charisma and for a fanbase that had seen every iteration of the Hogan in-ring comeback—Savage secured the final win only with Hogan's (illegal) assistance, and the two men celebrated together after the match.[3] It seemed as much a victory for the broader cause of Hulkamania as for Savage.

Savage the Good Guy was always seemingly presented as a sort of Hogan Junior—he was slightly smaller, significantly less epic, somewhat less bald—and the constant physical juxtaposition to Hogan didn't help change this perception. The majority of Savage's title reign saw him feuding with midtier pseudoluminaries—Bad News Brown, anyone?—while the real main event treatment went to Savage's tag team undertakings alongside Hogan. They battled against "Million Dollar Man" Ted DiBiase and Andre and later the porcine duo of Akeem (formerly the One Man Gang) and the Big Boss Man.

In a match against the latter pair, the soap operatic underpinnings of

---

3  Hogan and Andre the Giant had fought to a double disqualification in the tournament quarterfinals, eliminating them both from contention.

the Savage-Elizabeth relationship returned to the fore. When Savage was thrown outside the ring and onto Elizabeth, Hogan carried an injured Elizabeth to the back, abandoning Savage to the punishment of the Twin Towers. Upon the Hulkster's return, Savage was apoplectic, and he assaulted Hogan backstage after the match, igniting a feud that built toward a WrestleMania V collision wherein Hogan reclaimed the belt from Savage.

It's worth noting that the motivations at play in this storyline always seemed a few degrees off; Hogan's actions were presented as valiant and Savage's reactions to them unreasonable, but in part because Hogan was little more than statuary, personality-wise, and Savage came across as so deeply human (if unbalanced), their dispute never came off as cut-and-dried as the WWF of this era liked to play things. As with Savage's earlier abusive tendencies, there were well-defined tropes at play here, so we treated the Macho Man as the villain, but in retrospect it's hard to endorse Hogan's as the side for good here. Hofstadter could have been looking at Hogan through Savage's eyes when he wrote that "the enemy is clearly delineated: he is a perfect model of malice, a kind of amoral superman." Little wonder Savage was so paranoid.

As a face and a heel, Savage saw wrestling the way so many of us viewers did. He saw that every wrestler had an ulterior motive, that everyone was out for himself—that conspiracy theory was the only reasonable lens through which to perceive WWF reality. He was a canny viewer, sussing out all the angles. His paranoia was ours.[4]

Regardless, Hogan was the good guy and now he was back atop the mountain. Savage was left to redefine himself in a jumble of upper-midcard villains. After Savage dispatched the lukewarm "Hacksaw" Jim

---

**4** Conspiracy theory has played a fairly significant role in Savage's post-wrestling life, interestingly. There's a widespread Internet rumor that Savage deflowered a teenage Stephanie McMahon in the early '90s, and that accounts for his estrangement from the WWE since his departure. It's a compelling story, but it's been met with astonishment from less Internet-savvy figures like Hogan and tired shrugs from more plugged-in figures like Jim Ross; it seems just as likely that Savage's reclusiveness kept him remote enough from McMahon and the WWE to preclude a full-fledged reconciliation. And the WWE did work with Savage on a DVD collection and a video game shortly before his death.

Duggan, who was holding the WWF's "kingship" (passed down from Harley Race and Haku)—which, of course, demanded that the "king" at any given time wear a crown and robe, often to comical effect—Savage embraced the regality in his singularly lunatic manner, redubbing himself the "Macho King" and integrating a crown and scepter into his increasingly eclectic wardrobe: neon colors, faux leather, oversized sunglasses, and shirts heavy on the tassels. (It was, to be honest, a borderline iconic look.) Elizabeth disappeared and was replaced with the Sensational Sherri—sort of the anti-Elizabeth, an oversexualized, mascara-smeared freakshow.

Speaking of painted-up oddballs, it wasn't long before Savage crossed paths with the up-and-comer who would take his place as the heir apparent to Hogan, the Ultimate Warrior. When Warrior and then-champion Sgt. Slaughter were scheduled to meet up at Royal Rumble 1991, Slaughter promised Savage that he would be his first competition after the Rumble, should he retain the title. When Savage tried and failed to exact the same guarantee from the Warrior, the Warrior equivocated and Savage went apoplectic, attacking him before the Rumble match. (Again, his reaction here may have been unwarranted, but his motivation seemed oddly justifiable for a man being portrayed as the heel.)

Warrior and Savage finally faced off at WrestleMania VII, where both men put their careers on the line. Savage lost, putting him into "retirement" (that word in the world of wrestling is exactly as binding as it is in present-day boxing), but he won a greater victory that night: After his loss, Sherri came into the ring and berated him but, serendipitously, Elizabeth reappeared and dispatched her insufferable rival. The crowd loved it: Through no action of his own, Savage had been reverted to a fan favorite. All it took was the abiding love of his old squeeze.

His period of retirement saw Savage working as a color commentator. He eventually proposed to Elizabeth on air (just as their real-life marriage was falling apart), and they scheduled their nuptials for Summer-Slam 1991. (It was billed, rather brilliantly, as "The Match Made in Heaven.") It's unclear if there was more of a planned payoff for the wedding angle, but reality intervened and scuttled Savage's honeymoon.

Though Vince McMahon's obvious intention was to retire Savage to a permanent announcing role,[5] when he fired the Ultimate Warrior prior to SummerSlam, Savage was called back into active duty to fill his slot as the number-two babyface. He entered into a feud with Jake "The Snake" Roberts and his buddy the Undertaker when the two crashed Macho and Liz's wedding reception with a gift-wrapped cobra as their wedding present. (It's often forgotten that Roberts's beef with Savage stemmed from the fact that he was not allowed to attend the Macho Man's bachelor party. Seriously.) After Roberts loosed a real (but, in reality, devenomized) cobra on Savage in an in-ring confrontation, the WWF formally reinstated Savage so that he could formally deal with Roberts. He did.

Savage soon found himself tied up with Ric Flair, who had migrated from the NWA/WCW to try his hand at WWF stardom. In a notorious angle that presaged the contemporary era of the celebrity sex tape and that scandalized tweens the country over, Flair claimed to have "known" Liz before Savage had met her, and he had the photos to prove it. Macho, crazed with jealousy even as a good guy, battled Flair nominally to defend Elizabeth's honor but more realistically to defend his own lunatic ego. The payoff to the feud, in which it emerged that Flair had swiped pictures of Savage and Liz together and Photoshopped himself into them, was about as weird an ending as one could imagine. Even as a youth, I couldn't help but ask how Savage hadn't recognized Liz's poses from the photos in his own album. But looking for logic was a mug's game. The Macho Man's jealousy belonged more to the realm of paranoia than that of observable reality. We cheered when he overcame the libelous Flair threat—and rewon the heavyweight title—but there were plain symptoms that the Macho Man was going off the deep end.

It was roughly during this period that Savage began a memorable stint as the spokesman for Slim Jim beef jerky and solidified a place for himself in pop culture history. Despite that newfound notoriety, the remainder of his WWF tenure was unspectacular. He teamed up with a

......................................................................
**5** It has never been clear why Savage was deemed ready for retirement—or, for that matter, why he took to wearing shirts in the ring even though he appeared to be in good shape.

returning Ultimate Warrior and later split his time between announcing and feuding with the lesser lights of the WWF's baddie cavalry. He left the WWF in 1994 when it became clear they wanted him to transition into a permanent commentator's role while Savage thought his wrestling career should continue. (Vince McMahon, notoriously silent about business matters, wished Macho a surprisingly sincere farewell on the first broadcast without him.)

☆ ☆ ☆

Savage's next stop was WCW, where Hogan had previously migrated. Their notoriously tumultuous relationship was at the core of his reappearance—in interviews, Savage had ominously promised the Hulkster that he would "either shake his hand or slap his face." He was so unhinged—as evinced by his numerous turns over the preceding years, and by the pained efforts to make each turn more compelling than the last—that either option was viable. There was something poignant about this. His intentions were unreadable, and he now became opaque to the public that had once so thoroughly understood him. In the end, it may have been impossible to import a star of Savage's wattage as a villain, as the crowd would be likely to cheer his arrival regardless, but it was nevertheless a letdown when he returned to save Hogan from a beatdown by the milquetoast "Faces of Fear" stable. The crowd roared, but Savage was immediately sublimated once again to the Hogan mystique.

As Hogan wrestled as a special attraction, mostly away from the championship picture, Savage won the belt in a battle royal and then renewed his rivalry with Ric Flair, who too was back in WCW, and won the Heavyweight Championship, as the two swapped the belt back and forth.

Then came the formation of the nWo stable, where Hogan turned to the dark side for the first time in his mainstream career. He joined in on a beating of Savage to signal his reversal and, in constructing a new malevolent self, took on a good bit of the Savage persona. Savage dropped the title to Hogan and before long joined up with the nWo himself, splitting off with several others to form the nWo Wolfpac, and, well, the less said here is probably better.[6] Savage maintained a credible level of celebrity during this period, despite the zaniness of WCW booking, but soon he came to embody the midlife crisis that seemed to run through the bulk of WCW storytelling. He was suddenly overmuscled, and his hair was slicked back and dyed dark black, and, echoing and one-upping his association with Elizabeth, he was accompanied at all times by a trio of blond beauties: his real-life porn-star-esque girlfriend Gorgeous George,[7] female wrestler Madusa, and another wrestler in a ball gown and sash who went by "Miss Madness."[8]

Soon, though, WCW was near collapse and Savage's career was more or less over. He made a brief run in TNA wrestling, but afterward he retired into a seemingly complacent post-wrestling existence: He let his beard grow white. He put on weight. He avoided the life of autograph signings and high-school-gym appearances that befall so many others of his ilk. He married a longtime friend and settled into a fairly normal, if reclusive, lifestyle. Perhaps he was occasionally guilty of indulging in anti-Hogan conspiracy mongering in interviews, but even that stopped in his last years. For all outward appearances, Savage was the pro wrestling retirement success story. If we wrestling fans are inured to the notion of our childhood heroes dying prematurely, we were nonetheless optimistic that someone like Savage would be the exception.

Sadly he wouldn't be. On May 20, 2011, Savage suffered a massive heart attack while driving with his new wife, crashed into a tree, and died. (His wife was miraculously unharmed.) In an interview just after Savage died, Ric Flair painted Savage as a flawless performer but a man unable to ever get comfortable. And here is the marvel of Randy Savage: He was driven to greatness by the same paranoia that kept him from

......................................................................................
6  At this time, head writer Vince Russo was unintentionally taking the notion of nonlinear storytelling and free association to new heights of inanity.

7  No relation to the '50s icon, thankfully.

8  She would eventually reach slightly greater fame as the WWE's Molly Holly.

fully enjoying the fame that he accrued. Or to put it another way, the paranoia that made him so affecting in the ring was exactly what kept him from being relatable beyond the ropes. Hofstadter's famous piece ends aptly: "We are all sufferers from history, but the paranoid is a double sufferer, since he is afflicted not only by the real world, with the rest of us, but by his fantasies as well."

# THE WRESTLER AS PITCHMAN

"Art thou bored?" With those three syllables, "Macho Man" Randy Savage became, for the first time, a megastar. Up to that point, Savage had spent years toiling in the shadow of Hulk Hogan, both in the ring—though they shared storylines, Savage never got to fully share the spotlight—and out of it, where Hogan had the mainstream imprimatur stretching back to the MTV crossovers of the Rock 'n' Wrestling Era, plus a string of silly but still semi-legitimate kid-friendly movies. But now, in a commercial for a brand of beef jerky, Savage was cementing his star. He crashed through the wall of a boring high school play rehearsal, offered up some snacks, and with a brief, garbled koan—"Need a little excitement? Snap into a Slim Jim!"—made himself an icon, and made Slim Jims a part of pop culture. Savage was featured in a multitude of Slim Jim spots, tearing the door off a locker, crashing through piles of pizza boxes, beating up a mouthy snowboarder, beating up a mouthy rock climber, beating up a bag of potato chips, and, most wonderfully, rappelling in through the roof of a lamp-and-lightbulb store and shattering basically everything inside. When Savage left the WWF, he was replaced in the commercials by the Ultimate Warrior and, years later, by Edge. Neither had the cultural currency of the Savage run, but nonetheless a tradition long ensconced had reached its nadir. In pro wrestlers, advertisers had found a perfect mate: cheap celebrities with a flare for the dramatic.

Savage wasn't the first, by a long shot. In the late Territorial Era, good guys sometimes repped for local car lots and such; Texas standout "Iceman" King Parsons did a memorable (to me) commercial for Love Furniture Center in the 1980s, and the Ultimate Warrior himself—in his earlier Dingo Warrior character—did numerous commercials for Westway Ford of Irving, Texas. During the Rock 'n' Wrestling Era, Andre the Giant played a giant in a sweet, widely aired commercial for Honeycomb cereal.

Not to be outdone by Savage, Hogan appeared in a string of oddball commercials, pitching for everything from mainstream subjects like Right Guard deodorant, Arby's, the once-significant "10-10-220" long-distance service, and Rent-A-Center, to projects of his own imprimatur like Hulk Hogan vitamins, the Hulkamania Workout Set, and Hulk Hogan's Pastamania, a mall restaurant that obviously failed.

Most of the commercials wrestlers have starred in have been local affairs or spots specifically made to be aired during wrestling. Kurt Angle did a weird, low-budget spot for Pizza Outlet. Bret Hart did an embarrassing turn as spokesman for Humpty's omelettes. ("You know, Humpty," he said to the pillowy egg thing, "we should be a tag team.") WCW legend Sting was featured in a Sprite commercial. "Stone Cold" Steve Austin did one of the ironic ESPN *SportsCenter* commercials. John Cena shaved heartily and tormented his boss Vince McMahon in an ad for Gillette.

Most of the WWF/WWE-related campaigns have been results of corporate synergy; thus the several Slim Jim endorsers, and similarly with different series of spots for companies like 7-Eleven and Subway. There were also series of spots for Chef Boyardee (Big Show, Kane, the Rock, Mick Foley, and Booker T in separate spots), energy drink YJ Stinger (Cena, Triple H, the Undertaker, Eddie Guerrero), and nutritional supplement Stacker 2 (Cena, Kane).

It's a stunning thing to watch them all in sequence. The wrestlers are obviously better actors than the pro athletes that get these jobs more commonly on a national scale, more comfortable in front of the camera, and yet there's a disconnect. Perhaps it's the notion of fake people endorsing real products? The ignobility of these proud warriors shilling for pizza and omelettes? The reduction of a product always on the cusp of self-mockery to a laughable low-level consumerism?

Art thou bored? No, not really. Just confused.

# MISS ELIZABETH

When the lovely Miss Elizabeth debuted on WWF television
on the arm of her beau, "Macho Man" Randy Savage, she was serenaded
with effusive praise from the commentators as she slowly made her way
to the ring. *Oh my goodness... Is this a movie star? Who is this?... My
goodness... Take a look... What a surprise... I can't believe... Look at
this... What a beautiful woman... My goodness, she is absolutely gorgeous... That is a gorgeous, gorgeous lady.* It was almost as if they were
trying to talk themselves into it, into believing in her beauty. Certainly
they were trying to talk the audience into it. Because while Elizabeth
Ann Hulette was indeed a looker, she wasn't exactly Helen of Troy—and

that was the role for which she had been cast, the part she would play in WWF storylines in the coming years: the face that launched a thousand dropkicks.

Miss Elizabeth arrived in the WWF as the manager (with benefits, one assumes) of Savage, who himself came to the WWF to much acclaim. There began not just one love story for the ages but two: Savage and Liz's, of course, but also the love between Elizabeth and the WWF audience, as every male between the ages of five and seventy-five fell head over heels for this woman—or, at least, for the idea of her. We had been talked into it.

Despite her being within the provenance of the (then) dastardly Savage, soon every WWF viewer longed to be near Elizabeth, so they were given a surrogate in the form of an affable Neanderthal named George "The Animal" Steele. Adhering to the behavioral norms of pre-modern cartoon heroism, Steele didn't so much lust after Liz as he doted on her. And of course, this attention infuriated Savage to no end. Liz's tentative, fluctuating affection for the oafish Steele, though rather grotesque in retrospect, was as important for its symbolism as it was for storyline purposes. (Once, when confronted with video of Savage attacking "The Animal" after he gave a bouquet to Liz, Savage said, "We don't want to be associated with anything second class, ain't that right, Elizabeth? Right? Did you cause that? Yeah, by taking the flowers, didn't you? But that's all straightened out.") Sure, it cast Liz as a damsel in distress in the possession of a controlling Macho Man (he made her hold the ropes open for him as he entered the ring, for goodness' sake), but it also gave us a rooting interest in Liz's well-being and gave us a lens through which to imagine ourselves rescuing her.

Every fan was in love with her because, above all, Miss Elizabeth wasn't a woman. She was a symbol—a signifier of ideal beauty, of the perfect woman. Pro wrestling has long been a stage for Joseph Campbell–style heroics and for the telegraphic acting out of the oversized emotions of teenage boys, but now, in a new twist for the WrestleMania Era WWF, the standard Good vs. Evil morality plays could be balanced with archetypal love stories. There had been women in wrestling before her, and these roles had been previously explored, but there had never been a woman like Miss Elizabeth, a vessel into which viewers could pour their emotions. Little wonder that she was so uniquely popular or that her tenure coincided with such a high point in WWF history.

☆ ☆ ☆

Liz stuck by Macho through feuds with Ricky "The Dragon" Steamboat and the Honky Tonk Man, among others. When Savage became a fan favorite, their relationship was able to shift into grayer, more uncertain terrain. Just as Liz was a signifier for beauty and perfection, her relationship with good-guy Savage became a signifier for romance—for true love—with all of its highs and lows.

As the couple moved into what was arguably their career pinnacle—Savage's team-up (and later falling-out) with Hulk Hogan—the WWF kept the whole thing very conservative, but saucier subplots were there, bubbling underneath the surface, for anyone who cared to look. Liz was billed as "lovely" but never "sexy." She didn't ostentatiously seduce their opponents—like the "Million Dollar Man" Ted DiBiase and Andre the Giant—to gain an advantage, but she did flash some leg at ringside to help her men win. She didn't sleep with Hogan when Macho Man started showing signs of his old heelish behavior—but, rather, she was carried tenderly into the locker room by the Hulkster when she had been knocked out cold. Elizabeth's deliberation between the two alpha males was the subject of great on-screen intrigue, but at the end of the day, her uncertainty left her all alone—because Hogan didn't need a woman, and Savage was once again playing the bad guy.

We had already seen the dynamic of the evil Savage paired with the accommodating Elizabeth, so Liz was shunted off and replaced with the more sexual—and frightening—"Sensational" Sherri Martel. But when that relationship dissolved, of course, Liz was there to pick up the pieces. (Perhaps it was the abuse he suffered at Sherri's hands that finally allowed Savage to understand what he'd put Elizabeth through.) Their relationship thereafter was a romantic whirlwind: Savage proposed, and the two were married at SummerSlam 1991.

But somewhere along here the wheels came off the fantasy. The relationship had gone as far as it could go, storyline-wise, and the pair didn't ride off into the sunset. The magic was soon gone, and propriety went along with it: In a notorious angle, the lascivious "Nature Boy" Ric Flair claimed to have "been with" Liz before Savage had met her. So much for the fuzzy implications of years past. Liz's reputation was eventually restored, but the Age of Innocence had ended, and with it Miss Elizabeth's raison d'être. Her WWF career was soon over.

☆ ☆ ☆

Several years later, Elizabeth signed with WCW, as just about every wrestling star of her vintage and wattage did. She appeared there as a new woman—no longer in ball gowns but in a leather skirt and sleeveless top, her hair teased and frosted like a saucy forty-something midwestern newswoman. And once again, she was touted by the announcers—though not so much as a symbolic beauty as a symbol of the past. Her career there—and the inanity of WCW's booking during that period—is perfectly summed up in this Wikipedia synopsis:

> In January 1996, Miss Elizabeth returned to wrestling as a valet for Savage. She later turned against Savage and became Ric Flair's valet in the Four Horsemen. She later turned against the Four Horsemen and joined the New World Order (nWo) alongside Savage and Hogan. In June 1998, she parted ways with Savage once again by joining Hogan's side of the nWo, nWo Hollywood. Then, she accompanied Eric Bischoff on his way to the ring for the next few months.

The only real point of significance here was her pairing with Lex Luger because somewhere around this time the two started dating in real life. For the few true believers still out there, this may have signaled the end of the line for the Savage-Elizabeth fairy tale. Although Macho and Luger did eventually actually feud over Liz in WCW, it wasn't much of an epic by her earlier standards.

This was a modern era, and Liz was (nominally) a modern woman, liberated (somewhat) from the dependence of her Rapunzel youth. The art of wrestling storytelling had changed: Lex and Randy did not heroically vie for her love (or her "managerial duties"), and Lex did not win her hand, and he did not carry her off into some vision of chaste bliss.

☆　☆　☆

Though their real-world relationship continued, it did not end happily. In April 2003, Luger was charged with battery against Liz, and two months later (after several instances of erratic behavior on his part), Luger called 911 from the townhouse they shared in Marietta, Georgia, to report that Liz wasn't breathing. When paramedics arrived, she couldn't be revived. A medical examiner listed the cause of death as "acute toxicity," brought on by a mix of painkillers and vodka. Liz Hulette was forty-two years old.

With the possible exception of Vince McMahon or maybe Bobby "The Brain" Heenan, no on-air personality has ever meant more to the WWF without actually wrestling than Miss Elizabeth.[1] Liz held captive an audience of young men in a way that nobody did before and no one has since, not even in today's era of manufactured divas. For a few years in those simple, magical days, she was everything we ever wanted in a woman.

---

1 Both McMahon and Heenan did wrestle, of course, but their contributions minus those instances are still profound.

# WEDDINGS IN WRESTLING

The very mention of a wedding angle in wrestling is enough to make most fans anxious. It's a long tradition, but not a particularly proud one. If you delve into the history of WWE weddings, you see that they all follow the same basic script: Party A marries Party B by common will, trickery, or force; then Party C objects and/or physically intervenes, and hijinks ensue, tears are shed, punches are thrown.

The first on-screen marriage in the WWF was between Butcher Vachon and Ophelia in 1984. Captain Lou Albano ambled in and objected on the grounds that Vachon had been married "five or six times before," and because Ophelia was a virgin (although Vachon clarified that she was not, in fact, so pure, and Albano withdrew his objection). Then "Dr. D" David Schultz bodyslammed Vachon; later, at the reception, Schultz gave the bride a pie in the face as Vachon stood there passively. The best part was Vince McMahon's uncontrollable laughter at the drunken reception, and when the Samoan contingent forced midget wrestler Sky Low Low to sing with them. The 1985 marriage of Uncle Elmer, a Hillbilly Jim hanger-on, and Joyce was even more ridiculous, except that it was an actual wedding—as in, the two actually emerged a married couple—which goes contrary to the very fabric of pro wrestling.

The most famous wedding in WWF history was that of "Macho Man" Randy Savage and Miss Elizabeth. The pair was already married in real life, but because Savage played the heel and emotionally abused his ladyfriend, their on-screen union could only be consummated once Savage mended his evil ways. The WWF decided to play the in-ring ceremony totally straight, without interruption or other rasslin' contrivance—with the exception, of course, of Savage's ridiculous white-and-gold wedding gear in the ring and Bobby Heenan's snarky commentary. The reception, however, was famously crashed by Jake "The Snake" Roberts and the Undertaker, who had hidden a cobra in a gift box as a surprise for the groom, whom they loathed. During the toast, announcer "Mean" Gene Okerlund referred to "the new bride and groom, mister and missus Macho."

The latter-day weddings run in quick sequence, like a matrimonial fever dream. In 1999, Stephanie McMahon (daughter of Vince) was tied to a cross and forced to marry the Undertaker in a sort of pagan ritual until "Stone Cold" Steve Austin intervened. Later that year, Steph got the wedding of her dreams when she wed Test. Triple H derailed the proceedings when he informed the wedding party that he had married a comatose, post-bachelorette-party Stephanie at a Vegas drive-through chapel. This ceremony, such as it was, was really the high-water mark of the Attitude Era. It had implied kidnapping and rape, large-scale impropriety, and a healthy dose of Triple H's throaty sexual innuendo voice. It turned out that Triple H and Steph were in cahoots all along. They renewed their vows months later in an in-ring ceremony that needed no interference since Triple H hijacked it himself after learning that Stephanie had faked a pregnancy to keep his affection. "Stephanie," he said, "as I look into your eyes tonight, I see you for what you truly are: a no-good, lying bitch." And then he beat up Vince.

There have been many other weddings, all vulgar and nonsensical and wonderfully awful in their own ways: Lita married Kane and then almost Edge, and Edge married Vickie Guerrero; Dawn Marie married Torrie Wilson's dad and nobody cared; there was a gay marriage between Billy Gunn and Chuck Palumbo in 2002 that turned out to be a publicity stunt; SmackDown General Manager Teddy Long got married to Kristal in 2007 but had a Viagra-induced heart attack before the final "I do"; and Goldust married his protégée Aksana not too long ago, which was some sort of marriage of convenience, for either a Green Card for the bride or a beard for the pseudohomosexual groom.

WWE teased a wedding angle in 2012, when female wrestler-cum-groupie AJ proposed marriage to CM Punk, only to receive a counterproposal from Daniel Bryan, which she accepted. The AJ-Bryan wedding was interrupted by Vince McMahon, who appointed AJ to be *Raw*'s general manager. Bryan flew into a rage and destroyed the set. It may not have been true love, but hey, at least that was some passion.

# HAWK,
# OF THE ROAD WARRIORS

There's something to be said for the dramatic properties of elevation, particularly when there are monsters involved. King Kong scaled the Empire State Building and found himself on top of the world—and thus a target for military attack. At that great height, he was at once expressing dominance and exposing himself to harm. It's the former part that makes him a monster and the latter part that makes us care.

Elevation carries its own special thrill in professional wrestling, lending to the proceedings both a superhero aspect (Look! Up in the sky!) and an element of unfakeable danger. Wrestling has certainly seen its fair share of high-wire acts: Snuka leaping from the top of the cage;

Shawn Michaels's WrestleMania XII zip line entrance; various balcony spots in the gonzo ECW promotion; Mick Foley's masochistic Hell in a Cell tumbles; and of course the late Owen Hart's tragically ill-fated entrance as the Blue Blazer.

At NWA Starrcade in November 1986, something superheroic was certainly in the air. They called it "Night of the Skywalkers," and though Joseph Campbell certainly would have appreciated the *Star Wars* reference, the scene was more like something out of a comic book. The Road Warriors, Hawk and Animal, were facing their archrivals, the Midnight Express, in a scaffold match, which meant that the teams were to brawl on a plank two stories above the ground—a shockingly real sort of brawl, where life and limb were indisputably on the line.

It must be said that scaffold matches were, in retrospect, real almost to the point of boredom. The wrestlers were so consumed with safety—both their own and that of their opponents—that most of the combat took place in prone positions, and the punches and kicks were decidedly low-impact. But twenty or twenty-five years ago, through the semicredulous eyes of the premodern wrestling fan, those matches were stunning. To win the match, you had to knock your opponents—allow me to italicize—*off the platform and into the ring below*. On tape, you can see the kids and adults in the audience standing in awe, necks craned. The act was one part monster movie and one part Marvel Comics, and plainly very, very dangerous: No suspension of disbelief was necessary.

I first watched "Night of the Skywalkers" belatedly, on a homemade VHS compilation tape a buddy of mine had put together. The rolling lines of static only served to up the ante: I felt like I was watching a bootlegged copy of *Faces of Death*. It might not have been much of a match, but it took place thirty feet in the air, and it ended with the nefarious Midnight Express duo falling from the scaffold into the ring (each was hanging from the underside of the platform, monkey bars style, to minimize the distance of free fall). They were followed in their plummet by their insufferable manager, Jim Cornette, who stupidly climbed the scaffold after the match to escape the Warriors' manager, "Precious" Paul Ellering.

Cornette—nowhere near the experienced stuntman that his Midnighters were—blew out both knees when he landed in the ring.

Oh, and Hawk wrestled the match with a broken leg and never let on. But that's less surprising. The Road Warriors were forces of nature in the ring and two of the sport's true tough guys outside of it, muscled to their ears and notorious for working "stiff" in matches—wrestling parlance for not easing up on their various punches, chops, and stretches. Needless to say, they weren't the most popular team to go up against, but you can't tell a monster to take it easy—and you don't mess with that kind of popularity.

☆ ☆ ☆

Michael Hegstrand—who would come to be known the world over as Road Warrior Hawk—was a big kid from Minneapolis who fell under the tutelage of pro wrestling trainer Eddie Sharkey, who trained a metaphorical murderers' row of wrestlers: Hegstrand, Curt Hennig, Rick Rude, Barry Darsow (a.k.a. Krusher Khruschev, Smash of Demolition, and the Repo Man), and, of course, Joe Laurinaitis, who would become Hegstrand's tag team partner.

As wrestling writer Rick Scaia puts it: "Hegstrand was basically a bodybuilder in the early '80s: a time when bodybuilders [were] really coming into vogue in the wrestling business. The successes of Billy Graham and Jesse Ventura were fresh in everyone's minds, and a musclehead by the name of Hulk Hogan was just starting to turn heads." Hegstrand and his bodybuilder's physique debuted professionally in Vancouver. He went under the name Crusher Von Haig, and despite his build there was little in that first match to mark Hegstrand for any sort of greatness.

But what a difference some facepaint and a reverse mohawk make. Hegstrand and Laurinaitis were recruited to the Georgia territory to be part of manager Paul Ellering's new stable of behemoths to be called the Legion of Doom, the name (fittingly) swiped from a Justice League cartoon show. It certainly was a villains' all-star team: King Kong Bundy,

Jake "The Snake" Roberts, the Iron Sheik, the (original) Sheik, Arn Anderson, "Maniac" Matt Borne, and the Spoiler. Hegstrand and Laurinaitis—now Hawk and Animal—were dubbed the Road Warriors and modeled directly after the Mel Gibson movie. They wore simple, tribal-style facepaint, mohawk-style haircuts (Animal's a true mohawk and Hawk's a reverse mohawk that better suited his hairline), and leather-studded accoutrements. (It took a while to get the look right; at first, they more closely resembled patrons at a gay bondage bar than anything out of our dystopian future.)

The faction soon dissolved, but the "Legion of Doom" moniker would come to be synonymous with the Road Warriors for the rest of their careers. Right from the start, the Warriors' charisma was evident. They were nightmarish but cool—their extreme musculature, painted faces, and growling monologues set them apart from the then-standard wrestler. They were freakish next to the toughish-white-guy norm of the period—see their stablemates Jake Roberts and Arn Anderson for examples—but much sleeker and more electric than the pure monsters of the day, guys like Abdullah the Butcher and Kamala, who were garbling, corpulent grotesques whose peculiarity was such that no fan could root for them. But for the most part, the Road Warriors didn't scare fans away—they were gargantuan antiheroes, titans for a new era.

Their interview style was groundbreaking for two reasons: one, because the up-close format was the television viewer's first chance to really appreciate the He-Man physiques of the two men (particularly when they stood next to Ellering, who, though a serious bodybuilder in his day, was a shrimpy sort of guy), and two, because of their comic-book-villain intensity. Hegstrand excelled in these interviews, threatening the lives of his opponents-to-be in increasingly amusing and gory ways ("We'll rip your masks off Warrior-style—with your heads still in them!") and delivering the sort of catchphrases that would come to dominate wrestling in the coming decades: "We snack on danger and we dine on death," for instance, or, in closing every promo, "Ooooooooh, what a rush!!!"

Their in-ring style was brutal, and the audience probably perceived the too-real-to-be-fake grimaces on the faces of their poor opponents. Their no-punches-pulled routine actually started at the behest of Georgia Championship Wrestling booker Ole Anderson, who instructed the Warriors not to recoil at their opponents' assaults so as to disguise the fact that Hegstrand and Laurinaitis weren't skilled enough to realistically react. It was a winning gambit, and it became the Road Warriors' signature—they didn't show pain and couldn't have if they wanted to. Hawk in particular came to be known for "no-selling" his opponent's moves—even in later years, after his in-ring skills had improved considerably. Jim Ross says that when Hawk's opponents for the evening got to the arena, their first question would almost uniformly be "What kind of mood is Hawk in tonight?"

The Road Warriors ran through their Georgia competition and soon left for the greener pastures of the AWA. This was also the first hint of a pattern that would wind up defining the Warriors' career: Though their early days coincided with the tail end of the Territorial Era, they jumped from federation to federation, always leaving when their popularity was at its pinnacle. Whether this was shrewd business dealing, diva-style machination, or the unpredictable wanderings of untamed beasts is unclear—presumably, it was a little bit of all three.

It was in the AWA that the Road Warriors' irresistible popularity really took hold. People loved them, even if they were supposed to be the baddies. They were decidedly fresher than most of their competition there—they entered the ring in their facepaint and spikes to the strains of Black Sabbath's "Iron Man"—and their early opponents couldn't match their appeal. These were guys like Baron von Raschke, Dick the Bruiser, and the Crusher, who were all getting on in years and who looked rather like three guys from the Elks Lodge decked out in spandex. (The Crusher and Dick the Bruiser's entrance theme was "The Beer Barrel Polka.") The guys in charge took a look at the Road Warriors—oversized, ominous, and bizarre—and saw monsters, and monsters in pro wrestling were always bad guys. What they failed to see was that the Warriors were a new breed of baddie: more cartoonish and more human at the same time, and thus more compelling; the old guard saw Mothra when really they were looking at Batman. (The only time the Road Warriors earned real boos from the crowd was when they brutally attacked young golden boy Curt Hennig, who was local wrestling royalty. They nearly incited a riot.)

The Road Warriors soon became official fan favorites and feuded with the Fabulous Ones and the Fabulous Freebirds—underhanded brawlers from "Badstreet," Atlanta, who at SuperClash 1985, at Comiskey Park, emerged from the dugout wearing (highly questionable) stars-and-bars facepaint to simultaneously profess their Southernness and mock the Warriors' style.[1]

By 1986, though, the Road Warriors were such stars that one territory couldn't contain them. Their career over the next several years—and, really, over the next twenty—is difficult to reconstruct and, as is often the case in comic books and monster movies, highly repetitive. They shifted between the major and regional promotions frequently and feuded variously with just about every tag team of the era. They feuded in the NWA (which by then encompassed their old Georgia Championship stomping grounds—and which would eventually transform into WCW), squaring off with the unimaginatively named Russian Team (which included their old friend Krusher Khruschev). They feuded in Memphis against Jerry "The King" Lawler and Austin Idol.[2] They traveled everywhere, even doing a stint with the storied New Japan promotion, and wherever they went, they took their battering style with them, gaining fame and notoriety around the world with seeming ease.

It's not hard to see why: The Road Warriors were monstrosities and megastars; their physiques and personas were both overblown and yet,

--------

1  According to Freebird Michael Hayes, AWA owner Verne Gagne was skeptical that the Warriors would play as good guys despite the cheers they were getting—one can't help but see an echo of Gagne's earlier reluctance to push Hulk Hogan—and the Freebirds ended up leaving soon hereafter.

2  Lawler is an avid reader of comic books and so unsurprisingly was a huge fan of the Warriors.

for a generation that had grown up with cartoons and science fiction movies, relatable—and certainly a harbinger for the future of professional wrestling. When eventually they signed on exclusively with the NWA—the rest of the territories having more or less dried up—they brought a new sort of pop-culture legitimacy to the company, making the old-school, Southern-based organization more competitive with the zeitgeist-surfing WWF of the '80s. The stars of the NWA were happy to borrow on the cool quotient of the Warriors. Dusty Rhodes, who was both the top babyface there and the head booker at the time, quickly aligned himself with the Warriors, winning with them the NWA Six-Man Tag Team Championship and later fighting alongside them against the Four Horsemen.

Other notable feuds in their early NWA run were with the Midnight Express (see the aforementioned scaffold match) and with the Powers of Pain, a plain rip-off of the Warriors who had basically been running their shtick in the NWA before the originals got there (but to significantly less acclaim). In the territorial days of pro wrestling, the appropriation of storylines or gimmicks from another region was not at all unusual, but this was the end of that era and the beginning of national television deals, making the ersatz Road Warriors found in nearly every promotion particularly galling. The NWA's Powers of Pain (the Warlord and the Barbarian) were a sort of prehistoric Road Warriors; the Blade Runners (Justice and Flash, a.k.a. the Ultimate Warrior and Sting), who mimicked the act right down to the movie-title swipe and inhabited one of the outer reaches of the NWA kingdom, were the minor-league Road Warriors; and WWF's Demolition (Ax and Smash) were the Road Warriors gone corporate. There was even a weird British team that stole the name and about one percent of the aura; it's unclear how much they were influenced by Hawk and Animal, but it's fun to imagine that they were trying.

The Road Warriors' feud with the Powers of Pain amounted to little more than a steroid-addled pissing contest: The two teams actually had a weight-lifting competition that saw the otherwise feral Powers in matching Gold's Gym tank tops and the Warriors in gaudy Zubaz parachute pants.[3] Just when things began to turn serious—when the Powers of Pain heard that they were scheduled to compete against (and lose to) the Warriors in a series of scaffold matches—the imitators abruptly quit and signed on with the WWF.[4]

With all their foes vanquished, the Warriors eventually embraced their monstrous natures and turned to the dark side—and against their friend Dusty Rhodes, whom they attempted to "blind" with a spike from their shoulderpads. (Rhodes came up with the story but ended up losing his front-office job over it. The execs at TBS, which aired NWA shows, had demanded that they do away with on-air bleeding. One need only see the plenitude of scars on Rhodes's forehead to grasp how off-putting such a change would be for him.)

As the NWA transitioned into WCW—and into a truly national promotion—the Road Warriors remained prominent, but friction with new showrunner Jim Herd nudged the Warriors out the door in 1990. It was another instance of the Warriors walking out at the height of their popularity, but in this case, we have the first clear instance of a dispute with higher-ups causing their departure. This would become their new tradition. Hegstrand in particular was a serial collector of grievances; there was always a wrongheaded booker, some éminence grise holding the Warriors down.

☆ ☆ ☆

The pair quickly landed in the WWF, and it seemed like a perfect match. The WWF was the home of muscle-bound Technicolor, and the Warriors had long been WWF-style wrestlers operating outside the WWF. Their impact was immediate: The Powers of Pain split up to keep confusion at a minimum, and a feud with Demolition commenced. Due to the failing

---

**3**  Odd fact: The Road Warriors were actually the first investors in Zubaz, those neon animal-printed workout pants from the '80s. They insisted on appearing in them in TV sketches and in wrestling magazine photo shoots. Once Jim McMahon and his Chicago Bears teammates started wearing them, Zubaz became a certifiable national phenomenon.

**4**  They would soon be feuding with Demolition in the WWF, naturally.

health of Ax, Demolition had recently engaged a third member, Crush. The Road Warriors teamed up with the Ultimate Warrior, who, despite starting off as a Road Warriors ringer himself, had established himself as one of the WWF's top stars. At this point, Vince McMahon did away with the "Road Warriors" sobriquet and started referring to the team as the "Legion of Doom" to avoid confusion with his other Warrior.

The L.O.D. won the tag team titles from the Nasty Boys (a couple of silly street brawlers, two chubby white guys with mohawks, mullets, and black shirts splatter-painted in multicolor neon), which made them the only tag team to hold the belts in the WWF, WCW, and the AWA. But they lost the titles several months later to Money Inc.—the "Million Dollar Man" Ted DiBiase and his accountant, Irwin R. Schyster (a.k.a. Mike Rotunda)—whereupon they disappeared again, taking a leave of absence. When they returned, they had their old manager Paul Ellering back in tow, and for some reason, he had with him a ventriloquist dummy named Rocco, supposedly to bring inspiration to the team. The role of the manager for the monster wrestler (or tag team) is significant: He is an ambassador to the real world. Even when the monsters speak English, as the L.O.D. did, a manager can provide a human element—a plausible answer to the questions like "Does Hawk have a checking account?" But the addition of Rocco the puppet pushed the L.O.D. in the other direction, from cinematic realism to cartoon lunacy.

When L.O.D. faced Money Inc. at SummerSlam 1992, the trio rode motorcycles to the ring. According to Laurinaitis, Hawk was inebriated before the match and missed his parking spot outside the ring, forcing Animal to dismount on the wrong side of the bike and scald his leg on the exhaust pipe. He wrestled the match with his tights burned into his calf.

Any machismo bequeathed by those Harleys, though, was nullified by the fact that Ellering rode in with Rocco on his handlebars. Hegstrand was galled by the inanity of the storyline. And as was his wont, he quit the WWF in a huff. What's notable is that he did so without discussing it with Laurinaitis. (Animal stayed in the WWF to try to finish out the L.O.D.'s obligations there, but a back injury derailed his plan.) No longer were the Road Warriors underappreciated in Hegstrand's mind; now it was just Hawk who was underappreciated. Hegstrand's decision-making, always prone to fits of pique, was becoming increasingly bizarre, and the stories of his substance abuse multiplied. At that point, the AWA was a shadow of its former self; options were diminishing, and Hegstrand's temperament was threatening to become his Kryptonite. He traveled alone to Japan, where he replicated the Road Warriors gimmick sans Animal, teaming up with a famous (and similarly itinerant) wrestler named Kensuke Sasaki.

Hegstrand was a huge draw in Japan, as have been many other overgrown Americans. Such achievement evinces a sort of circus-mirror inverse of the state of U.S.-Japanese relations at that point. While the American economy of the '80s and '90s was ravenous for Japanese electronics and automobiles, the only American export that the Japanese had any interest in were white giants like Hawk. The country that decades earlier brought us Godzilla and Mothra was now more than happy to take our monsters back in trade.

Hegstrand soon turned up again in WCW, wrestling solo and later in a loose tag team with former imitator Sting, and in the new and growing federation ECW. He could never really make the singles career work, though. (Nor could Animal, who made a go of it in WWE after Hawk's death.) Like so many tag teams that achieve massive success, the Road Warriors were necessarily plural. Even megastars have a niche. Fans wouldn't take Hawk fully seriously as a solo act if he didn't evolve beyond the old gimmick, but the old gimmick was too popular to give up. Animal finally returned to the scene, and the Road Warriors reunited in WCW and made their way through various disputes with the Faces of Fear (Meng and their old foe the Barbarian), the team of Sting and Lex Luger, the Steiner Brothers, and Harlem Heat. They left WCW six months after the reunion and returned to the WWF. It was the start of the Monday Night Wars, and WCW was in the midst of hiring away loads of WWF talent. Vince McMahon was glad to take something away from his deep-pocketed rivals, even if it meant forgiving Hegstrand for walking out several years before. In the WWF, Hawk and Animal teamed up with "Stone Cold" Steve Austin against the militant Canadian Hart Foundation stable.

For two decades, the Road Warriors had been cutting-edge, futuristic in style and fashion-forward in affect. In the '90s, other acts began to catch up, and against the upstart New Age Outlaws, their vintage was finally beginning to show. The Outlaws embodied the WWE's Attitude Era, and their crass stylings, sing-along catchphrases, and almost comical movesets indicated a new age of pro wrestling. The L.O.D.'s time had come; they certainly weren't the monsters they used to be.

One night on a pay-per-view preshow, during a live interview with Vader, Hawk accidentally walked through a nearby door in the background, realized his error, and recoiled comically. It was a moment's lapse, but in retrospect it serves as a metaphor for the death of Hawk's mystique.

☆ ☆ ☆

After another brief hiatus, the L.O.D. was repackaged in WWE as L.O.D. 2000, the Legion for the new millennium, their old medieval armor replaced by shiny silver shoulderpads and metallic hockey helmets. The immutability that had long been the Warriors' calling card was discarded, and their aura seemed to go along with it. Hawk's displeasure with the redesign was obvious: He tossed his helmet into the crowd, and it was never seen again. The team soon took on a third member, Darren Drozdov, who was going by the name "Puke," and the storyline pivoted to focus on Hawk's alcoholism, an unsubtle reference to Hegstrand's real-life substance-abuse issues. This sort of after-school-special storytelling was common in those days, but the L.O.D.'s old-school personas stood at extreme odds with the earnestness of the angle. So did Hegstrand's notorious pride. The story led to a despondent Hawk climbing atop the big-screen "Titantron" above the entrance ramp and "attempting suicide" by jumping off to the floor below. Fans groaned, and Hegstrand felt slighted—legitimately, this time. The L.O.D. quit the WWE soon after.

Post-WWE, Hegstrand reportedly descended further into his self-abusive behaviors. In 1999, however, both he and Laurinaitis became born-again Christians, and Hegstrand cleaned up his life. The duo appeared on some of the Christian wrestling events of Ted DiBiase—the former "Million Dollar Man"—and on TNA Wrestling a couple of times, and then one final time on *WWE Raw* in May 2003. They were hoping to parlay that appearance into a full-time contract. They didn't get one.

Five months later, Hegstrand died of a heart attack at his new house in Florida. At the time of his death, he and Laurinaitis were working on a book about their careers.

☆ ☆ ☆

The Road Warriors never truly evolved with the times—at first because they were never in any one place long enough *to* evolve, but moreover because they never really had to. In the Territorial Era, they were the future incarnate, but in the Modern Era they were the last of the territorial wrestlers, dinosaurs migrating from place to place—perhaps ill-suited for long-form, postmodern storytelling but wildly popular nonetheless. When they appeared for the first time in TNA, they got the biggest cheer of the night—an eruption that could only be described as a "Road Warrior pop," as TNA announcer Jeremy Borash put it. They got bigger cheers than anyone else because they represented everything to the crowds: the present, the future, and the past. The Road Warriors were by then both timeless and comfortably dated, and their wanderings around wrestling's demimonde hinted at very human neuroses and vulnerabilities. They were antiheroes for a Marvelized audience that had acclimated itself to rooting for eccentric baddies. They were beasts we could love, Calibans forever straining at Prospero's leash.

# THE FABULOUS KANGAROOS: THE FIRST GREAT TAG TEAM

When one thinks of international villainy—especially in the grotes-querie of the wrestling world—one rarely thinks of Australia. But it was indeed a couple of brutes from Australia who ushered in the modern heyday of tag team wrestling. There were foreign menaces before them, and there were certainly tag team matches, but no team codified the concept of the tag team as we know it until the Fabulous Kangaroos came along.

When Aussie Al Costello conjured up the idea of a nationalist Australian gimmick in 1957 to buoy his lackluster career, he men-tioned it to promoter Joe Blanchard, who suggested he pair up with Roy Heffernan ("Australian rules" was already established as a syn-onym for a tag team match, so perhaps wrestling as a tandem was unavoidable), and the two made their debut soon thereafter in Stu Hart's Stampede Wrestling.

The Kangaroos were huge stars everywhere they went. (And, for the record, they were tougher than they sounded. They were Australians in the hardened, island-of-criminals sense.) They were arrogant, aggressive, and vicious in the ring. One night in Madison Square Garden, the crowd became so incensed at the Kangaroos' underhanded tactics against fan favorites Antonino Rocca and Miguel Perez that people started throwing fruit into the ring. When the audience was on the verge of riot, the houselights went up and the PA system starting playing the (American) national anthem—which someone apparently decided was the most effective calming mechanism to a jingoistic mob. The ire the Kangaroos engendered was valuable, though: That card supposedly drew 20,000 fans and earned a then-whopping $63,000 at the gate.

One night in Winnipeg, the fans started throwing their chairs at the Kangaroos (and their partner that night, Stan Stasiak), resulting in stitches in the head and leg for Costello and broken ribs for Heffernan. The villains took refuge under the ring, and the fans tried to set the ring on fire to smoke them out before calm was restored. (No word on the presence of the Canadian national anthem that night.)

It's not hard to see the Kangaroos' legacy in the decades of tag team wrestling that followed. They predated the defining characteristics of the greatest teams throughout the history of the sport: the brutality of Dick the Bruiser and the Crusher, the "otherness" of the Assassins, the teamwork of Arn Anderson and Tully Blanchard or the Midnight Express, the haughtiness of the Fabulous Ones, and the savagery of the Wild Samoans. Unlike other teams that had come before, they were two parts of the same whole: This wasn't two wrestlers teaming up; this was a team in and of itself. Ironically, this made the men themselves not just subordinate to the gimmick but disposable too—a turn we've seen over the years in some of the most successful tag teams, like the Midnight Express and Demolition—as Heffernan was eventually replaced by Roy St. Clair and later the American Don Kent, and after that the team marched on without either original.

But the Kangaroos' greatest innovation might have been self-promotion. They stalked to the ring with a banner bearing their team name, wore bush hats to underscore their foreignness, put marketing flyers crassly extolling their accomplishments in every seat at their first Madison Square Garden show, and, perhaps most notably, made cardboard boomerangs with their names and pictures and tossed them into the crowd. Because even villains need publicity.

# "RAVISHING" RICK RUDE

The Super Posedown at Royal Rumble 1989 wasn't much of a bodybuilding expo, but it was probably close to the average person's idea of one: On one side stood the chiseled and oiled "Ravishing" Rick Rude, flexing and diabolically gyrating his hips; across the ring loomed the Ultimate Warrior, the WWF's grotesquely muscle-bound comer, grunting and shaking and nominally "posing" for the audience.

Warrior certainly had the crowd on his side, but then, so did anyone standing opposite Rude, arguably the most loathed bad guy of his era.

It's not hard to hate a guy with his own face airbrushed on the crotch of his pants, after all. But Rude's act—the classic Lothario shtick with the volume turned up to 11—wasn't as simple as it seemed.

☆ ☆ ☆

Rude was born Richard Erwin Rood in Minnesota at a time when the state was a fertile ground for wrestling talent. He went to high school with Tom Zenk and Nikita Koloff and trained with Eddie Sharkey, who also trained the Road Warriors, Curt Hennig, and Barry Darsow.

Rude worked early on in Canada, Georgia, and Memphis, mostly as an insignificant babyface, but his turn as an evildoer in Jim Crockett Promotions in 1983 determined his life's purpose. He made a return to the Memphis territory in '84, and it was there that Jerry Jarrett gave him the nickname "Ravishing" and helped define the role Rude would inhabit for much of the rest of his life.

Rude came along at a cultural moment when image—read: physical perfection—was at a premium in the wrestling biz. But he wasn't all mustache and musculature: Contra most of the statuesque brutes of his day, Rude was actually a considerable in-ring technician. His sojourn through the South saw him forge a new archetype for the pretty boy bad guy. Early playboys of that sort were bleached, tanned jerks who projected their churlishness broadly, in the manner of the oversized masks of ancient Greek theater, so that they would be at least as detestable from the back row as from the front. This was, after all—in the words of Barthes—"where the most socially-inspired nuances of passion (conceit, rightfulness, refined cruelty, a sense of 'paying one's debts') always felicitously find the clearest sign which can receive them, express them and triumphantly carry them to the confines of the hall."

Rick Rude descended from a long line of these oiled-up alpha males, defined not so much by the jealousy they inspired in others as by the esteem they assumed for themselves. From the legendary Gorgeous George to "Nature Boy" Buddy Rogers, they played on a trope that falls somewhere between the philandering star quarterback and the macho beachcomber who kicks sand in your face and steals your girl.[1] Rude refined this role into a lewd, chiseled Casanova—his disgustingly obvious sexiness as much a part of his antiappeal as his disdain for the average Joes in the crowd. To drive the point home, throughout his career, Rude was constantly presented in stark physical juxtaposition, both to his fan-favorite, pot-bellied, common-man opponents—guys like Jerry Lawler, Tommy Rich, Dusty Rhodes, Jake "The Snake" Roberts—and to a series of slovenly or slight (or plainly unimpressive) managers—scrawny Jimmy Hart, obese Percy Pringle, clinically unkempt Paul Heyman, and the embodiment of annoyance, Bobby Heenan. "Here's you," the contrast seemed to be reminding audiences, "and here's *him*."

His time in Texas's World Class Championship Wrestling—where he was managed by Pringle and where he feuded with their unusually comely everymen, guys like "Gentleman" Chris Adams and the Von Erichs—focused his act and honed his '80s-pornstar-chic image. In the ascendant era of wrestling in the late '80s, he was the bridge between the old pompous pretty boys and the new chemically enhanced poseurs—between the cockiness of the old and the physique of the new. He briefly teamed there with his future rival Jim Hellwig, a.k.a. the Ultimate Warrior (who was then the Dingo Warrior).

☆ ☆ ☆

His star power was conspicuous in the charisma-deprived ranks of WCCW, and it wasn't long before he moved back to the Jim Crockett territory—then basically the entire NWA—in search of greater things. He formed a team with stocky tough guy Manny Fernandez under the guidance of Paul Jones. They called themselves the "Awesome Twosome," which, it should be said, was about a hundred times more fitting a moniker than that of the team with which they'd soon feud, a megapopular duo of underdeveloped oddballs who'd caught fire as the Rock 'n' Roll

---

1  The other offshoot of this archetype is the "Adorable" Adrian Adonis–style gay baddie. If Buddy Rogers was the guy that male fans could call a fag under their breath, Adonis and his ilk just played the fag. If you will.

Express, despite the fact that their only ties to rock 'n' roll were mullets and bandanna-trimmed tights. In the midst of this rivalry, though, Rude got the call-up from the WWF.

☆ ☆ ☆

Rude's foray into the big time was nothing short of a mode shift in the pro wrestling world. Previous WWF heels were bad guys by virtue of being vaguely discourteous, antagonistic toward fan favorites, and abusive toward the referees; Rude feuded with the fans themselves and unsubtly questioned the manhood of his opponents. Rather than just emasculate us, Rude found a more insidious, intelligent means of questioning our manhood. He engaged us directly, narrating his own ring entrance as he walked from the back in a sequined robe, microphone in hand, and he insisted that all the fat, out-of-shape "couch slobs" in the audience sit down and shut up while he showed them what a real sexy man was supposed to look like. It was about as concisely obnoxious as heel shtick would ever get. He institutionalized the in-ring sketch by having Heenan bring a "lucky lady" from the local crowd into the ring to get a kiss from the heelish heartthrob. The audience booed, the woman in the ring swooned, and then Rude ditched her and posed, laughing, hips gyrating.

It was a distillation of the amoral narcissist; Rude wasn't so much a heel who happened to be attractive as he was a 100 percent pure concentrate of machismo and self-absorption, a Lothario for his own sake. He could have any woman he wanted, but his objective was never love or even lust; it was heterosexual avidity purely for show. And he seemed not so much to objectify women as to coolly demean them. The object of his affection was solely himself. It was hardcore pornography minus the sex.[2]

It's probably not too much to say that at times he seemed to prefer grappling with other underdressed men to any sort of meaningful female

----

**2** Years later, the WWF would introduce a character named Val Venis who basically aped Rude's whole act, only without the subtlety: He was actually supposed to be a porn star.

embrace. He handled the women offered to him with disregard; only his rivals were able to affect Rude on a primal, emotional level. Conspicuously, the kiss he would lay on female fans and the reverse neckbreaker with which he dispatched his opponents were both called the "Rude Awakening."

This, more than anything, hits at the core of our hatred of Rude. Consider his hip thrusts, his mustache, his washboard stomach, and his overapplication of baby oil—not to mention the fact that he seemed to be both dramatically oversensitive to hits to the crotch (his wincing, wobbling reaction to inverted atomic drops was classic) and oddly prone to getting pantsed in the ring. Rude embodied all the nudge-nudge jokes about pro wrestling. With Rude in the ring, perhaps for the first time, the sport's homoeroticism was undeniable. Little wonder the crowds booed him.

☆ ☆ ☆

After one match, Rude approached a conspicuously seated woman in the crowd who seemed unimpressed with his routine. Rude was pure preening bully, demanding her attention—and affection—and, when rejected, Rude asked whom, if not him, she was there to see. She answered that she was there to see her husband, Jake "The Snake" Roberts. An argument ensued. Rude grabbed Cheryl Roberts by the wrist, and Jake stormed down the aisle to intervene. An epic rivalry was born as the two men fought violently: Jake because his wife had been dishonored and Rude because he had been rejected.

Rude had long worn his pant-length spandex in varieties of airbrushed splendor, with catchphrases and/or tough guy imagery (incongruously) depicted in various shades of neon. When his feud with Roberts reached fever pitch, Rude began airbrushing his tights—his crotch—with Cheryl's face. After one match, when Rude dropped trou to reveal the special-edition Cheryl tights, Roberts ran into the ring and yanked them off him. The audience erupted at the sight of Rude disrobed down to his briefs; the home audience saw only a postproduction hazy black blotch, creating the firm impression that Rude had been left naked—left as bare as he laid our pastime.

Not long after, Rude began decorating his tights with his own face, a level of narcissism previously unmatched even in wrestling's ego parade.[3] To be self-absorbed and overconfident was perhaps an act of sensible egomania; to paint one's own treasured visage with one's crotch as canvas was an unprecedented affront to our wrestling sensibilities. Previously, ring gear had largely been an afterthought, a series of unspectacular minibillboards reminding us of things like nicknames ("Mr. #1derful") and the names of special moves ("Thump"). If anything, such sewn-on words distracted us from the fact that we were looking at a man's pelvic region. Rude's attention-grabbing ensembles inverted such convention. They underscored the fundamentally homoerotic nature of the enterprise: His comeliness was indistinguishable from his physique and also from his, ahem, manhood. The masturbatory allusion was not ambiguous. When Rude rotated his hips in the ring, hands behind his head, he wasn't showing off for the crowd or playing mind games with his opponent: He was sucking his own dick.

★ ★ ★

After his feud with Roberts wound down, Rude returned to self-adulation and put out an open challenge for a flexing competition, naively assuming that no one could match his physique. He was shocked—*shocked!*—when his invitation was accepted by the Ultimate Warrior. The posedown at the Royal Rumble ended with Rude attacking Warrior with his warm-up bar, and a new feud was started.

The Warrior was wildly popular with the crowds and was quickly climbing the ranks of the WWF despite the fact that he was very limited in the ring, and Rude—as stated, a much better grappler than most other muscleheads of his era—was tasked with carrying him through a series of matches. They feuded through much of 1989, with Rude taking the

---

**3**  To be fair, airbrush technology was just reaching its golden age.

intercontinental title from the Warrior at WrestleMania and dropping it back to him in August. They feuded again in 1990 after the Warrior had become heavyweight champ—their most notable fight was in a steel cage match at SummerSlam—but in this later iteration, Rude was never presented as a credible threat to the ascendant Warrior. By that fall, a dispute with the front office had sent Rude packing. He had just started a feud with the Big Boss Man; WWF on-screen president Jack Tunney explained to viewers that Rude had been suspended for sleeping with the Boss Man's mother.

☆ ☆ ☆

Rude's following run in WCW is interesting simply because of how well he fit in. The WCW product was still basically an outgrowth of its predecessor, the NWA—a gritty, old-school Southern counterpart to the WWF's antic play fighting. It's a tribute to Rude's versatility that he could tweak his character—turning down the gigolo, turning up the tough guy—so as to work himself seamlessly into the WCW counterculture. On some level, this was because, despite the excessiveness of his WWF persona, the core conceit of the Rick Rude character was so basic, and so universally deplorable.

Rude soon won the U.S. Championship—the counterpart to the intercontinental belt that Rude had long held in the WWF—and a couple of years after his debut he defeated Ric Flair for the heavyweight strap. It was significant again in juxtaposition to his WWF run—despite his high profile there, he never threatened Hulk Hogan's title reign, and his heavyweight feud with the Warrior petered out until he was left feuding with second-tier faces like Big Boss Man.[4] After Rude beat Flair, he feuded with fan-favorite Sting. In 1994, during a match with Sting in Japan, Rude was dropped awkwardly—some would say recklessly—onto the edge of a steel platform outside the ring and injured his neck,

......................................................................................

**4** Rumors abound that Hogan refused to work with Rude, though it should be said that in certain quarters such Hogan rumors abound like stories of UFO sightings.

functionally ending his wrestling career. He started collecting on a Lloyd's of London insurance policy and faded from view.

☆ ☆ ☆

Rude's later act—the Lothario in winter—would be sad if it weren't so forgettable. The remainder of his career was a strange sequence of brand hopping. He still seemed to be in immaculate shape, but because of lingering neck issues—and/or an inclination to continue collecting insurance payments—he couldn't compete. He turned up in ECW in 1996 and teased an in-ring return, but he never wrestled. He went back to the WWF the next year as a bodyguard for Shawn Michaels and Triple H's new D-Generation X faction, and the crowd popped memorably when he first appeared.

With his history, he was a perfect fit for the promotion's new generation of sex-obsessed disorderlies, but rather than play off his persona, he was mostly content to stand by as hired muscle, significant only as an echo of his old self: the physical specimen now reduced to department-store mannequin.[5]

The one truly memorable part of this era was his November 1997 defection to WCW. The two promotions were deeply involved in their battle over Monday night viewership at the time, and WCW saw in Rude a chance to score a puckish point. WWF's Monday night shows were pre-taped every other week, and Rude—paid by appearance—didn't have a long-term contract. So on November 17, mere moments after Rude appeared with DX on the WWF's taped show, he turned up live on WCW's *Monday Nitro* with his beard trimmed down to a mustache—the classic Rude look—to underscore the difference in time stamp.

But just as with DX, Rude was just a prop. WCW had no real plans for him.[6] He joined the nWo, managed his old friend Curt Hennig, and the

---

**5**  If he lacked the oiled homophilia of his earlier incarnation, his slim-cut, double-breasted suits and perpetual nine o'clock shadow subtly affected a certain International Male vibe.

**6**  If one were to be snarky, one might point out that WCW had no real plans for most of the roster.

two were soon embroiled in the endless inanities of nWo infighting. He last appeared on WCW television in 1998, and he died a year later while purportedly training for a WWF in-ring return.[7]

☆ ☆ ☆

In his heyday, Rude was a foil of the highest order and a legitimate spectacle; it was nearly impossible to turn away when he was on the screen. But more important than the way we watched him was his effect on the way we watched wrestling. In a metaphorical sense, Rude pulled wrestling's pants down and revealed it for what it was. It was a necessary development in the sport's evolution. The audience was increasingly in on the joke—that wrestling was scripted—but still willfully oblivious to the *other* joke. It was this revelation that made Rude so entirely detestable to the wrestling audience; by putting his face on his crotch and then putting his crotch in our face, he made the homoeroticism far too evident. That he wasn't played for a buffoon like Adrian Adonis with his feather boas or Goldust with his platinum wigs only made matters worse for fans: He was a credible tough guy. He was unignorable, and so he was insufferable.

---

7    The cause was heart failure possibly brought on by an overdose of mixed medications.

# THE "BRITISH BULLDOG" DAVEY BOY SMITH

On Saturday afternoons in the '70s, at around four, England watched the latest chapter in the ongoing rivalry of expanding waistlines between the nefarious, leviathan farmhand Haystacks Calhoun and the blond, beer-gutted hero of the British working class Big Daddy. It was on ITV's *World of Sport*, the weekly sports show that drew in wide audiences with its coverage of British mainstays like football, cricket, snooker, darts, and, of course, pro wrestling. It was on that program on September 2, 1978, that a rangy fifteen-year-old called Young David went to a draw with an old hand named Bernie Wright. Young David was probably 150 pounds, which was beyond scrawny compared to Big Daddy and his ilk and, for those familiar with David's own frame fifteen years later, might come as something of a shock.

Despite his slight stature, when Davey Boy Smith[1] walked into class on Monday, his secret hobby wasn't a secret anymore; he was a certifiable famous professional wrestler, and now everybody knew it. He'd never be an average bloke again.

He and his cousin Tom Billington, known widely as the Dynamite Kid, would go on to team extensively on ITV, and when Billington was recruited to Stu Hart's Stampede Wrestling in Canada, Smith came along for the ride; he lived at Stu's son Bret Hart's house since he was still a minor. By 1983, when Smith was nineteen, he and Billington were splitting their time between Canada and Japan, the mecca of the international wrestling world. A year later, Vince McMahon bought out Stampede Wrestling, and the British Bulldogs were soon stars all over the world.

Davey Boy Smith was only twenty years old.

☆ ☆ ☆

A brief step backward here. That to the mainstream wrestling fan Davey Boy Smith is the bigger star of the British Bulldogs is not exactly pro wrestling sacrilege, but it certainly is a hole in the institutional memory of the enterprise. Many wrestlers—Bret Hart and, of course, Davey Boy Smith, most notable among them—have called the Dynamite Kid the greatest pound-for-pound wrestler of all time, which is to say that he'd be the best in the world if he weren't so short. (He was billed as being 5-foot-8 but was probably closer to 5-foot-6.) What Billington lacked in height, he made up for in tenacity; from rough-and-tumble Lancashire, England, he was

---

1 Contrary to popular usage, "Boy" is a family name treated as a middle name, and should rightly be treated as the first part of a hyphenate—for instance, the Dynamite Kid refers to him as "Boy Smith" in interviews—but since everybody in the United States assumed that "Davey Boy" was a nickname version of "David," I'm going to hew to that line for readability's sake.

raised by an ex-boxer father and trained to be not just a pro wrestler but rather a stout "real" fighter. Perhaps it was partly him overcompensating for his height or maybe it was simply his desire to succeed in life and stay out of the mining work that his father had fallen into, but the severity of his technique—the damage frequently inflicted in the practice of pantomime violence on his opponents and on himself as well—is the memory about Billington that persists most widely to this day.

But that wasn't the whole of his skill. His matches with Tiger Mask in Japan in those early years are (justifiably) the stuff of wrestling-industry legend. Watching the matches in the context of their time, they seemed to incorporate the entire history of the sport and evolve into a new, electric thing. For Dynamite, it was a revelation to be working for the first time with guys who could keep up with him. Watching the early British Bulldogs matches in the WWF, one is struck by the athleticism and technical skill that *both* of the Bulldogs employ: Davey Boy was clearly inspired to greatness by his cousin—in his later years, Smith said of Billington that he "looked up to him like he was a god"—and the Dynamite Kid was seemingly driven to some sort of masochistic perfection by something deep inside of him. For lack of a less obvious diagnosis, you can almost see the Napoleon complex working itself out in the ring. He dominated his opponents with a stiff, unrelenting frenzy when he was in command and brutalized himself with his high-wire performance, flinging himself (literally) headfirst into whatever position would make each move look most impressive.

Billington's abandon and his lunatic desire for success were always intertwined, so when, on a tour through Germany in 1983, the Junkyard Dog supposedly turned him on to anabolic steroids, he jumped headfirst into that as well. And later, back in Calgary, when Jake "The Snake" Roberts supposedly got him into speed,[2] it was a natural fit. Insomuch as Smith was influenced by Billington in the ring, he was certainly influenced toward such illegal predilections outside of the ring as well.

......................................................................................................

**2**   This fact will come as no surprise to many wrestling fans, who well know Jake to be the industry's most famous substance abuser.

Nothing in Davey Boy's career can be considered minus this lens: Despite being half a foot taller, he was always toiling for respect in the Dynamite Kid's shadow.

☆ ☆ ☆

In the WWF, Smith and Billington feuded with the Hart Foundation—Bret Hart and Jim "The Anvil" Neidhart—who had also come over from Stampede,[3] as well as the "Dream Team" of Greg "The Hammer" Valentine and Brutus "The Barber" Beefcake, from whom the Bulldogs finally claimed the WWF tag team championships after a yearlong pursuit at WrestleMania 2. The late '80s were the halcyon days of tag team wrestling in the WWF, a period when a shared land of origin and matching flashy outfits were all the characterization a duo needed, and a minor grievance was all the beef necessary to send two teams on a months-long rivalry.

In 1986, on the night Hulk Hogan battled King Kong Bundy inside a steel cage, the British Bulldogs were ascendant in the tag team world. They were among the biggest stars of the era. Despite the nasty breakup, the American soul still holds a candle for its British ex. How else to explain how a Canadian impersonating a Scotsman like "Rowdy" Roddy Piper would naturally be a heel while a prickish judo-kicking Brit like "Gentleman" Chris Adams would be the toast of Texas wrestling—or how a pair of brawny Brits could be one of the most popular tag teams of the '80s and '90s?

Sadly, their reign wouldn't last long: During a more or less insignificant match in December 1986 against "Cowboy" Bob Orton and Don Muraco, the Dynamite Kid leapfrogged awkwardly over Orton—in the midst of the most pedestrian of moves—and landed with a severely injured back. He lay on the ground getting pummeled by his opponents before anyone in the ring could comprehend what had happened. It's hard to blame anybody there: It wasn't a bad fall or a hard hit, just an

---

3   Bret and Billington had themselves been tag team partners in Stampede.

odd twist to a body that had been so tortured over time by night-in, night-out wrestling, the extra burden of steroidal muscles, and drug abuse. Billington eventually dragged himself along the bottom rope to the corner and tagged in Smith and then was carted to the back in a stretcher. He had back surgery and yet improbably returned the next month to lose the titles to the Hart Foundation. Davey Boy carried him to the ring piggyback, and a supposed hit to the head from Hart Foundation manager Jimmy Hart's ever-present megaphone left Dynamite lying prone at ringside throughout the match. It was an odd sight, particularly in a sport where participants often recover from the most brutal attacks in mere moments. As the match dragged on, and Smith held his own against both Hart and Neidhart, who were double-teaming him at the allowance of corrupt referee Danny Davis for what seemed like ages, the camera regularly cut back to the Dynamite Kid pitifully squirming on the floor. He was writhing while the match was proceeding in a sort of reverse suspension of disbelief: Suddenly, mortality was part of the storyline.

When Billington returned to real action, the Bulldogs had fully embraced literalism as they were newly accompanied to the ring with a pet bulldog named Matilda.[4] If the whole company was skewing in the direction of cartoon buffoonery, it was technically proficient guys like the Bulldogs whom the trend hit hardest. Neither of them were great actors, but their promos with Matilda were laughable; one can almost see Billington roll his eyes as Smith orates.

The Bulldogs didn't last much longer in the WWF. Billington was a notorious asshole. Backstage, despite his size, he bullied wrestlers whom he didn't respect, and played sometimes cruel pranks even on the people he liked. After Billington had supposedly pestered Jacques Rougeau of the Canadian tag team the Rougeau Brothers for months, Jacques hit him in the mouth with a roll of quarters in his fist. Billington lost four teeth, and purportedly because so many in the locker room were happy to see him finally get his comeuppance, the WWF didn't punish the

---

**4** Matilda would later be replaced by another bulldog named Winston.

Rougeaus. The Bulldogs quit in protest. It would be the first of many odd exits in Smith's career.

☆ ☆ ☆

Back in Stampede,[5] the Bulldogs didn't provide significant star wattage, so the promotion split them up to feud against each other.[6] And as happens so often in pro wrestling, life would imitate art: Smith and Billington's relationship began to deteriorate in earnest. As if he needed any more real-life metaphor to distance himself from his previous life, in 1989, Davey Boy was in a car full of wrestlers[7] when it crashed, sending Smith headfirst into the windshield, through it, and then twenty-five feet through the air. He needed 135 stitches, but his wrestling career continued.

In 1990, Smith went back to the WWF alone. He had personally trademarked "British Bulldogs" during their earlier WWF run, so he claimed the moniker as his own upon his WWF return. By this time, his relationship with Billington had fallen apart, and Smith supposedly threatened promoters in Europe, where Dynamite was wrestling at the time, with legal action if they used any reference to the British Bulldogs in promoting his cousin.

Smith was reintroduced not just as a singles competitor but as a wholly new man: He was noticeably bigger, deeply tanned, and his short hair had become a mane of dreadlock-style braids. The WWF was expanding its reach into Europe and had a regular spot in England on Sky TV, and Smith was the centerpiece there. He was never given a run at the heavyweight belt, but he was conferred high-profile second-tier wins in battles royal and the like. The apex of this run was in 1992, when the WWF held the SummerSlam pay-per-view event at Wembley Stadium in London. It was one of the biggest houses in WWF history, with a

---

**5** Though the WWF bought Stampede in 1984, McMahon was only interested in its assets and sold the company back (minus the wrestlers) in 1985.

**6** Due to their popularity in Japan, they still worked as a team in their continuing runs there.

**7** Including Chris Benoit.

reported 80,000 people filling the arena to see Davey Boy defeat his old friend[8] Bret Hart for the Intercontinental Championship. The match was the main event, despite it being for the company's secondary title.[9]

It was the best match of Smith's singles career, and it was a thrilling moment to see him celebrate in front of his countrymen, but the thrill would be fleeting. Smith lost the title to Shawn Michaels a month and a half later. He was released shortly thereafter (along with the Ultimate Warrior) for receiving shipments of human growth hormone from a British doctor.

He turned up next in WCW, where he feuded with Big Van Vader and Sid Vicious, but he got into a bar fight when a man supposedly hit on his wife, whereafter Smith supposedly powerbombed said man and broke his back.[10] When the aftermath got too litigious, WCW dumped Smith.

He returned to the WWF in 1994 as part of the burgeoning Hart family drama that pitted Bret against his jealous younger brother Owen. Smith returned to the tag team scene, pairing up with similarly over-muscled American Lex Luger as the Allied Powers—a pretty brilliant name, but a lousy team—and then with his brother-in-law Owen, with whom he passably recaptured some portion of the magic he had shared with the Dynamite Kid. There's a rumor that he was poised to jump ship back to WCW to be the fourth member of the nWo but instead re-signed with the WWF after McMahon made a load of promises that, if the story is true, he never kept.

After the infamous Montreal Screwjob in 1997,[11] all of the Hart family, except for Owen, left WWF for WCW, where Smith teamed with Bret's

......................................................................................................

**8**  And, by this point, his brother-in-law. Smith had married Bret's sister Diana in 1984.

**9**  For whatever reason, the World Championship match between the Ultimate Warrior and Randy Savage went on third to last. Second to last was the Undertaker vs. the "Ugandan Giant" Kamala.

**10**  This is likely apocryphal; if it's true, it's probably the only time a powerbomb has been used in an actual fight.

**11**  Wherein the heavyweight title was surreptitiously stolen from Smith's brother-in-law Bret via collusion by Vince McMahon, Hart's opponent Shawn Michaels, and the referee. See the chapter on Owen Hart on page 305.

former partner Jim Neidhart.[12] During a match at 1998's Fall Brawl, Smith landed on his back awkwardly; it turned out that WCW had installed a trap door for the Ultimate Warrior's special entrance later in the night and not told any of the other wrestlers.[13] Smith contracted a staph infection in his spine, and he was fired, via FedEx, while lying in a hospital bed recuperating from back surgery.

Even if he hadn't already been abusing drugs—and certainly, his physique hadn't regressed since his HGH bust—the surgery left him addicted to morphine. Soon after Owen Hart died in a WWF ring, Smith was back in the WWF, wearing jeans instead of spandex, but his ringwork was notably faltering. In 2000 he went into rehab, paid for by the WWF, and divorced his wife.

His last match was an independent show alongside his son Harry, who was breaking into the business. In 2002, while on vacation with his girlfriend, Davey Boy Smith died of a heart attack. His brother-in-law Bruce Hart straightforwardly said that "Davey paid the price with steroid cocktails and human growth hormones."

☆ ☆ ☆

For his part, the Dynamite Kid continued wrestling, but his self-destructive ring style—and his own penchant for hard drugs—left him in tatters. Back and leg injuries cut short his career. His last match was in a showcase match in Japan, called "Legends of High Flying," featuring other fading stars like Mil Máscaras and Billington's old foe Tiger Mask. Billington was such a shadow of his former self that it's hard to watch in a way that betrays the hyperbole of other "hard-to-watch" matches. Today he's paralyzed in one leg and wheelchair-bound, largely a shut-in.

........................................................................

**12** Also a Hart family brother-in-law.

**13** For the record, the (not entirely reliable) Ultimate Warrior disputes this claim, pointing out that Smith could hardly walk normally by this point, which is true, and that he and Neidhart were smoking crack regularly in those days, which is totally plausible but utterly unprovable.

He occasionally gives interviews about the cruelty of the wrestling industry.

The dream of almost every tag team wrestler is to reach glory as a singles competitor. Davey Boy Smith reached his mark, though his success as a singles wrestler was always in the context of—and so always subjugated to—his earlier success as one half of a seminal tag team. And although Smith was undeniably the bigger star to emerge from the Bulldogs, his legend is tempered to this day by the comparison to his partner. In the '80s and '90s, Smith's physique pegged him as the breakout star, but in today's wrestling world, not only are a generation of wrestlers indebted to the Dynamite Kid's revolutionary ringwork, but a crop of diminutive wrestlers—none much bigger than Billington—have found stardom. Which is to say that now he would have had a chance, and Smith might not have gotten his third, fourth, or fifth chances.

But he did, and he was the biggest international wrestling star of the '80s and '90s, an international hero who charmed American audiences with a British accent. A sort of real-life James Bond—on steroids, as they say.

# "MR. PERFECT"
# CURT HENNIG

Between November 1991 and January 1993, the WWF's
flagship show, *Prime Time Wrestling*, became a bizarre experiment in pugilistic cross talk. Since debuting in the early '80s, *Prime Time* had seen
several incarnations—it was best known as the recap studio show hosted
by the legendary duo of Gorilla Monsoon and Bobby Heenan, and probably best forgotten for the subsequent talk-show-style show helmed by

Vince McMahon and Heenan.[1] After that setup fizzled, the show mutated into a roundtable-style show, with McMahon at the head of the table, and two wrestlers on either side of him, two nominal good guys—Gorilla Monsoon and Hillbilly Jim, say—and two from the heel division; Heenan was, of course, a regular on that side.

The WWF has always had an impulse to be anything but a wrestling company: It costumes its shows as talk shows and ESPN-style studio shows, it clings to mainstream endorsement (like the imprimatur of MTV during the Rock 'n' Wrestling Era) in a sometimes needy way, and the company has occasionally become preoccupied with nonwrestling endeavors: a music label, a movie studio, the XFL. It's a corollary of the wrestling industry's penchant of employing "legitimate" athletes to buoy its roster of presumably inauthentic grapplers. Over the years, the WWF has employed Olympic weight lifters like Ken Patera and Mark Henry, Olympic wrestlers like Kurt Angle, and MMA fighters like Ken Shamrock and Brock Lesnar, and, for brief runs, sports stars like Lawrence Taylor and Mike Tyson. (And even in the case of career pro wrestlers, announcers often make more noise about their college athletic records than their in-ring accomplishments.) In each of these cases, it's an unsubtle cry for legitimacy from a sport too often guffawed at.

Even so, the roundtable format of the last years of *PTW* is slightly galling when one confronts this line from Wikipedia: "This format appears to have been inspired by the PBS series *The McLaughlin Group*, which was growing in popularity at this time." Some things are simply beyond parody. Nevertheless, the show was an often entertaining forum for its talking heads—if not so much for the wrestling matches. When the show was at its best, the babyfaces were bland and befuddled and the heels were given free rein to enliven the proceedings. And the best heel duo on that show was Bobby "The Brain" Heenan and "Mr. Perfect" Curt Hennig. Heenan was bombastic and grating, and Hennig was all smarm and sarcasm.

---

**1** This was not the first attempt at the talk show format by the WWF; *Tuesday Night Titans*, a straightforward *Tonight Show* rip-off, though occasionally leavened by evident parodic elements, aired from 1984 to 1986.

Whereas Heenan could never leave well enough alone in an argument, always pursuing a point until cut off by commercials, Hennig was the king of the one-liner, jabs that were often punctuated by him angling his chair toward the camera, smiling broadly, and, almost absentmindedly, flipping a pencil into the air and catching it without looking. It was an act built upon poignant insinuation; nobody could pull off that pencil toss bit except Hennig, and that was all the physicality he needed to express his dominance.[2] There are few examples of pure heel distillation as memorable as that Mr. Perfect pencil-toss-and-grin. Sadly, his presence there had less to do with his charisma and more to do with his tendency to get injured; Hennig's WWF tenure was largely spent on the Injured Reserve.

But when he was in the ring, it could be a spectacular sight. Hennig was a top-shelf in-ring technician, and his résumé reads like a *Who's Who* of wrestling talent in the late '80s and '90s. The son of Territorial Era brute Larry "The Axe" Hennig, he entered the wrestling world in the AWA, a scrawny, half-awkward shadow of his future self and yet still a powerful emergence in the star-depleted world of Minnesota wrestling. His second-generation credentials also placed him (favorably) in stark contrast with AWA owner Verne Gagne's son, Greg: From the start, Hennig felt like nothing less than a formal apology for Verne's overpushing his son. As Hennig would prove, second-generation wrestlers weren't necessarily destined to fail.

In short order, Hennig held the AWA World Tag Team Championship with fellow future superstar Scott Hall, who was working a persona that was more of an anabolic Magnum, P.I., than the Razor Ramon shtick that would make him famous.

When the territorial system began collapsing around the AWA, and with much of their top-level talent absconded to the WWF, Hennig was positioned as the last great hope of the AWA. He beat the iconic Nick Bockwinkel for the AWA heavyweight title—a feat Hulk Hogan and many others never achieved—and lost it to Jerry "The King" Lawler when Gagne and the Memphis wrestling promotion that Lawler and

---

2   As a ringside color commentator, Hennig did it numerous times on live TV as well.

Jerry Jarrett ran teamed up to try to stave off the coming tide of WWF expansion.[3] As great as Lawler was, he was lucky that he was the most prominent champion standing after all of the others on or above his level had already decamped for the WWF or Crockett's NWA. A couple of years later, there would be no question that Hennig was the superior star.

☆  ☆  ☆

After Hennig relinquished the AWA title, he followed Hulk Hogan and many other former AWA stars to the greener pastures of the WWF. Prior to his AWA run, he had wrestled for a couple of years in the WWF, never reaching any great acclaim. And in his first matches back in New York, the signs didn't point toward him surpassing his old record; if he was more muscular and a little more confident, he was basically the same Curt Hennig. He came to the ring with an '80s Chyron dubbing him "Mr. Perfect" Curt Hennig, but there wasn't much substance to the act. Soon, though, he was pulled off TV and reintroduced through a series of video packages that redefined his career.

Mr. Perfect—his real name from thenceforth was only acknowledged offhandedly by announcers and stray graphics—was delivered to the WWF audience as a flawless all-around athlete in commercial-length videos that showed him doing honestly impressive things (bowling a strike, hitting a home run, throwing a bull's-eye in darts) and feats of camera-trickery (hitting every shot in a basketball drill, throwing a football a field length to himself), along with oddly comical odds and ends (a diving board backflip, a moderately impressive golf putt, a competent horseshoe toss). He was often accompanied by a real star of the sport at hand—Wade Boggs for baseball, Pervis Ellison for basketball, Mike Modano for hockey—who attested to the greatness of Mr. Perfect. The

--------

**3**  Many consider this a borderline coup on Lawler's part; after winning, he basically decided to keep it as a trophy around his waist and refused to defend the belt in the AWA, staying in Tennessee with the mainstream title belt and bragging rights that had long eluded him. He was eventually stripped of the title by the AWA, though he held on to the physical belt and continued to proclaim his supremacy on Tennessee TV.

videos, which aired on every WWF television show for weeks on end, were the—ahem—perfect mix of comedy and competence, of arrogance and self-consciousness. The power was in the athletic feat, but the potency was in the borderline ridiculousness of it all: Finally, the WWF fans said, an asshole who doesn't take himself so seriously.

It goes unsaid that those videos were as much a testament to the power of steroids, tanning beds, and hair bleach as anything else. In his first matches back, he was only scraping the surface of the Perfect character; he was basically the AWA Hennig with a nickname. Now, suddenly, Hennig looked the part of a top-tier pro wrestler, and it seemed that by osmosis he'd absorbed the power of character that went with them. Walking to the ring, he would toss his towel over his shoulder from behind his back and catch it without looking. He would spit out his gum and swat it away without difficulty. They were minor affectations but significant ones. Everything he did was expertly queued to make him look like an ideal.

To this day, his contemporaries attest to Hennig's excellence in nearly everything he did. He really did excel in horseshoes and darts and bowling and billiards and whatever else he tried. And for months the WWF booked him so as to underscore his perfection: He went undefeated for a year, even beating Bret Hart with an illicit pull-of-the-tights roll-up. He was paired up with the Genius, a graduation-robe-and-mortarboard-clad blowhard formerly known as "Leaping" Lanny Poffo.[4] Before long, Perfect and the Genius were feuding with Hulk Hogan, and Hennig's future was looking bright: Tellingly, even though Hogan pinned him at a few untelevised house shows,[5] those losses were never reported on air. The desire to keep him unblemished was paramount. Apparently always in the market for an upgrade in association, Perfect took on Bobby

....................................................................................................

**4** The real-life brother of "Macho Man" Randy Savage.

**5** Once televised wrestling—and, moreover, live telecasts—became the norm in the industry, the term *house show* was used to refer to the nontelevised shows, off-night (often small-town) events where the feuds of the day are presented but where storylines almost never advance. (That's saved for TV and megashows.) A corollary is the "dark match," which is a nontelevised match that occurs on the night of a TV show before the taping begins.

Heenan as his manager and captured the Intercontinental Championship. And then he got injured.

They were mere "nagging injuries" in wrestling terminology, but they would be debilitating to anyone else: He had bulging disks in his back and a broken tailbone when he lost the title to Bret Hart. After trying to continue on after dropping the belt, he took over a year off to recover. It's a bit ironic that a company with such a love for authentic athletes finally found one and had the wisdom to market him as such, only to be betrayed by the bane of the real athlete: injury. It's not that wrestlers don't get injured; they do, often. But it's poignant that, in an artificial world, a wrestler as "legit" as Hennig could be bitten with injuries of such severity and frequency.

During his recuperation time, the WWF started using him as a color commentator, and Hennig found a second calling. He acted as Ric Flair's second when Flair made his triumphant (and ultimately disappointing) jump to the WWF and worked side by side in the announcer's booth with Vince McMahon, tossing that pencil or pen and catching it flawlessly whenever the camera was on him. His running buddy Heenan ultimately provided the vehicle for Hennig's return to the ring, when Heenan scoffed when Randy Savage asked Perfect to team with him against Flair and (Hennig's AWA partner) Razor Ramon. In reality, Hennig was healed enough to return to combat; in the storyline, he was motivated solely by pride. He poured a pitcher of water over Heenan's head, and fellow panelists McMahon, "Hacksaw" Jim Duggan, and Hillbilly Jim cheered.

He was back, and then within a year, he was back on the shelf. When his spine problems reemerged, he was suddenly a guest referee, an announcer on numerous shows, and a manager to Hunter Hearst Helmsley—later shortened to Triple H—in his first big WWF push. During this stretch, Hennig was receiving payouts from Lloyd's of London, with whom he'd taken out a sizable insurance policy,[6] which may have delayed his return to the ring and definitely made his WWF appearances in-

---

**6** As had his friend Rick Rude.

creasingly sporadic. Despite his potency as a talker, with his physical excellence sidetracked, there was nowhere for him to go. What good is the perfect athlete, after all, when he can't play the game?

☆  ☆  ☆

In 1997 Hennig turned up in WCW, as was the norm for stars of his era. He was still brawny and tanned and blond, and if his physical gifts were still extant, they were no longer central; he was significant almost solely for his history. He was a former WWF superstar, and it was that fame that buoyed him in WCW. The company was more focused on star power than wrestling ability—its biggest stars were prone to giving speeches in the main event instead of wrestling—and even someone with Hennig's ability was sublimated to the strictures of the pro wrestling fame game.

After an unnecessary stint in the formerly cutting-edge nWo—wherein Hennig's middle-aged girth seemed to be a metaphor for the nWo's increasing bloat—he was recast as the leader of the heel West Texas Rednecks, a gang of cowboy types that existed predominantly to feud with rapper Master P and his appointed crew of semiexperienced grapplers. It was truly one of the most idiotic angles in latter-day WCW, and that's saying a lot; the idea that the Southern wrestling fans who still made up a large portion of the WCW fanbase would cheer for an interloping rapper over a crew of experienced ring hands with country-music proclivities was inane. When the Rednecks sang their signature song, "Rap Is Crap," the fans had a hard time not cheering. If Hennig seemed an odd fit for the troupe, well, he was, although he was a country music fan—his AWA-era tights were modeled on country and western wear—and he embraced his role as the band's lead singer more convincingly than the other (more authentic) cowboys embraced their roles as rhythm guitarists.

Despite his willingness in that angle, anything short of "Mr. Perfect" was perceived by fans as a waste of his talents. So the crowd swooned when soon thereafter he reappeared in the WWF, back in the garb and mantle of Mr. Perfect. He returned at the Royal Rumble in 2002, entering the ring when its only two occupants were "Stone Cold" Steve Austin and Triple H. If this was his introduction to the Attitude Era, he was being welcomed in as a headline talent.

But it was not to be. After a couple of brief feuds, there came an event known in wrestling lore as the "Plane Ride from Hell." Imagine, if you will, an airplane filled entirely with wrestlers and exhaustion and alcohol. They were flying back from a big show in London, the whole roster on the plane. The story goes that much alcohol was consumed and things quickly got uncomfortable: Hennig and Scott Hall went wild with some shaving cream; Dustin Rhodes awkwardly serenaded his ex-wife, Terri; the legendary wrestler turned booker Michael "P.S." Hayes got punched out by JBL and later, after he had fallen asleep, had his ponytail chopped off by Sean Waltman; Ric Flair paraded in front of a flight attendant in nothing but his sequined ring robe; and, to top it all off, Hennig challenged collegiate wrestling star (and WWE golden boy) Brock Lesnar to a Greco-Roman wrestling match that ended when Lesnar tackled Hennig into the exit door, and they were pulled apart just before they jeopardized the flight. Of course, this is all thirdhand hearsay, but what's concrete is that Hennig was fired afterward, the sacrificial lamb for the transgressions of the roster at large.[7] (Because he took the fall, Hennig took to calling himself "the Pete Rose of wrestling," which might have been apropos had there not already been a Pete Rose of wrestling: Pete Rose.) Once again, Hennig was rendered expendable in comparison to guys whom he was better than. This time, he probably deserved it.

He appeared briefly in TNA Wrestling, the wannabe replacement for WCW's counterbalancing force, in 2002 and early 2003. On February 10, 2003, Hennig was found dead in his hotel room. It was cocaine, painkillers, steroids: the diet of the WrestleMania Era superstar. You

---

7   Scott Hall was also fired, though he slept through much of the flight; it was reported that he had been in "bad shape" for the entire UK tour, and his release probably had as much to do with his ongoing substance-abuse issues as anything that happened on the plane.

take the steroids to make you a star, the painkillers to get you through the aches of nightly matches,[8] and the cocaine to get you back up from the painkiller malaise. Your heart takes the toll for the drugs keeping you normal.

☆ ☆ ☆

*Normal* is an odd word to use in reference to Hennig. He was pushed as being perfect, after all. But he wasn't a monster, or a god, or even a sports star. "Mr. Perfect" was the best at everything you'd ever do in life—the best at normal things. He was your coolest friend. But he was never godly enough to climb to the top of the WWF.

Hennig inhabited his character more fully than any wrestler this side of Kamala. He *was* "Mr. Perfect." Because in the ring, in his prime, Hennig had a magic that couldn't be duplicated and that can hardly be defined. His persona wasn't kitschy like Rick Rude's playboy act or absurdly contrived like Ted DiBiase's "Million Dollar Man" gimmick. Hennig was an asshole whom fans secretly loved, the show-off who was emulated by a cohort of little boys. We wanted to be just like Mr. Perfect, even if we didn't know why. And this adoration, which so many secretly harbored, came from a generation that simply did not root for the bad guy. Hennig's charisma defied that. He didn't even change his character when he occasionally morphed into a good guy—he just started fighting bad guys.

Little wonder, then, that those young boys grew up to be the generation of assholes. Mr. Perfect epitomized everything we wanted to be years before we could put it into words. (The prominent bulge in the front of his tights probably didn't hurt matters.) He was the harbinger for a generation of jackassery, of smart-guy sarcasm and holier-than-thou

......................................................................................................

**8** Studies have suggested that participating in a wrestling match is more or less equal to playing offensive line in a football game. Pro linemen play once a week, sixteen weeks a year, though, and wrestlers regularly go at it 200 nights a year.

snark—of Internet machismo, Tucker Max, Bill Simmons, and Deadspin .com. We are the Mr. Perfect generation.

He never achieved top billing, but that hardly matters. It was all about attitude. You have the balls to toss your pencil into the air on live TV, it almost doesn't matter if you catch it. Hennig did, but that's beside the point.

# INTERLUDE

## ★ THE ULTIMATE ★
## WARRIOR

When the Ultimate Warrior made his shocking (and final) return to the ring on *WCW Monday Nitro* in Fall 1998—and I use *shocking* here loosely since "shocking" returns became, over the years, as much a part of the Warrior's shtick as the facepaint and tassels—Hulk Hogan's response was "I . . . I thought you were dead." He wasn't the only one. The question going through the mind of the curious wrestling fan was more pointed: Well, yeah, me too. Was that even the original Ultimate Warrior at all?

Since his first "shocking" return in 1992 at WrestleMania VIII, when he rescued Hulk Hogan from a beatdown at the hands of Sid Justice and Papa Shango, the pro wrestling world had been abuzz with an urban legend: that the Ultimate Warrior had disappeared from the WWF in August 1991 because he had died, and upon his return the character was being portrayed by a new wrestler.

The evidence was circumstantial but, in the way of conspiracy theories, somewhat compelling. This new Ultimate Warrior had a shorter haircut, blonder hair, and a fleshier, less-defined physique.[1] And under that mop of hair and behind his unmistakable, all-obscuring facepaint, half of the bodybuilders on Muscle Beach probably could have done a convincing impersonation. The Ultimate Warrior's frantic style and garbled speech, though unique in that era of wrestling, wouldn't have been too difficult to imitate.[2] Just imagine: The Warrior's signature music plays, some imposter of a muscleman scuttles to the ring, the crowd goes

....................................................................................................

**1**  Sometimes he even wore a singlet, flesh-toned and airbrushed with veins and striations to approximate the old Warrior's musculature.

**2**  In the WWE-produced *The Self-Destruction of the Ultimate Warrior* DVD, both Edge and Christian do passable impressions.

wild—one can easily imagine Vince McMahon thinking he could pull off such a ruse . . . and the entire audience falling for it.

☆ ☆ ☆

Jim Hellwig, the man who would go on to become the Ultimate Warrior, started off as a bodybuilder—he won the title of Mr. Georgia in 1984 and placed fifth in the 1985 Junior USA competition—but he abandoned that calling as a member of a group of bodybuilders who jumped into pro wrestling as a stable called Powerteam USA. Soon, Hellwig defected from the troupe along with another Powerteam member named Steve Borden (who would go on to a long, successful career under the name Sting) to form a tag team in Jerry Jarrett's Continental Wrestling Association. They debuted as the Freedom Fighters and were slated to be good guys, but in the Jerry Lawler–Bill Dundee days of the CWA, the crowd was accustomed to cheering for pudgy tough guys, and Hellwig and Borden's chiseled physiques soon were drawing boos.

They renamed themselves the Blade Runners, a point-for-point knockoff of the Road Warriors (right down to the facepaint and the movie-title team name), and they soon took that act to Mid-South wrestling (which soon became the UWF), where they found some success. Eventually, though, Hellwig struck out on his own and left for the Von Erichs' WCCW territory. He dubbed himself the Dingo Warrior and modified his facepaint to a tribal, full-face style that would stay with Hellwig throughout his career.

He briefly tagged with Lance Von Erich (who was himself, one could say, a fake brought in to replace a dead man) and competed individually for the Texas Heavyweight Championship. What is most significant about this period is that he began fully fleshing out the character that would soon be known as the Ultimate Warrior—and the further into the character he descended, the further "Jim Hellwig" faded into the background. Here again, though, the Warrior's tenure was brief. He left WCCW in 1987 for the big leagues of the WWF.

Almost immediately upon his arrival, the Warrior—the *Ultimate* Warrior now, to set him above the Road Warriors, who were not yet WWF property—became a sensation. His in-ring shortcomings were effectively hidden behind a frenetic match style and mostly short, decisive brawls. He was not so much a man as he was a force of nature, and he was no longer billed as being from Queens, New York, as was the Dingo Warrior—he was now from "Parts Unknown." He feuded with Mr. Perfect, "Ravishing" Rick Rude, and the Honky Tonk Man, from whom he won his first Intercontinental Championship.

During this period, the Warrior began to hone his signature interview style; low on coherence and heavy on growling mysticism, it was a sort of carefully cultivated inanity. And as the years wore on, the Warrior's promos became idiosyncratically obsessed with death and preoccupied with theories of the afterlife—often touching on issues of masochism, destiny, and messianic visions. He described the feeling of seeing a fan in facepaint like his thusly: "I know that that warrior is ready to make that sacrifice so that I shall live." He was unique—incredibly strange and off-key for his era.

Before long, the ecstatic crowd response made it inevitable that the Warrior would rise to the top of the ranks in the WWF, and indeed, he was chosen to be the heir to Hulk Hogan and his successor as World Heavyweight Champion. The two megastars squared off at WrestleMania VI with both title belts on the line. The stakes were not just grand but also dire: The Warrior gave an interview before the match in which he talked darkly about going into the cockpit of Hogan's plane, taking the controls, and crashing it. The Ultimate Warrior emerged victorious—earning a handshake from the fallen Hogan after the match—and the proverbial torch had been passed. As Hogan stepped back from the limelight (to dedicate himself fully to his Hollywood career), it seemed that the Warrior Era had begun.

But his reign didn't prove to be as durable as his predecessor's—despite the hype and despite the Warrior's self-professed "destiny," it's almost laughable in comparison. As an insurgent, the Ultimate Warrior was irrepressible, but as a champion he was dull. The eccentricity that once made him stand out made him seem dark and bizarre in comparison to the shining light of Hulkamania. When Hogan rallied his little Hulkamaniacs to his cause, it seemed a joyous army; when the Warrior spoke to his "little warriors," he seemed to be preaching to a cult. If Hogan was the wrestling Billy Graham (the evangelist, that is, not the actual wrestler), the Warrior was Jim Jones.

He lost the belt less than a year later to Sgt. Slaughter, who at that juncture—during the first Gulf War—was a nefarious, over-the-hill Iraqi sympathizer. Hogan returned to feud with Slaughter and retake his position atop the WWF, while the Warrior was relegated to a fatalistic feud with the Undertaker in which the Undertaker shut the Warrior inside a coffin, suffocating him. (He was revived, thankfully, by EMTs.) A corollary storyline with Jake "The Snake" Roberts saw the Warrior buried alive and (in a separate incident) bitten by a king cobra; it was a wonderfully dark yarn that saw Warrior approach Jake to help him conquer his fears—the only chink in the Warrior's armor—only to have Jake submit him to further psychological torture. The culmination of the snakebite scene—wherein Jake is revealed to be working for the Undertaker and explains himself by saying, "Never trust a snake"—was rivetingly sinister. At SummerSlam 1991, the Warrior revisited his feud with Sgt. Slaughter and his Ba'ath Party compatriots, Colonel Mustafa and General Adnan, as he teamed with Hogan to dispatch the baddies.

And then the Ultimate Warrior disappeared.

☆ ☆ ☆

It was said later to be the result of a contractual dispute, that the Warrior felt he was owed money by Vince McMahon and that Vince disagreed and fired him. But whatever the case, the Warrior would make his aforementioned first (shocking) return at WrestleMania VIII, when he came to Hogan's aid.

And so the Ultimate Warrior was back, picking up where he left off. Or was he? If this new man wasn't the old Ultimate Warrior, then who was he? Kerry Von Erich? Jim Powers? Some unknown 6-foot-2 muscleman? After all, the WWF has pulled similar switches over the years. The Killer Bees' whole gimmick was based on their masquerading as each other; there was the Dave/Earl Hebner switcheroo at WrestleMania III; the Undertaker (Mark Calaway) was replaced for a stretch by Brian Lee (known lovingly to fans as the "Underfaker"); Jim Ross brought impostter versions of Diesel and Razor Ramon to *Raw* after Kevin Nash and Scott Hall, the men who originally played the roles, defected to WCW in 1996.

Which is all to say that even if rumors of the Warrior's actual death were unfounded, the idea of replacing him wasn't at all unlikely.

And for anyone looking for clues, the Ultimate Warrior's career sent off many more signal flares than did all of the Beatles' album art and reversed tracks after Paul McCartney "died." There were the thanatophilic promos, the morbid feud with the Undertaker, and now, upon his return, a new grudge against voodoo doctor Papa Shango, another mystical overseer of the hereafter. Shango cast a spell on the Ultimate Warrior that left him vomiting multicolored bile and "possessed" him at one point, causing a blood-like ooze to trickle down from his scalp during an interview.

Although much of this "Warrior is dead" theorizing occurred prior to the heyday of Internet message boards, there are glimpses across the web of various Hellwig death theories: that he died of liver failure due to years of steroid abuse, or that his tasseled armbands cut off his blood circulation. Every time an "establishment" source entertains the theory long enough to joke about it only reaffirms the conspiracy theorist's mind-set.

☆ ☆ ☆

Whoever it was underneath the paint, the Ultimate Warrior's career was intermittent at best from that point on. Around this time he legally changed his name to "Warrior." It has been sold as a defiant act of copyright protection, and that may well be true. But one is left to wonder if it didn't also conveniently put "Jim Hellwig"—and any lingering questions about the identity of the man behind the character—to rest.

In 1995, in an odd turn of events, WWF rival WCW, then the home of Hogan, introduced a "new" character called the Renegade[3]—a fighter whose entire gimmick, although it was never stated as such on air, was that he impersonated the Warrior. Hogan proudly proclaimed Renegade to be his *"ultimate* weapon"—wink, wink.

The WCW audience was at once energized and perplexed. And for those convinced that the Warrior had been replaced all those years before, this was further proof that it could be done. It may have been a case of WCW trying to cash in on the persistent popularity of the Warrior without having to pay the actual man. But pro wrestling is a strange, incestuous world where innumerable character names and countless storylines are veiled references to offscreen stories. Many fans are aware of these traditions—it's part of the game, and the WWF (and other federations) has conditioned its viewers to be conscious of this sort of signifier. The story of the Ultimate Warrior, whether or not you take his death as fact, is one of these metatextual games—it's basically Nabokov with muscles and facepaint. And at the time, there were certainly whispers that with the Renegade, WCW was trying to make a comment about the Warrior's authenticity.

The "real" Ultimate Warrior returned (again) to the WWF in 1996, but this stint was even briefer than before—only about four months. After another money-related dispute, the Warrior said his final farewell to the WWF.

He turned up in WCW in 1998 for a poorly planned feud with his old nemesis Hogan. In one sequence, Hogan looked into a backstage mirror and saw the Ultimate Warrior looking back at him. This is supposedly a storyline idea that the Warrior came up with himself. It was intended to symbolize that the Warrior had gotten into Hogan's head, but one wonders whether the Warrior himself was trying to broach the subject of his very existence. Did the Warrior only exist in the imagination of his foes?

--------

**3** Real name: Rick Wilson.

☆ ☆ ☆

Hellwig—or whoever it was—certainly emerged from wrestling a different man—the animalistic bodybuilding egotist of yore is today a clean-cut, buttoned-down conservative speech giver.

Only his fascination with death seems to have remained constant. In various online outpourings, the Warrior has made light of Michael Jackson's death ("Well, you gotta give him credit for one thing. He spent all his money [and then some] before he died"), said that Heath Ledger was "better off dead," and advised Hulk Hogan to do himself in as well. When asked about the wrestlers who have died in recent years, the Warrior was brusque: "I'm not like some of the idiots I used to work with. . . . I don't have any sympathy for them." On his blog, he makes dismissive but telling remarks about Martin Luther King Jr. and Jesus—both spiritual leaders who were killed before their time.

In his heyday, the Ultimate Warrior vociferously defined himself as more than a lone man. He was a symbol for a creed, a lifestyle—and, at times, it certainly sounded like he was talking about some sort of suicide pact or death cult. Little wonder that questions about the Warrior's transience became so prevalent. That fans to this day are uncertain about the Warrior's survival speaks to both the gravity of the supposition and to the tenacity of the conspiracy theorist's mind-set. And, of course, the cult of death that has sadly come to define the wrestling world.

It should be said that these rumors are false; reports of the Warrior's death have been greatly exaggerated. The conservative crank and sometime steroid denialist of today is the same Jim Hellwig who quivered and growled in the ring throughout the '80s and '90s. There's really no evidence to the contrary. But, hey, it makes a good story. That's what pro wrestling is about.

And what of Renegade, the Warrior's WCW doppelgänger? Rick Wilson was released by WCW in 1998. His fate was all too real: Deep in a battle with depression, he committed suicide in February 1999.

# THE

## ☆ MODERN ☆

# ERA

In 1993, the WWF's *Prime Time Wrestling* show was killed off due to low ratings and replaced with a new concept show called *Monday Night Raw*. Whereas *Prime Time* leaned on the WWF's cult of personalities, featuring pretaped matches from house shows, overdubbed with commentary by the legendary announce team of Gorilla Monsoon and Bobby "The Brain" Heenan, *Raw* featured live matches filmed in a small studio.[1] This was no small thing: In the *Prime Time* era, the wrestling action was secondary to the commentary, and the outcomes almost always plainly preordained. On *Raw*, the machinations of mainstream wrestling entered real time.

It goes without saying that this format wasn't entirely a revolution; it borrowed heavily from the format of the rival NWA/WCW shows of the era, with live audiences[2] interacting with the matches in a way that finally—for the WWF—acknowledged the crowd's necessary participatory role in the wrestling enterprise. But the thing that really set it apart was the combination of the WWF's cartoonery combined with the format's reality. The various NWA shows focused on wrestling's rough realism, but the WWF, with its neon spandex and immaculate production values, rendered the sport a new thing, a model of pop-cultural excess. By adapting the format of its old-school rivals, the WWF found the path to the future.

......................................................................................

1   It originally aired from the Manhattan Center's Grand Ballroom, which would later be the site of many memorable ECW and Ring of Honor indie wrestling events.

2   This is "live" as in "live to tape." The WWF had long aired footage of individual matches in segments from a remote studio, while the NWA kept to the old-school format of running an entire TV program, from start to finish, from within the confines of the arena, basically filming an episode in one take. It was cheaper and easier that way, and despite McMahon's impulse to evolve, it was the way that wrestling fans preferred their product: immediate, interconnected, earnest.

Meanwhile, although Ted Turner had been eager to purchase WCW,[3] he didn't have the time or expertise to be much of a hands-on owner. He left the operations to a series of vice presidents and showrunners, none of whom found a stride that accommodated both the ardent fans of the old NWA and the Turner network heads. After middling seasons under the guidance of Ole Anderson and Dusty Rhodes that did little to grow the promotion to national, WWF-level popularity, and finally after a disastrous run with former Mid-South promoter Bill Watts running things, a dictate was given that WCW would never again hire a "wrestling guy" to run the show. But the nonwrestling heads who had been previously tasked with running things—like Kip Frey and Jim Herd—hadn't been able to acclimate to the particulars of the wrestling world, and turned off more fans than they attracted. So, perhaps bereft of other options, WCW was handed over to a man named Eric Bischoff, an announcer with the company who had also worked in sales and marketing at Minnesota's AWA.[4] Bischoff wooed the Turner brass by emphasizing his marketing skills, and they in turn liked his vision and perceived creativity.

Although his first year in WCW (starting in 1993) wasn't significant outside of the in-ring return from the WWF of WCW mainstay Ric Flair,[5] Bischoff came in with a sort of Hollywood slickness that the wrestling world—and WCW in particular—hadn't seen. On advice from

---

**3**  Vince McMahon often tells the story of Turner calling him and saying, "Vince, I'm in the rasslin' business," to which McMahon replied, "That's nice, Ted. I'm in the entertainment business."

**4**  He had also been an announcer in the latter days of the AWA. Prior to that he had been an all-around gofer for the promotion and, as numerous insider jokes imply, apparently mowed Verne Gagne's lawn on occasion. He supposedly got the interviewer's gig when then-announcer Larry Nelson was arrested on suspicion of driving under the influence, and Bischoff was the only guy wearing a suit at the office that day.

**5**  Due to a noncompete in his WWF contract, Flair spent much of his first year back hosting an often uncomfortable '80s-bachelor-pad interview show called *A Flair for the Gold*, which was also the name he gave to his pursuit of Harley Race's championship in 1983.

Mike Graham,[6] who was then employed in the WCW front office, Bischoff initiated a pursuit of Hulk Hogan, who was on one of his numerous periods of leave from the WWF (this time filming the television show *Thunder in Paradise*, which was basically *Magnum, P.I.* with muscles and boats) and was for the first time open to working for the competition. Eager to see his wrestling venture compete with the WWF, Ted Turner anted up the money to acquire Hogan—and, soon thereafter, Randy Savage—and, on Bischoff's request, gave WCW a prime-time Monday night spot on his TNT network,[7] airing head-to-head with *WWF Monday Night Raw*.

☆ ☆ ☆

The Territorial Era had been defined by the old-school NWA style—a rougher, gruffer, more reality-based (or at least reality-insistent) form— and when the WWF rose to prominence, it was with a product largely defined in contrast, with an emphasis on pop-culture tie-ins and slick production. And so when the WCW unequivocally appropriated the WWF formula in 1994, it signaled the end of the old school in the wrestling mainstream. In 1991, the remaining NWA promoters had been fully alienated by WCW's growing superiority, and when the NWA began making demands of WCW and its champion, WCW pulled out of the NWA altogether.

In 1994 in Philadelphia, the last NWA affiliate of any significance solidified the shift. Eastern Championship Wrestling owner Tod Gordon— who had just hired as his head booker a former WCW manager named Paul Heyman[8]—was approached by former Mid-Atlantic promoter Jim

........................................................................................

6  Onetime wrestler and son of Eddie Graham, who owned and starred in the NWA's Florida territory.

7  The resultant show was *WCW Monday Nitro*, beginning in September 1995.

8  Known in WCW—and frequently in ECW, though usage varied—as Paul E. Dangerously, a reference to Michael Keaton's gangster character in *Johnny Dangerously*, he actually played more of an Alex P. Keaton role, a loudmouth yuppie with a giant cell phone always in hand.

Crockett[9] about holding an NWA title tournament to reestablish the legitimacy of the dwindling confederation.[10] Gordon agreed, but when NWA president Dennis Coralluzzo started trying to exert influence, Gordon got peeved and turned to his booker for advice. Heyman hatched a plan that would upset the power balance in the wrestling world. ECW staple Shane Douglas won the NWA title tournament and then—on orders from the ECW brain trust—cursed the belt, threw it down, and grabbed an ECW belt from ringside. He declared himself champion of "Extreme Championship Wrestling." And so ended the reign of pro wrestling's old guard.

It could have been just another death rattle from an increasingly illegitimate NWA. But Heyman's vision was broader: He was attempting nothing short of a revolution—a pro wrestling version of the grunge music movement.[11]

★ ★ ★

The tenor of the WWF-WCW Monday showdown was evident from the very start. The inaugural episode of the unsubtly named *WCW Monday Nitro* (which aired for an hour in September 1995—the show was subsequently expanded to two full hours) was filmed in the Mall of America and featured the surprise return to WCW of Lex Luger. Luger had just been with WWF, and though his contract had expired, his defection was a shock—especially because, unlike *Raw*, which was taped live but aired on later dates (this was less expensive since you could tape multiple shows on one day or weekend and spread the products out over the following months), *Nitro* was airing fully live, like an actual sporting event. To the average

---

**9**  Crockett himself had just been freed from the noncompete that stemmed from his sale of WCW to Turner.

**10**  The NWA, the former national powerhouse in the wrestling world, had been reduced to near nothingness after its divorce from WCW, and ECW, small-time as it was, was probably its most prominent outpost.

**11**  He literally referred to it as such, which kind of diminishes the point, but still.

fan, it appeared that Luger had been wrestling for the WWF the night before. The era of the surprise appearance in pro wrestling had begun.

In May, Scott Hall, who had until eight days before been known as WWF star Razor Ramon, appeared unannounced on an episode of *Nitro* in "street clothes"—jeans and a denim vest—and interrupted a match, evincing a subtle disregard for the kayfabe code, and said to a confused audience, "You all know who I am, but you don't know why I'm here." He was joined in the following weeks by Kevin Nash, who was known to wrestling fans as the WWF's Diesel. They were presented not as Razor and Diesel—although Hall was still using his faux-Cuban Ramon voice— but as the actual guys behind the characters: Kevin and Scott, two regular dudes setting out to break the fourth wall. Their arrival wasn't billed as a talent signing (although both would later say that it was the guarantees of huge amounts of money that attracted them); it was implied that the duo were usurpers from the WWF—"up north," they'd say, with deliberate vagueness—bent on destroying WCW from within: It was a parable of WWF's industry dominance, and through this storyline based around WWF stars, WCW planned to wrest control of the wrestling world from the competition.

On July 7, 1996, at WCW's Bash at the Beach PPV, Hulk Hogan came to the ring to save Randy Savage from a beatdown at the hands of the "Outsiders"—as Hall and Nash had come to be known—who had also dispatched WCW's other two headliners, Sting and Luger. But Hogan, in one of the most shocking moments in wrestling history, joined in the attack on Savage and aligned himself with Hall and Nash, announcing to the wild boos of the crowd and the buffoonish indignation from the announcers, that they were establishing a "new world order" in wrestling.[12] While the nWo[13] was a gimmick borrowed from New Japan wrestling, it proved to be a game changer for American wrestling. Seemingly overnight,

---

12 Actually, Hogan said "new world organization," but this was immediately edited to say "order" whenever the footage was reaired. In instances of confusion such as this, it's easier to go with wrestling unreality than reality so as not to get too bogged down.

13 The odd capitalization was a design element that infiltrated the grammatical world just as the nWo infiltrated WCW.

wrestling storylines went from elementary Good vs. Evil rehashings to postmodern meditations on the nature of the sport.

☆ ☆ ☆

What was emerging meanwhile in ECW was certainly revolutionary, even if the term is defined down within the context of play fighting. In a landscape suddenly wanting for a different direction, ECW was a thumb to the eye of the status quo. The wrestlers looked different, to be sure—rather than the baby-oiled muscleheads common in the WWF and WCW in those days, ECW wrestlers were often fully clothed, beer-bellied brawlers. The style of fighting—eventually dubbed "hardcore"—was rough and frequently bloody. Weaponry of all sorts—from folding chairs to stop signs to household cutlery—was allowed; referees were present but largely irrelevant. Wrestlers were sent crashing through folding tables, sometimes towers of them, into the metal ring railings or ropes of barbed wire. These matches, with the nothing-fake-about-it injuries the wrestlers suffered, undeniably felt genuine, and they went a long way toward discrediting the increasingly campy style of WWF programming in the eyes of many fans.

Just as the bloody matches upset the conventions of the sport, ECW storylines frequently blurred the distinction between the real world and wrestling unreality. Douglas damning the NWA belt was just the start. Other highlights included the time Tommy Dreamer "accidentally" "blinded" the Sandman with a cigarette—and then, upon realizing what he had done, seemingly broke character and apologized profusely. WCW castoffs Steve Austin and Brian Pillman appeared at different times between major league jobs, seemingly off their respective rockers and intent on sabotaging their own careers with irreverence (in the case of Austin) and insanity (in the case of Pillman). Once, hardcore legend Mick Foley saw a (presumably sarcastic) sign that read "Cane Dewey"—a call for hitting Foley's young son Dewey with a "Singapore cane," one of the traditional weapons of the genre—and excoriated ECW fans for demanding violence. Moments like these garnered ECW attention from savvy fans of the mainstream promotions and from the WWF and WCW themselves, by brutally breaking down the fourth wall. To the wrestling traditionalists, this was sacrilege, but slaughtering sacred cows was ECW's ritual: That was the way they did business.

And just as WWF and WCW were moving to large-scale stadium shows as the home for their television tapings, ECW embraced the small-venue ambiance and the intimacy with (and ardency of) their crowds; the famous chants that emanated from ECW audiences ("Ho-lee shit! Ho-lee shit!") formalized an interactive nature of the product in the wrestling world that hadn't been seen since the Territorial Era heyday.

ECW wasn't competition to WCW or the WWF by a long shot—it didn't even have a national television deal[14]—but in the growing Internet era, awareness of the ECW among serious wrestling fans was growing rapidly. And as the predominant independent American operation, it functioned as a petri dish for talent and ideas to develop. In a battle for viewers, with WCW and WWF rosters depleted by expanded programming time (both companies eventually ballooned to around six hours of television a week) and poaching each other's talent, the major leagues would take notice.

☆ ☆ ☆

Meanwhile, the WWF was struggling to develop an identity that could rival that of the insurgent WCW megalith. What they had stumbled into was "Attitude," an ethos of crass language and lewd innuendo that was ushered in by the incredibly compelling adolescent antics of Shawn Michaels and Triple H—known as D-Generation X. DX is often seen as the WWF's answer to the nWo, but there are subtle differences: DX grew much more accidentally and organically and was, in the end, much more real. Michaels and Triple H often pushed the line of actually getting themselves fired, while Hall and Nash's faux corporate takeover only

--------

14 ECW would eventually have TV shows on two different cable networks, but neither was a big success.

entrenched them in the WCW power structure. While the nWo was the going issue on-screen in WCW, DX's unexpected success was changing the WWF behind the scenes. As McMahon was dragged grudgingly into accepting the DX ethos, some old-school personalities disapproved— none more so than champion Bret Hart.

If WWF found its new identity in "Attitude," the era had its seminal moment, almost accidentally, on November 9, 1997, at their Survivor Series PPV. It was the moment where Attitude met reality, and a new wrestling world was born. The year before, WCW had tried to lure Bret Hart—the WWF's de facto flag bearer since the defection of Hogan— away from the WWF with a three-year, $9 million offer.[15] Hart chose to stay with the WWF, which signed him to an unprecedented twenty-year deal. A year later, however, competition with WCW had left the WWF near financial shambles and the company's lowbrow turn had cast Bret, ever the moralist, as the odd man out. Vince pled financial distress to Bret, telling him he couldn't afford to live up to the deal he'd agreed to just a year before, and suggested he contact WCW to see if he could still get a big contract from them. Bret did—WCW head Eric Bischoff apparently had no idea McMahon had steered Hart to WCW—and agreed to decamp for WCW in the coming weeks. The only problem was that Bret was the WWF champion, and the last week of his tenure took them on a tour through his home country of Canada.

The facts here aren't so much unclear as they are itchily contradictory. McMahon wanted Bret to drop the title to Shawn Michaels—who was the other major star of the WWF at that point and who, through his lewd jokes and overt sexuality, represented the depravity of the new movement, and who, moreover, had a long-standing real-life beef with Hart—at Survivor Series in Montreal. Bret didn't want to drop the belt to Shawn, and he definitely didn't want to lose in his last big WWF match in his home country. The WWF's story is that solution after solution was shot down by Bret, and McMahon and company were left without a choice.

....................................................................................................

15 Flush with Turner's money, Bischoff paid exorbitant amounts to the wrestlers he poached.

Bret's take is that McMahon took Bret's reluctance as a guarantee and, instead of working for another solution, decided to sneak the championship away from him. What all parties agree upon is that McMahon conspired with Shawn and referee Earl Hebner so that when Shawn locked Bret in his own finisher,[16] which was part of the script Bret had agreed to, Hebner would call for the bell as if Bret had tapped out.

It should come as little surprise that when this transpired, Bret did not take kindly to it. He stood up, spat expertly in the face of McMahon, who was standing ringside, and proceeded to wreck the announcers' tables. Backstage, he punched McMahon in the face. Left without any option but to acknowledge the truth, WWF embraced it.

It wasn't just an inversion of kayfabe—it was the one night where reality indisputably reigned. For wrestling fans, unreality is our passion but reality is our drug. And the wrestling world did not implode. Instead, at the moment when these men first became fully human to us, kayfabe evolved, and the next night a newly evil Vince McMahon—formerly an on-screen announcer but now known as "Mr. McMahon," the owner (presumably a character closer to reality than his previous one)— explained to the WWF audience that "Bret screwed Bret." Reality was being written into wrestling's revisionist history.

✫ ✫ ✫

Meanwhile, WCW was collapsing under the weight of its own monolith. All the talent signings had come to pass, every heel turn and face turn had been done and done over, and without any more shocks, story progression went into a tailspin. Along with the high-dollar contracts, some of the top-tier hires were given contractual storyline control, which obviously becomes a problem when more than one person has it, especially when you're trying to navigate such intricacies in the context of five hours of live television a week. Despite all their accumulated talent, there was nowhere to go but nowhere. To attract viewers, both

16 A submission hold called the Sharpshooter.

companies scheduled main event matches between major stars—a departure from a previous dependence on promos and "squash matches"[17]—but WCW became increasingly dependent on fourth-wall-scratching promos and false finishes: shocks for their own sake. Every episode of WCW seemed to end with a much-hyped megamatch, and every week that megamatch would end inconclusively, with other wrestlers interrupting the proceedings (if the match even started in the first place). This stood in stark contrast to ECW, which prided itself on having decisive finishes (the crowd would chant the "One...two...three" along with the ref's count), and the WWF, which was realizing the value of definitiveness. The WCW audience grew disaffected.

The WWF, with a newfound vigor epitomized by Mr. McMahon and new stars like "Stone Cold" Steve Austin, the Rock, Triple H, and Mick Foley, was suddenly cruising. One Monday night in January 1999, Foley—who had wrestled over the years as Cactus Jack, Mankind, and recently, Dude Love—won the WWF championship. Foley was a longtime midtier wrestler, a pear-shaped masochist known for his bloody brawls, his passion for the sport, and his also-ran status. The match was taped six days before airing, so WCW, still puckish about the rivalry, sent announcer Tony Schiavone out that night to preempt the news: "Fans, if you're even thinking about changing the channel to our competition, do not. We understand that Mick Foley, who wrestled here at one time as Cactus Jack, is gonna win their world title. Ha! That's gonna put some butts in the seats." Fans turned over to WWF en masse, and WCW's eighteen-month choke hold on the ratings charts ended permanently.[18]

........................................................................................

**17** A match that features one star and one nobody, where the ending isn't in question, which serves solely as hype for the star involved.

**18** One of the long-standing jousts the two companies would have was the "overrun" of the show. Since they aired live, they would go an extra minute or two over the supposed end time, and when the two Monday night shows went head-to-head, their overruns became longer and longer, each company trying to grab two minutes of undivided viewership away from its opponent. WCW had more leeway on this front since the network was a part-owner. Even so, once the tide was turned, no amount of overrun could save it.

☆ ☆ ☆

Despite losing talent to both of the major federations, ECW's profile was growing steadily. But that very prominence spelled out the end for ECW. It had succeeded to the extent that it was decidedly not WWF and WCW; the closer ECW got to the wrestling mainstream, however, the more its identity was thrown into question. When ECW finally got a national television deal with TNN,[19] its drift to the mainstream seemed complete. But here in particular ECW was too successful for its own good. Seeing how well wrestling programming was performing for the network, TNN signed up the WWF—the big leagues—to take ECW's place. Despite the ever-expanding world of cable television, ECW couldn't find another home quickly enough—its reputation for violence dissuaded many a network—and in 2001, in debt to both creditors and wrestlers, Heyman declared bankruptcy and the WWF bought all of ECW's assets. Heyman, who went to work for the WWF as an announcer, has often called ECW "the first victim" of the Monday Night Wars.

On March 23, 2001, WWE bought WCW and, in doing so, swallowed its only competition. This transaction happened, as things often do in pro wrestling, both in real life and on-screen. WCW was bought by Vince McMahon's company for a mere $3 million due to the fact that parent company AOL/Time Warner had decided to stop airing WCW broadcasts and that without a TV deal there weren't many serious offers.[20] On television, news of McMahon's takeover—which had trickled out into the mainstream—was preempted by his son, Shane, who appeared live on *WCW Monday Nitro* to inform his dad that he'd been outmaneuvered. (In reality, it was McMahon outmaneuvering the expectations of the fans, who were expecting only a triumphant Vince.) This led to a famously underwhelming storyline in which Shane's WCW stable—

........................................................................................

**19** The Nashville Network, later the National Network, and later still Spike TV. The deal was a three-year contract, which TNN tore up about a year in to instead make the deal with the WWF.

**20** Bischoff had attempted to buy the promotion, but without a TV deal, his financing fell apart.

already diminished because WWE chose not to take on the onerous contracts of stars like Kevin Nash, Ric Flair, and Bill Goldberg—joined forces with a reunited ECW posse, under the "ownership" of sister Stephanie McMahon, to challenge Vince and the WWE stalwarts. Dubbed the "Invasion," it quickly petered out when wrestlers began haphazardly switching teams, and it became clear that this was not the clash of civilizations fans had been dreaming of.

To be fair, there was no way WWE could have lived up to the expectations of its fans, who had been fantasizing about a WWE vs. WCW war since the Outsiders first appeared on WCW. And of course, many fans had been waiting much longer than that. Prior to the WrestleMania Era in the late 1980s, talent sharing between regional federations was the norm, and it produced feuds like the acclaimed Dusty Rhodes vs. "Superstar" Billy Graham series that sold out Madison Square Garden several times in the 1970s. But since then, the industry model had changed and such crossover bouts stopped occurring, as rival companies like WWF and NWA had no desire to acknowledge the other's existence, let alone to work together.

For years, wrestling fans dreamed of matchups like Hogan-Flair and Sting-Savage and argued about the relative merits of the companies. But it wasn't until the inception of the nWo that reality started bending to the point that anything seemed possible again, and it wasn't until five years later that McMahon's acquisition of WCW made it a reality. But even then, it wasn't the reality that fans had dreamed it would be. It couldn't be—there's seemingly something about wrestling that demands two opposite poles for either to be appreciated. The WCW Invasion could have been handled better, but its failure was preordained.

As soon as WWE swallowed its chief competitor and assumed the mantle of wrestling's lone megapower, the company seemed to fall into an identity crisis. The McMahon family is the on-screen representation of WWE's brain, and when the family is divided, as it was in 2001, WWE fans are forced to process not just the obvious Oedipal fracas but an odd uncertainty about the stability of that brain. With no competition left, the McMahons had only each other to fight with. As the Invasion storyline fizzled and WCW was fully subsumed into the mother company, WWE, seemingly hungry to re-create the duality that characterized so much of the company's history, split *Monday Night Raw* and its Friday show, *SmackDown*. The two shows became separate "brands," with different wrestlers, different announcers, and even, briefly, separate pay-per-view events. The two shows only crossed over at the annual draft lottery, in which wrestlers were "randomly" swapped to boost ratings and freshen storylines.

The separation proved untenable, if only because WWE was (understandably) more interested in ratings than in adherence to logic: Why limit their biggest stars to one show a week? Why hamstring storytelling by segregating your talent pool? It wasn't long before the borders of the brands became fuzzy, and eventually, *Raw* formally reverted to an everybody-is-invited event.

And yet, duality persists. A second-tier federation called TNA Wrestling emerged, snapping up some of the era's lesser free agents and combining them with up-and-coming stars of the independent scene. It even hired Bischoff and Hogan—who was, at this point, not able to wrestle due to age and accumulated injuries—and briefly aired its show on Monday nights to try to re-create the Monday Night Wars aura, but that never caught on. "Super independent" promotions like Ring of Honor and Chikara have taken ECW's indie-rock mantle, each finding a following in the Internet age despite not having a truly national TV show upon which to base itself.

And yet WWE—which changed its name from WWF in 2002 to distinguish itself from the World Wildlife Fund[21]—persists. Wrestling may never again be the widespread cultural force it was in the television era of the '50s, or the WrestleMania Era of the '80s, or the Monday Night

---

21 McMahon and company made a misguided decision in the early '90s, while distracted by a lawsuit alleging that they trafficked steroids to their talent, to allow the World Wildlife Fund to operate as "WWF" everywhere except America, wherein McMahon's company would be known as the WWF. (Outside of their realms, the companies would have to use their full names.) In the next decade, as Internet-driven globalization made such sequestration untenable, McMahon made the decision to simply change the name of his company.

Wars Era of the '90s—but it's fair to wonder whether anything in a world of 500 TV channels and infinite Internet distractions could ever have the level of informational solidarity that wrestling once exerted.

☆ ☆ ☆

On June 27, 2011, a wrestler named CM Punk—with his tattoos, ragged facial hair, and decidedly unenhanced physique, the antithesis of the Hogan mode of wrestler iconography—interfered in the main event on *Raw*, costing present-day lead-actor John Cena his match. With Cena lying half-broken in the ring, Punk walked to the top of the entrance ramp, sat down cross-legged, and proceeded to issue one of the most defiant fourth-wall-breaking monologues in wrestling history.[22]

He started off by calling himself the "best in the world" and called Cena and Hulk Hogan and the Rock ass-kissers. He said that the fans' complicity in the whole commercial enterprise is what drove him over the edge. He threatened to win the title at the next pay-per-view event and take the belt with him to New Japan or Ring of Honor. The coup de grâce was when he said that "I'd like to think that maybe this company would be better after Vince McMahon is dead, but the fact is it's gonna get taken over by his idiotic daughter and his doofus son-in-law"—that's headline wrestler Triple H, for the uninitiated—"and the rest of his stupid family." And then the mic went dead and the screen went black.

It wasn't for real—it was a "worked shoot" promo, a pro wrestling trope featured heavily in ECW and WCW during the preceding era, in which a wrestler seemingly goes off script and speaks truth to the audience (a "shoot") but the whole thing is in fact scripted (thus it's "worked"). But nonetheless it was one of the biggest moments in modern wrestling history. The "worked shoot" is a vital part of wrestling. Fans are in on the joke—they always have been, more or less—but in the Modern Era, it's necessary to wink a little more, to give the audience assurance that you're in on this together.

........................................................................................................

[22] Punk actually said "Oops, I'm breaking the fourth wall" during the speech.

Wrestling's come a long way since ECW and the early days of *Raw*, when the crowd was embraced as a coequal partner in the enterprise. It's come a long way since Jack Pfefer "outed" the industry as a less-than-honest sport. And guys in spandex are still beating each other up in the ring, and we still know it's fake, and we still don't mind.

# THE ATTITUDE ERA: A DIGRESSION

On June 7, 1999, the Corporate Ministry—a semisatanic posse fronted by the Undertaker, long a devilish sort but only newly a brawny Antichrist—gathered in the ring to present to the world their Higher Power (alternatingly known as the "Greater Power"), the mysterious person from whom they'd been taking their cues since their inception early that year. The Corporate Ministry was an amal-gamation of the Corporation, the WWF's institutional front-office menace, and the Ministry of Darkness, the Undertaker's demonic troupe. The Corporation had been established by Vince McMahon in his feud against "Stone Cold" Steve Austin but had since been taken over by Vince's usurping son, Shane, leaving Vince to battle along-side the company's top babyfaces—Austin and the Rock—to try to topple the Shane-'Taker army of devils and suits.

The night's surprise was the most obvious turn one could have imagined, and yet it was the only truly fulfilling one: When the comi-cally oversized druid's hood was pulled back, the Higher Power was revealed to be Vince himself, who had been stringing his erstwhile heroic foils along all this time. "It's me, Austin! It was me all along!" he said, to which announcer Jim Ross replied with a combination of revulsion and boredom: "Aw, son of a bitch."

It was a couple of years into the WWF's famed Attitude Era, but rewatching the video, it somehow feels as if the whole movement was building up to this moment. Nothing better encapsulates the intrinsic egotism of the Attitude Era than Vince's simple statement: "It was me all along" wasn't just assertion of authority; it was a proclamation of masturbatory volition. The secret force that had been governing the company over the proceeding few years wasn't a mysterious godfather; it was the "me" of self-involvement, "me" in the broadest sense possible. The Attitude Era was the era of ego.

☆ ☆ ☆

On June 23, 1996, the WWF held its annual King of the Ring PPV. That night, an up-and-coming Austin took on Jake "The Snake" Roberts, a megastar of the WrestleMania Era returning for a second shot at glory in a WWF sorely wanting for star power. Sadly, this did not turn out to be the Roberts fans had come to love years prior; the Machiavellian snake handler had been replaced by a Bible-thumping, sober-living, tubby shell of his former self. (He now wore a sleeveless snakeskin-print shirt, which was obviously a functional decision to hide his middle-age gut but which also served metaphorically as a serpentine hair shirt, an act of penance on the part of the God-fearing Jake for his prodigal heyday.) In a postmatch interview, a victorious Austin went on a tirade, famously saying, "You sit there and you thump your Bible, and you say your prayers, and it didn't get you anywhere. Talk about your Psalms, talk about John 3:16—Austin 3:16 says, 'I just whipped your ass!'"

That, for my money, was the inciting incident of the Attitude Era, the moment in which irreverence became a catchphrase. It was the moment when everything was subsumed into the advancement of the product, and the product was the self. Jesus Christ be damned, this was Austin's moment.

The era that followed saw the WWF turn away from its kid-friendly past and tear headlong into a crass, PG-13-rated parade of sacrilege.

There was a sexual revolution—from the button-pushing idiosyncrasy of Goldust's transvestite homoerotics to the *Maxim*-style processions of scantily clad Amazons like Sunny and Sable (not to mention the bygone tradition of a Diva appearing in *Playboy* at WrestleMania time)—that rendered incomprehensible the implication-laden chastity of Miss Elizabeth and her ilk. There was violence—starting the prior year with Brian Pillman pulling a gun on Austin and culminating in the Undertaker tossing Mick Foley off of a steel cage and through the announcers' table—to which even the grittiest bullrope matches and parking lot brawls of earlier years paled in comparison.

On December 15, 1997, some time after such deviancy had become the wildly successful norm, Vince appeared in a commercial on an episode of *Raw*, formally explicating and defending the new direction his company had taken. "It has been said that anything can happen here in the World Wrestling Federation, but now more than ever, truer words have never been spoken," he said, speaking from a nebulous backstage area, outfitted in a WWF-logoed letterman's jacket. "This is a conscious effort on our part to open the creative envelope, so to speak, in order to entertain you in a more contemporary manner. Even though we call ourselves 'Sports Entertainment' because of the athleticism involved, the key word in that phrase is *Entertainment*. . . . We borrow from such program niches like soap operas like *Days of Our Lives*, or music videos such as those on MTV, daytime talk shows like *Jerry Springer* and others, cartoons like *The King of the Hill* on FOX, sitcoms like *Seinfeld*, and other widely accepted forms of television entertainment. We, in the WWF, think that you the audience are quite frankly tired of having your intelligence insulted. We also think that you're tired of the same old simplistic theory of 'Good Guys vs. Bad Guys.' Surely the era of the superhero urging you to say your prayers and take your vitamins is definitely passé." That last line was a direct assault on Hulk Hogan and his '80s-era role-modeling, which, of course, Vince himself had scripted. In justifying the bawdy turn his company had taken, McMahon had sacrificed himself at the altar, condemning his '80s-era masterwork as retrograde in this new era of ribald mythmaking.

Of course, the platform upon which he made this pronouncement—that of the owner of the company—was something of a novelty. Even though he had been the public face of the organization for years, it was only a couple of months earlier, at the Survivor Series, that McMahon had been revealed on-screen to be the owner. (Previously he had been a mere announcer. In retrospect it's easy to see his announcer role only as micromanagement, but it's still stunning that he could sublimate the glory that comes with ownership to the minor celebrity of the commentary gig.) When Vince appeared the night after the Screwjob to plaintively explain what had transpired the night before, he might as well have said "It was me all along!" because that, more than the watered-down details of the fracas with Bret, was the real reveal.

It was a difficult time for McMahon and the WWF, as they were struggling in a ratings war against rival fed WCW, and Bret's departure after the Survivor Series might have been the nail in the coffin. But if the road toward eventual victory would be paved with cuss words, bloody foreheads, and underboob, the most pivotal moment in the turn toward this brave new world occurred when McMahon outed himself as himself and let his ego run wild.

And such egoism would manifest itself in the supplication of the id of the wrestling fanbase. Of course, the most offensive bits were more often than not mere allusions. The ribald troupe D-Generation X trafficked almost wholly in heterosexual innuendo—their gang sign was the crotch chop, which involves one making X-shaped indications toward one's genitals—even though their physical associations seemed to be only with each other and a brawny, Neanderthal-jawed woman named Chyna. Their proclamations of sexual prowess were little more than metaphorical masturbation. Similarly, the forays into gratuitous nudity on the parts of the more traditional beauties on the roster always ended in thongs and bras—though this happened with incredible frequency—except for one instance in which Sable appeared with black paint covering just the nipples of her cartoonishly immobile breasts. Such gestures didn't deliver so much on their implicit promises as they did draw attention to the guarantor.

The exploration of the id wasn't limited to that of the audience, and this was probably the most lasting contribution of the era—that wrestlers' personalities took on a level of depth and reality to coincide with the increasing grittiness of their environs. The Undertaker went from comic book zombie to gruesome satanist—and was confronted with a walking id in the form of his "half brother," Kane—but more importantly he was revealed to be a corporate peon, ultimately always answering to McMahon. Mick Foley embraced all three parts of the personality in different on-screen forms: Mankind, Cactus Jack, and Dude Love were id, ego, and superego. Innumerable real-life issues became storyline fodder, and the celebrity of the noncombatant wasn't limited to McMahon, as other backstage characters—most prominently head writer Vince Russo—became celebrities in and of themselves in the minds of the fanbase.

The biggest stars of the era—Austin, Foley, the Rock, Triple H, even the Undertaker during his phase as a leather-and-denim-clad biker—abandoned "characters" such as they had been heretofore known as in favor of outsize versions of their own personalities, and all of them embodied the "Me" ethos of the period to a T; with the exception of Foley, who was basking in a much-deserved reign atop the industry, the others embraced their celebrity with catchphrases that amounted to lyrical "fuck yous."

The most commercially significant moment of the Attitude Era was Mike Tyson's involvement in WrestleMania XIV. He was introduced into storylines by Austin flipping him the bird, and his deciding role in the Austin-Michaels main event boiled down to Tyson deciding which of the competitors was cooler. He sided with Austin, and Michaels was gone from the fed the next day. Without hipster bragging rights, after all, what was the point of continuing?

☆ ☆ ☆

It's ironic that the final valedictory in the WWF's campaign against WCW came in the form of an old-school wrestling win, the traditional tale of a benighted hero finally making it to the top. On the same night that WCW most wrongheadedly chose shock over substance (in a much-hyped main event, Kevin Nash relinquished the title to his stablemate Hulk Hogan in a match that saw Hogan barely touch Nash, who then comically lay prone for Hogan to beat him—it's known infamously as the "Fingerpoke of Doom"), the WWF put its belt on Mick Foley, the long-suffering fanboy turned human pincushion who had emerged in that era of ego as the fans' proxy.

The Attitude Era was one of the greatest periods in wrestling history, but those aspects that came to define it weren't its best features. So much of that time can be summed up in pleas for attention—"Look at my tits," "Look at my dick," "Look at me bleed"—but in the end, wrestling matches and simple stories of triumph proved decisive.

After he revealed himself as the Higher Power, McMahon ridiculed all those who had bought his act of penance: "Every damn one of you were made fools of!" Which is about as good an epitaph for fans of the era as I can imagine. The WWF had cut its product with transitory crack, and we all enjoyed the high.

# BRIAN "CRUSH"
# ADAMS

Brian Adams's mainstream wrestling career started in medias res. A former soldier who'd learned how to grapple while stationed in Japan, Adams was plucked out of the indie scene of the Pacific Northwest in 1990 and thrust into top-level WWF storylines as the third member of Demolition, one of the most successful acts in the WWF. Demolition was a semisanitized, commercialized version of the Road Warriors—smaller spikes, less anabolically grotesque physiques—and the connection was perhaps even stronger than that. The members of Demolition swiped their look directly from the character Lord Humungus of *Mad Max 2: The Road Warrior*, the very film from which Hawk and Animal had years earlier lifted their postapocalyptic shtick.[1]

While the addition of a third member to their crowd-pleasing rough-neck S&M routine was an interesting twist, it chiefly served to reestablish Demolition as a villainous stable. They had debuted as baddies, but—just as with the Road Warriors before them—their unique and brutal style made them fan favorites in relatively short order. After WrestleMania VI, though, they had brawled their way through all of the legitimate heel opposition, and the decision was made to bring them back over to the dark side. And so came Crush. Demolition was so domi-nant it hardly seemed fair—Ax and Smash were huge, and Crush was the biggest of the three—but that was exactly the point: It was just a case of monsters being monsters.

There's some minor dispute as to the real reason for Crush's addition to Demolition. It's usually accepted that Ax (Bill Eadie), the team's elder statesman, was getting older and steering toward a backstage role in the company—although there's also some question over whether he agreed to the plan or whether it was forced upon him—but there are other re-ports that cite things such as a serious shellfish allergy as the cause of Eadie's semidemotion. Either way, Demolition invoked the Freebird Rule—named for the legendary Fabulous Freebirds—wherein a three-man squad can defend the tag belts with any two members on any given night. And, as if that weren't enough, they proceeded to flout even those tenuously legal rules by regularly switching the nonactive member into the match in dire situations.

This was, it must be said, a point of serious consternation for the more earnest young fan. All three members dressed alike and had full face-paint, but their paint patterns were distinct and their physiques were

--------

1  Incidentally, there was a wrestler—or, rather, several wrestlers—who went by the name "Lord Humongous" in Mid-South (where star-promoter Jerry Lawler was notori-ous for swiping pop-cultural characters) and the CWA and probably a bunch of other places. They all looked exactly like the guy from the movie, except when promoters got lazy and it was just a guy in a hockey mask. Sid Vicious, who would later be a major head-liner, played Humongous at one time, as did—allegedly—Scott Hall.

significantly dissimilar. It was only through the willful negligence of the referees that these shenanigans were possible, though it goes without saying that such negligence is at the core of a high percentage of bad guy in-ring machinations.

In retrospect, Crush's whole run with Demolition was the only time his career made sense. He was a creature of wrestling's 1990s; nobody better embodied the gonzo eclecticism of the day. He played so many archetypes of '90s wrestling mythology that he became legendary at none of them, moving from persona to persona without ever fully leaving the last behind, though no real mention of his previous lives was ever made. He was a man without a history, unstuck in time.

☆ ☆ ☆

Demolition battled against the cream of the fan-favorite crop—the Rockers, the Hart Foundation—before the team found itself at odds with its forebear, the Road Warriors, who had finally arrived in the WWF, going by the Legion of Doom. This was a big moment for wrestling. Many wizened wrestling fans were eager to see the copycats get their comeuppance, but even to the less-worldly fan who didn't know that Demolition was a knockoff of the Warriors, both teams were famous enough that this rivalry seemed inevitable even when they were contractually and geographically detached. To finally see them face-to-face was exhilarating.

Unfortunately, the feud crumbled under the weight of its own hype. Both teams were competent, but neither was built around technical wrestling mastery. And while either faction could cut growling, threatening promos with the best of them, there was something unimpressive and almost laughable about hearing them growl so monotonously at each other. Each team had built its legend by having an everyman duo to stand in opposition. The Demolition–L.O.D. feud had all the hype of *King Kong vs. Godzilla* and the payoff of *Alien vs. Predator*.

Although it was never said aloud, the final confrontation was basically an old-school Loser Leaves Town match: Once dispatched by the

L.O.D., Demolition's fate in the WWF was all but sealed. The team hung around for a while after, but soon Ax, Smash, and Crush went their separate ways.

☆  ☆  ☆

Adams reappeared in the WWF soon after, still going by Crush but otherwise completely repackaged. He was now a blandly straightforward babyface: fluorescent orange tights, bleached tips on his mullet, golden tan, and an easygoing Hawaiian surfer disposition. They called him Kona Crush, and to drive the point home he did the traditional surfer's "hang loose" hand gesture. If he was less easygoing in the ring, it was mostly to comical effect: His finishing move—wherein he grabbed either side of his opponent's head, lifted him off the ground, and then smashed him back down—was called the Coconut Crush.[2] He soon began a feud with Barry Darsow, formerly Crush's old Demolition running buddy Smash, who was now portraying a wrestling repo man called, unimaginatively, the Repo Man.

It was at this point in Adams's career that the repackaging became something of a gimmick in and of itself. Wrestling fans are persistently willing to turn a blind eye to familiar players in new garb; whereas one might think that keeping the "Crush" moniker would establish some sort of "reality-based" consistency, in fact it did little more than confuse the whole structure of wrestling reality. Were we supposed to recognize this new character as Crush from Demolition? Were we supposed to pretend that the former iteration had never existed? If fans reacted less than exuberantly to Crush's re-debut, perhaps it was because they were busy trying to sort out the schism. The storyline was edging toward the meta; Crush was changing clothes and speech patterns with every chapter while the background remained stubbornly immutable. He had become the middling protagonist in a Philip K. Dick paradox.

........................................................................................................

**2** This isn't to be confused with the seminal moment when "Rowdy" Roddy Piper crushed a coconut on the head of "Superfly" Jimmy Snuka in 1984.

The only memorable part of Crush's Hawaiian-heritage run—and I guess it bears mention that Adams actually was from Hawaii, though he wasn't discernibly ethnically Polynesian, and his Kona Crush persona was so inauthentic as to render that fact almost irrelevant—was his feud with the evil clown Doink. If it's not clear by now that this was an era of unbearably Philistine wrestling personas in the WWE, let it be known that Doink wasn't just a wacky creation of the WWF think tank that was bestowed upon some unknown schlub; it was a character given to "Maniac" Matt Borne, a borderline legend of the '80s indie scene.[3] (One imagines Vince McMahon seeing Borne's psychopathic cackle and saying, "Has anybody seen that Stephen King movie with the clown?") Crush fell victim to an attack from Doink's prosthetic arm—he had all his natural limbs; the prosthetic was a gag—and later, at WrestleMania IX, he was double-teamed by Doink and a Doink look-alike, the latter of whom, as if to add to the mirroring effect, also attacked Crush with a prosthetic arm.

After falling victim to a sternum-crushing attack at the hands of Yokozuna, Crush disappeared for several months. He returned as a heel, shockingly aligning himself with Yokozuna and manager Mr. Fuji and bristling at his former friend Randy Savage for not contacting him during his recuperation. This was taken (for whatever reason) as nothing less than an attack on America itself. Crush fashioned himself an anti-American Japan sympathizer, now with darkened hair, a goatee, black-and-purple tights, and a return to facepaint (naturally). If the switchover to the dark side didn't pass the groan test, again, that was beside the point—why simply reposition Crush when a complete and inexplicable makeover would do? And while you're at it, why not have a native Hawaiian take up the banner of Japan? It's a mindfuck on the order of *The Man in the High Castle*. Crush feuded with Savage through WrestleMania X and then faded from the main event scene until late 1995, when he was arrested in Hawaii for carrying an illegal firearm and purchasing steroids, which landed him briefly in jail.

......................................................................................................

**3** After Borne was fired, though, others played the Doink role without missing a clown-shoed step.

While this might have spelled the end for a lesser (read: smaller) performer, Crush was welcomed back to the WWF in 1996, probably in large part due to the beginning of the WWF's Monday night showdown with WCW and WCW's consequent raid of the WWF roster. With ECW's indie success and Scott Hall and Kevin Nash's "invasion" of WCW as the Outsiders, this was an increasingly "reality-based" period in pro wrestling. And so, as if to prove beyond a shadow of a doubt that the WWF didn't quite get it, Adams was brought back in a new role that maintained his continually unacknowledged backstory but also capitalized on his newfound lawbreaker status: Crush was now an ex-con—and a grizzled caricature of an ex-con, to be sure.[4] He was still called Crush, of course—and while he was portrayed as a man changed by his recent past, the specifics of his previous incarnations were left for the most part unmentioned.

This was an odd era of WWF programming, one in which every wrestler seemed to be part of a gang or faction, so Crush was lumped into the antiestablishment group the Nation of Domination (which would later become a more straightforwardly Black Power outfit) and then subsequently put in his own quartet of bikers called the Disciples of Apocalypse, or, for short, DOA. He was joined by Brian Lee, formerly the infamous fake Undertaker, and the Harris twins, who both sported shaved heads. If that and the motorcycles and the tattoos didn't evoke a vague sense of white nationalism, the Disciples' subsequent feuds with the (now all-black) Nation of Domination and the Puerto Rican nationalist posse Los Boricuas made the insinuation plain. But the gang-warfare era petered out, and so did Crush's renaissance. Soon after, supposedly in reaction to Bret Hart's treatment at the infamous Montreal Screwjob, Adams left the WWF.

☆ ☆ ☆

He materialized soon thereafter in WCW, under his real name—the norm for WCW, which had pushed "reality" programming to its

---

4   His manager upon his return was his lawyer, and he proclaimed the injustice done to Crush by the American legal system.

thudding end point, although as with every other real name, "Brian Adams" was just a wink-wink way for WCW to imply "Crush" without violating copyright. He debuted to fairly significant but momentary acclaim. This too was the standard in WCW: introduce a familiar face, put him in street clothes, have the announcers scream things like "That's Brian Adams!! What on earth is he doing here?!?" and then bury him in the back of a crowded in-ring promo two weeks later, seldom to be heard from again. (Sorry, spoiler alert.) Adams teased an alliance with Bret Hart, then betrayed him and joined the nWo's villainous platoon, and basically disappeared from the spotlight.

He had a brief resurgence in 2000 as part of the tag team KroniK alongside Bryan Clark. In this tweaked persona, Adams seemed to have adopted his real-life buddy Randy Savage's style regimen of that day: minimal body fat, bulging muscles, black-dyed hair, and sunglasses fit for an asshole teenager. KroniK was basically mercenary, which meant Adams and Clark switched allegiance for little or no reason, which ironically rendered them the most internally consistent characters in all of WCW's helter-skelter storytelling. When Vince McMahon bought WCW a year or so later, KroniK had a brief feud with the Undertaker and Kane, but, the (real-life) story goes, their performance in the payoff pay-per-view match was so lackluster that the Undertaker lit into them backstage, and neither member of KroniK was asked to return thereafter. The duo did some work in Japan, but that functionally spelled the end of both of their mainstream wrestling careers.

☆ ☆ ☆

Soon, Adams was trying his hand at pro boxing. He had been a boxer during his military days, and he seemed to be serious about a second ring career, even if having Randy Savage as his hypeman made it all seem rather silly.[5] But Adams injured himself in training and called it a career.

---

**5** Adams also worked in real life as Savage's bodyguard at times, though one has to chuckle at the image of a fake fighter being protected by another fake fighter.

He settled down and collected on a Lloyd's of London insurance policy—a station of the cross for the wrestler in decline—and thought about opening a gym (another station of the cross) in Florida. Sadly, that never got past the planning stages. He died just two months after Chris Benoit murdered his family and took his own life, so Adams's death, at age forty-three, was covered widely in the mainstream media—notably on ESPN—which lost interest in dead wrestlers almost immediately thereafter.

Extreme as it was, Benoit's case was taken in the mainstream press as somehow pervasively illuminating of the wrestling world, whereas Adams's death was merely a footnote. In a lot of ways, that gets things exactly backward. Crush was as pure a product of his era and his sport as any professional wrestler. If you want the short-form version of the modern wrestling career arc, in all its weird glory, look no further than Brian Adams. He was, in order, a paint-faced monster; a neon-clad, bleached-blond do-gooder; an unpatriotic scoundrel; a gritty ex-con biker; and a black-clad nWo turncoat. He wrestled in the territories, in Japan, in the indies, in the WWF, and in WCW. He was American; he was a tropical exotic; he was un-American; he was a beast from Parts Unknown. Outside the ring, Brian Adams was a military man, a bodyguard, a wannabe boxer, and a prospective gym owner; post-career, he lived off the dividends of his insurance policy. And then he died in his bed, having swallowed a bad mixture of painkillers and muscle relaxers that he took for his lingering back injury.

We know this story by heart even if we didn't know the man, and there's something both pathetic and heartbreaking in that. He was everything he could have been, for better and for worse. He was a stereotype right down to his sad end. For all the incoherence of his in-ring career, his life outside the ring played exactly and tragically to type.

# GEOPOLITICS IN WRESTLING

The pro wrestling world has rarely shied away from borrowing from the arena of current affairs in crafting its on-screen politics, the brawny egoism of faux fisticuffs working as the stand-in for geo-political conflict in the same way that it does, at other moments, for love and hate or good and evil. From the early days of the Territorial Era, crowds filled with World War II veterans gathered to ceremonially berate the phony Nazi Krauts and scurrilous Japs who paraded to the ring in mock splendor.

In the early '50s, Boston promoter Paul Bowser—himself a German, but a capitalist first and foremost—repackaged a Quebecer named Guy Larose as German malcontent Hans Schmidt. Soon the "Teuton Terror," as he was known, was riling up crowds all over the country and, most famously, on the earliest days of nationwide television, on the DuMont Network; in the mid-'50s, Schmidt may have been the most recognizable German villain in the world after Adolf Hitler. His denunciation of the American concept of good sportsmanship earned him a mention in an op-ed in an August 1953 issue of *The Oneonta Star* newspaper in New York—"This country has no place for a sports figure who refuses to recognize the code which made this country great"—and his general despicableness earned him a few stab wounds and more than a few wild punches from irate wrestling fans. This was an indelible sign of success. By 1960, rings the nation over were regularly populated by the likes of Karl von Hess, Ludwig von Krupp, and, of course, Fritz Von Erich.

Von Hess started a riot one night at the Capitol Arena in DC when he choked Wildman Fargo (who would go on to be known as Jackie Fargo of Memphis fame) with a wire and attacked the referee. When the local government sought to regulate away wrestling's seeming lawlessness, promoter Vincent J. McMahon did his best to publicly walk back the villainy of the episode. "Von Hess is no Nazi," he said. "He uses that silly salute to point up the act he is the villain. Each wrestling exhibition has a hero and a villain. Von Hess isn't much wrestler so he must use props or gimmicks. . . . Half an hour after the people thought Wildman Fargo was fighting for his life in a hospital somewhere as a result of being strangled with a piece of wire, Fargo was in Goldie Ahearn's restaurant polishing off an inch thick steak that was almost a foot wide."

When Von Erich returned to his home state of Texas, eventually to become the scion of Texas's wrestling royalty, he switched sides, embracing his home country but not forsaking his German alias. It was semisymbolic, proof that in the unreal world of wrestling, even an evil foreigner could assimilate just like any other immigrant.

☆ ☆ ☆

The Japanese wave of wrestling baddies lagged behind their Axis power cohorts, probably due more to the lack of availability than anything else. When they did finally come ashore, they walked a fine line between being vague geopolitical scourges and foreign beasts, indiscernible masters of steely resolve and mystical manipulation. Two early baddies of this sort were fearsome martial artists Toru Tanaka and Mr. Fuji. Though both were born in Hawaii—the home-place of a great number of faux Japanese, both in wrestling and in Hollywood—they played Japanese foils in the 1960s, drawing jeers by throwing salt in their opponents' eyes. They were followed by such symbols of a growing Asian market dominance as the Great Kabuki, who terrorized the United States starting in the '70s, had a painted face, and spat green mist into his opponents' faces; and the Great Muta, who used the same gimmick when he debuted in the NWA in 1989. After his wrestling career wound down, Mr. Fuji became the WWF's go-to manager for foreign (or otherwise frightening) menaces of just about any sort. It was almost a devolution of the caricature: His previous Japanese martial artistry was replaced with a bowler hat and bow tie, a Jerry Lewis sketch into perpetuity. Over the years he sired to the ring such Asian caricatures as the Orient Express (Tanaka and Sato), the Hawaiian Japanese sympathizer Crush, and the sumo behemoth Yokozuna. Yokozuna—actually a Hawaiian named Rodney Anoa'i—was a major player in the WWF for several years, but his prominence can't exactly be called political correctness. When he first became WWF champion by beating Bret Hart at WrestleMania IX in 1993, Fuji threw salt in Hart's eyes to allow Yokozuna to get the win.

☆ ☆ ☆

In the '60s and '70s, the looming threat of the USSR on the national scene resulted in a quick immigration of Russian surnames and beards into the wrestling ring. A pair of "brothers" named the Kalmikoffs first emerged in the '50s in Texas, but the next decade would see a more significant Soviet menace as the Russian threat continued to mount. Boris Malenko—an American named Lawrence Simon posing as a Russian—fought Buddy Rogers for his championship in 1961. In 1967, Canadian Jim Parras, who had previously competed as an Irishman named Red McNulty, adopted the moniker of the "Russian Bear" Ivan Koloff, and by 1970 he was embroiled in a heated feud with WWWF champ Bruno Sammartino. In January 1971, Koloff beat Sammartino for the title, ushering in a new era of anti-Soviet fearmongering that was only slightly less fearsome than the Red Scare in real life. A red singlet, a goatee, a bearish growl—rarely has villainy been so easy to manufacture. Koloff lost the belt a few weeks later to the new hero du jour, Pedro Morales. Morales was a Puerto Rican and Sammartino was Italian, but that didn't make them necessarily bad; like the Axis holdouts who came before him, Koloff wasn't bad because he was foreign but because he was that certain kind of diabolical, dream-crushing foreigner that only international conflict can scare up. (And what's more, Morales and Sammartino had important ticket-buying constituencies in the New York market.) With his shaved head, geometric beard, and stocky, utilitarian physique, Koloff set the mold for the wrestling Russians who followed. He also shepherded in a new generation of Russian baddies in the '80s, as his "nephew" Nikita Koloff (né Scott Simpson) and confederate Krusher Khruschev (Barry Darsow) ran roughshod over the NWA under Koloff's guidance. (Khruschev was later replaced by the "Russian Assassin" Vladimir Petrov, whose real name was Al Blake.)

There were others—Canadian Pierre Lafleur became the Russian Stomper; Jim Harrell (who had previously wrestled as the military man Pvt. Jim Nelson) became Boris Zhukov in the AWA; and of course, there was the Croatian Josip Peruzović, who comically terrorized American audiences in the WWF's '80s heyday as Nikolai Volkoff—but perhaps none had the cultural impact of the younger Koloff, who was feuding with all-American pretty boy Magnum T.A. in the NWA in 1986 when a car wreck ended Magnum's career. Expediency trumped political fervor; the lack of another top-tier babyface to take Magnum's spot led to Nikita himself seeing the light and defecting to team up with Magnum's old friend Dusty Rhodes. What's most incredible was the audience's quick acceptance of the erstwhile Russian scourge. It was five full years before the fall of the Soviet Union, but it was just after the first throes of perestroika. If the rise of glasnost was a harbinger for the USSR's fall, Koloff's emergence as a hero in the Southern United States was perhaps an early sign that the Soviet Union's geopolitical villainy was on its way out.

When the Soviet Union finally headed toward dissolution and the Berlin Wall came down in 1990, the Russian infrastructure in the wrestling world began to unravel along with it. In 1992, longtime baddie Nikolai Volkoff split with his partner, Boris Zhukov; embraced America (the country had been so good to him all these years, after all); and was embraced, in turn, by the American fans.

✰ ✰ ✰

That year, as the United States was gearing up to go to war in Iraq, a familiar face made his return to WWF television: Sgt. Slaughter, former WWF and AWA star and living G.I. Joe figure. (He actually appeared on the G.I. Joe cartoon.) In years previous, Slaughter had often been the actor through whom American political muscle was deployed in the squared circle, as he feuded against any number of foreign invaders. But the Slaughter that appeared in 1990 was not the same guy. This new Slaughter was disgusted by the fact that fans had accepted Volkoff after so many years of misdeeds, and so he had become disillusioned with his country. He became an Iraqi sympathizer during the Gulf War, and he was accompanied to the ring by two apparent Iraqi military men: General Adnan (formerly known to wrestling fans as Sheik Adnan Al-Kaissie) and Colonel Mustafa (who was very obviously the previously-Iranian Iron Sheik). Villainy overrides accuracy in such cases, one assumes.

The wrestling world was thrown for a loop—we had suffered losses at the hands of foreigners before, but never had we lost one of our own, never had we lost the *ideological* fight. In the ring, Slaughter was set against the Ultimate Warrior and Hulk Hogan, the stalwarts of the American Way. In real life, Slaughter was receiving death threats. And why not? Before, guys like Slaughter defended us from our global rivals; now that Slaughter had turned, how could we trust anyone to defend us? In the end, Hogan and Warrior got the job done and dispatched the Iraqi delegation. A short while later, Slaughter reembraced his Americanness and all was right with the world.

The next time America went to war, following the attacks of 9/11, the WWF couldn't resist engaging once again with the jingoism of the zeitgeist. But our scourge this time around wouldn't be strictly a foreign insurgent or even an American turncoat. It was worse: It would be an embodiment of the prejudices that led us into war. In late 2004, wrestling fans were introduced to Muhammad Hassan and Khosrow Daivari, two Muslim Americans (Hassan was an Italian American from New Jersey named Mark Copani; Daivari was actually an American of Persian descent named Shawn Daivari) who were outraged at the biases that had emerged against them since 9/11. They questioned our motives along with our national manhood and praised Allah to boot. In the end, it was probably too high-concept a tack, and certainly too much for the audience psyche, and Hassan and Daivari were rejiggered into more or less straightforward al-Qaeda symps, through whose evildoings the crowd could justify its own prejudices, and who were routinely beaten up by Shawn Michaels and, of course, Hulk Hogan. Despite this unprecedented assault, the American Way managed to stay intact. Later, Hassan and Daivari feuded with the Undertaker. If it weren't clear enough by then that Hassan's character had traded in idiosyncrasy for one-dimensionality, he sent a team of ski-masked, cargo-pantsed terrorist-types to beat up 'Taker one night. The show was pretaped, but it aired on the night of the London bombings, when terrorism fervor was again at a high pitch. Public outcry was severe. Never mind the fact that wrestling characters regularly imply such high crimes as assault, rape, and murder. The geopolitical realm was a bridge too far, and the world had evolved as wrestling's fakery became mainstream knowledge. Whereas with Slaughter, death threats were in order, Hassan's major misdeed was one not of villainy but of impropriety, and public admonishment from a few media outlets was enough to get him tossed off the air. Hassan eventually parted ways with the company and quit wrestling; Daivari stuck around to help other wrestlers get booed.

☆ ☆ ☆

In the years that followed, WWE stayed mostly above the political fray; certainly some of this has to do with the fallout of the Hassan angle, and one could probably pin some of it on former WWE CEO Linda McMahon's burgeoning political career also. But at the same time, the jingoistic American psyche is worn out from years of military activity in the Middle East, and there'd be little stomaching regular heel tirades against the American colonialist impulse. Our country's politics have become much more obsessed with Mexican immigration than with the wars we're fighting. In early 2013, WWE reintroduced Jack Swagger, an all-American collegiate wrestling star, as a sort of Tea Party caricature. (For much of his career, Swagger has been called the "All-American American," which may be a nod to John McCain's "the American president Americans have been waiting for" motto from 2008.) With a scraggly beard and newly shaggy hair hanging from his 6-foot-6 frame, he looked like a survivalist Übermensch, and his entrance music sounded like it was lifted from a Fox News show. He also had a new mouthpiece in Zeb Colter, a Vietnam vet and militiaman who directed the brunt of his patriotic fury at undocumented Mexican immigrants who "steal" jobs from hardworking Americans. The point was to use them to score points for then-champ Alberto Del Rio—a Mexican national— and to ridicule the self-styled patriot in the same way that foreigners had been ridiculed for decades prior, much to the pleasure of fans. The WWE's audience is increasingly Hispanic, and young where the Tea Party is old. And far be it from a wrestling promoter to let ideology stand in the way of making a buck.

# THE BIG BOSS MAN
# (RAY TRAYLOR)

Ray Traylor started his wrestling career in the most unremarkable of ways: as a jobber—"enhancement talent," in gentler parlance. He was one of the average Joes sent out to get clobbered by the
stars. For the majority of jobbers, this was the end of the story—they
wrestled some matches, they lost some matches, they went back to their
day jobs with a story to tell. Ray Traylor wasn't destined for greatness
any more than a thousand other guys. And yet there was something
about him. Dusty Rhodes (who knows a thing or two about the common
man and, for that matter, the American dream) was the head booker in

1985 in WCW, where Ray Traylor was jerking proverbial curtains, and he saw that something. After watching Traylor lose a few squash matches, Dusty pulled him off television and made him over as a bullying enforcer called Big Bubba Rogers. What name could be more perfect for an over-stuffed average Joe from Georgia? Big Bubba would soon be feuding with Dusty himself—then the promotion's top babyface—and Traylor's rise from nothing to something was confirmed. The monstrous Big Bubba Rogers, who stalked to the ring in a suit and tie like a mafia enforcer or the doorman at an underworld club, was a villain, but in playing him, Traylor was living the American dream.

He and Dusty traded wins back and forth, but after Dusty got the decisive victory in a series-ending steel cage match, Bubba was sent packing. He went over to the UWF—formerly Bill Watts's legendary Mid-South promotion—which the Crocketts had purchased ten days prior. As an unofficial emissary from the new parent company, he immediately won the UWF championship from the One Man Gang, who was leaving to join the WWF.[1] Big Bubba lost the title to local favorite "Dr. Death" Steve Williams—just as Traylor himself was called up to New York,[2] where Vince McMahon and company repackaged him as the Big Boss Man, a wrestling prison guard.

Or unpackaged, rather. Because even as the idea of the wrestling law officer fed neatly into the play of good and evil at the heart of pro wrestling, it was also a reference to real life, as Traylor himself had been a corrections officer in Cobb County, Georgia, prior to falling into the wrestling trade. In his heyday, "Stone Cold" Steve Austin was fond of saying that the best characters in pro wrestling are the wrestlers who just play themselves but with the volume turned up. The Big Boss Man followed this model—he was little more than the WWF-trademarked version of Ray Traylor—but perhaps this was a foregone conclusion.

.....................................................................

**1** Once Traylor followed him there, the two ovoid bruisers would eventually form a tag team called the Twin Towers, which, regardless of their respective heights, always seemed to be pointing out the wrong measure of their physical distinction.

**2** In continuing the regional designations of the Territorial Era, WWF/WWE is to this day called "New York" by industry insiders, and WCW was always called "Atlanta."

Traylor didn't have it in him to play a monster like Abdullah the Butcher or even the Earthquake, another big-boned regular guy turned into a seismic beast. Traylor was too average, too unaffected (and, by all accounts, a total sweetheart backstage). Ray Traylor was destined, it seems, to be Ray Traylor. Even as a bad guy, he was a God-fearing, tax-paying citizen of the world: He was unremarkable, and that was his indelible appeal.

☆ ☆ ☆

The Big Boss Man began his WWF career in a wholly pedestrian way too: He beat Koko B. Ware—the bedazzled, macaw-toting mild fan favorite famous for getting beat up by ascendant baddies—in his first pay-per-view match at SummerSlam 1988. But the WWF writers soon saw the same spark in Traylor that Dusty had seen before, and in short order the Boss Man was feuding with the anything-but-regular Hulk Hogan. It turned out to be a sort of back-burner grudge for Hogan: He fought Boss Man at untelevised house shows and on the weekly TV shows, but Hogan spent the majority of his time in those days dealing with his dissolving friendship with "Macho Man" Randy Savage. The Boss Man bided his time teaming up with fellow big man Akeem the African Dream (formerly the One Man Gang),[3] under the "tutelage" of the huckster manager Slick,[4] against top good-guy duos like the Rockers and Demolition. But his simmering dispute with Hogan culminated in a near-legendary cage match on *Saturday Night's Main Event*, wherein Hogan superplexed Boss Man—all 350 pounds of him—off the cage and into the ring.

(You can find the video on the web, but let me warn you: It's probably not as impressive as it sounds and definitely not nearly as incredible as it seemed at the time, especially viewed today through the hardened eyes

---

**3** While often regarded as at best befuddling or at worst racist, the white Akeem character was actually a dig at Dusty Rhodes, who was a fat guy who talked and jived like a black man, or so the thinking went. The "African Dream" was a play on Rhodes's "American Dream" moniker.

**4** Slick would eventually retire and become a preacher in Texas.

of a wrestling fan who lived through ECW's high-flying routines of the late '90s, but for the time it was good enough to be incredible. Especially for a regular guy.)

This was the pinnacle of Traylor's career, the summit of how far his simple appeal would let him climb. When the average wrestling fan looks at his reflection and appraises himself honestly, he probably doesn't see Hulk Hogan staring back at him. But consider the Big Boss Man: He's overweight, he's got a crew cut and goatee, he's Southern, he's blue-collar. This is the everyman, to a large portion of the WWF audience. "Justice will be served," he would say, and wrestling fans heard within it a deeper truth—that was precisely what they wanted from wrestling, and what they wanted from the universe. In his pants and (tucked-in) shirt, the Big Boss Man was Willy Loman in the funhouse mirror of pro wrestling: big and burly, sure, but a man of principle at his core—and yet an under-achiever, a man not wired for greatness. He was the archetypal mid-carder, almost unremarkable, but somehow—and this can only be to Traylor's credit—entirely unforgettable.

☆ ☆ ☆

When the Big Boss Man became a good guy, it was (of course) in the most commonplace sort of way: Bad Guy rediscovered his conscience and fell out with other baddies. But in this case it was portrayed perfectly. Jake "The Snake" Roberts, you see, had been feuding with the "Million Dollar Man" Ted DiBiase, and Roberts had taken possession of DiBiase's self-made "Million Dollar Championship Belt" and stowed it for good measure in the bag that his pet python Damien called home. Since DiBiase was petrified of snakes, as everyone who feuded with Roberts (all too coincidentally) was, and since he had the money to blow, the Million Dollar Man paid Boss Man—via manager Slick[5]—to retrieve the belt. Boss Man indeed got the bag—and was glad to since the belt was stolen

---

**5**  Any incidental instance of a pro wrestling manager actually performing real-world managerial duties and not just provoking opponents is worth pointing out.

property and such matters were his jurisdiction. But once he realized that Slick had accepted payment for the job, Boss Man did an about-face. His moral code would not be compromised. He returned the bag to Roberts, defiantly staring down both Slick and DiBiase.

In a matter of mere moments, played out with incredible drama on national television, the Boss Man went from the most diabolical of men to a fan favorite without betraying his character—and we cheered loudly, because we understood him, because he was one of us. Little wonder that in an era in which half of the wrestling superstars on WWF TV were assigned unglamorous middle-class careers "outside" the wrestling world—the garbage man, the hog farmer, the accountant, the repo man— the Big Boss Man was the only prole to achieve any lasting fame. He worked not because he acted like one of us but because he *was* one of us.

The Boss Man would soon feud with his old partner Akeem, and then with a heelish lawman from north of the border called the Mountie (played by the wildly underrated Jacques Rougeau).[6] This latter feud was notable because it featured the Mountie attacking the Boss Man with a cattle prod (complete with overdubbed electric shocking noises) and culminated in a match in which the loser had to "spend the night" in the county jail. (Where two or more wrestling lawmen are gathered, a paddy wagon match is sure to follow.)

This started the Big Boss Man down a path of increasingly bizarre and ridiculous storylines. For the everyman, this was a sort of ignominy, but it made a certain sense—the Boss Man wasn't the superhero commanding an audience's awe solely by the flexing of his sculpted arms. No, he was a (sort of) real person, only with unreal problems. This was underscored by the fact that most of the feuds that would follow were based on cultural grievances or things that happened outside the ring in the backstory lives—as with the aforementioned wrestling accountant.[7]

---

6   The same guy who coldcocked the Dynamite Kid with a roll of quarters.

7   Usually called by his guffaw-inducing initials, IRS, Schyster was the standout grappler Mike Rotunda functionally repackaged as Ted DiBiase's financial planner. Indisputably his best angle was the time he took issue with Native American wrestler Tatanka for failing to pay taxes on a ceremonial headdress.

It was the workaday stiff vs. the grabby hands of Uncle Sam—which probably encapsulates the everyman dream as well as anything else Traylor did. He warred memorably with an ex-con named Nailz, who, the storyline went, claimed that Boss Man beat him in his cell when he was incarcerated. We fans assumed that Nailz was lying, of course, but once that's decided, the origin of Nailz's ire is difficult to discern, as are Boss Man's counterarguments, which relied less on straightforward denial as on legalese—and a bizarre element of introspective admission that the system around which he'd based his life wasn't perfect: "I've read the police report, I've looked through your files, I've seen the psychological review. I know that you're a crazy man, that you should be locked up for the rest of your life. That's just showin' that sometimes the system don't work, that they have to let out trash like you. Just a technical error. But the plain and simple fact is that law, order, and justice have been around since the beginning of time, and it's gonna be around [till] the end of time."

One can't but help hear the echo of Barthes: "But what wrestling is above all meant to portray is a purely moral concept: that of justice." If the reading of the rap sheet seems a little bit off-subject to the principle of wrestling, well, that was sort of the point. This was a common man, with real-life issues. He just happened to be afforded the unique ability to settle his workplace disputes in a sanctioned wrestling ring.

☆　☆　☆

When Traylor left the WWF for WCW in 1993, he abandoned law and order for vigilante justice and became known as the Guardian Angel, complete with red beret, but when that personage failed to catch on, he reverted to his old Big Bubba Rogers persona, and then again to his real name. (This was mid-'90s WCW after all.) In his return to the WWF[8] (and to the Boss Man character), the storylines only got stranger. Despite

--------

**8**　He was a low-level poaching pitched as a big deal; WCW was stealing WWF stars in those days with huge contract offers that WWF couldn't match, so with funds otherwise depleted, it lured in Ray Traylor types with promises of increased screen time.

the privilege of feuding with Steve Austin, D-Generation X, and the Undertaker, there was no real glory; that last conflict ended in a Hell in a Cell match that saw the Boss Man hanged by a noose in the center of the ring. (This was so baldly offensive that the announcer immediately tried his best to disavow the play lynching by screaming "Is it symbolic?!?" over and over, even as Traylor played dead.) A grudge against Al Snow, another regular Joe type, hinged on the Boss Man killing Snow's pet Chihuahua and serving it to an unaware Snow for dinner. The Boss Man then battled the Big Show for the WWF championship in a storyline in which the Boss Man crashed the funeral of the Big Show's father and made off with the coffin, driving off with it chained to the back of his car.

Needless to say, perhaps, there really wasn't anywhere to go from there. Traylor's WWF tenure ended not long thereafter. His last match was against another preeminent wrestling everyman, ECW legend Tommy Dreamer. That was the last we saw of the Boss Man. He died the next year at forty-one years old at his Georgia home of a heart attack.

☆   ☆   ☆

Wrestling legend has it that there was a segment on *America's Most Wanted* in which the criminal in the filmed reenactment of a heist bore an uncanny resemblance to none other than Ray Traylor. The story goes that wrestling fans nationwide called into the hotline with the same tip: You can find your perp at the WWF show on Monday night—he'll be wearing a police uni, and they call him the Big Boss Man. That Ray Traylor could so convincingly be mistaken for someone else speaks loudly to his everyman credentials. And in the end, that the everyman, the chubby guy with the goatee, made it as far as he did speaks volumes about Ray Traylor's talent.

# OWEN HART

On May 23, 1999, at the WWE's Over the Edge pay-per-view event, Owen Hart died in a wrestling ring. He was playing a character called the Blue Blazer, a farcical masked superhero, though it can more accurately be stated that Owen Hart—who had, for much of his career, exploited wrestling's interplay between reality and unreality—was portraying "Owen Hart" masquerading as the Blue Blazer. On this night, Owen was being lowered to the ring in a harness to approximate superhuman flight. The harness malfunctioned; a clasp gave way, and he fell seventy feet onto the ring ropes, which severed his aorta and killed him almost instantly. At that moment, the difference between Owen, "Owen," and the Blue Blazer was rendered tragically immaterial. Wrestling had lost one of its greats.

In the modern world of pro wrestling, even when you're ostensibly playing yourself, you're really playing a character. On-screen, "Owen" always denied that he and the Blazer were the same person, even though it was comically obvious that they were one and the same. (His buddy Jeff Jarrett wrestled in the Blazer garb while Owen sat by on commentary to "prove" they were separate, and Koko B. Ware even took a turn under the blue mask for a similar gag; the ruse was more than obvious due to the skin pigmentation differences between Ware and Hart, and the audience was happily in on the joke.) Owen had played the Blue Blazer character earnestly early in his career, mostly in Japan and Mexico, where such masked personas are customary. Such a character from his past was an ideal vessel for what would be, in its 1999 iteration, an antimodern crusade. The Blue Blazer was at once a masked alter ego and a manifestation of Owen's superego—the Blue Blazer was a remnant of a simpler era, standing opposed to the excesses of the WWE's Attitude Era, the crass sex- and violence-obsessed style that took over WWE programming in the late '90s. Owen the person had long been quietly uncomfortable with the direction the company was heading—he notably refused to work a storyline that had him in an affair with Jarrett's on-screen companion, Debra McMichael, for fear that his children would watch and believe it was true—and now Owen the character was exorcising the demons of his own discomfort and deconstructing such depravities within the context of Attitude Era programming. It was a winning ploy; many wrestlers were at that point playing outsize versions of themselves to great success, and Owen joining the fray as the movement's antihero was borderline-inspired storytelling. That he was playing it for comic effect didn't necessarily undermine its agenda—championship-level feuds in those days were often marked by dick jokes—and neither did the audience's heckling subjugate the message: Owen was playing the heel, a pariah loudly extolling integrity and moral rectitude, so the jeers were part of the routine; and besides, the good guy–bad guy continuum had been turned on its head by the ascent of "Stone Cold" Steve Austin and other ideological "tweeners." When the Blazer ran to the ring with his arms outstretched, like a kid imitating his favorite cartoon character, or when he was lowered from the rafters, arms flailing, the crowd laughed in unison.

It would have been a conceivable punch line to send the beleaguered superhero—or a mannequin dressed to look like him—crashing down from the rafters into the ring. Such attention-grabbing stunts were common in those days. Wrestling is based on the premise of fake injury, of course, but pro wrestling in the modern age has been ever intent on pushing the boundaries in such a way as to simultaneously shock viewers and yet underline the ridiculousness of it all. It was clear from the crowd's reaction that when Owen fell, at least briefly, they thought the fall was part of the act.

And why shouldn't they? The boundary between real life and fake life was irreparably blurred by that point thanks to any number of fourth-wall-breaking storylines, but the Blue Blazer angle—Real Owen playing Fake Owen playing a masked avenger fighting for Real Owen's honor—was surely the pinnacle of such multilayered surrealism.

✩ ✩ ✩

Owen's storyline wasn't always pitched at such a meta level. He was born into wrestling, as the youngest child in the legendary Hart family, son of Stu Hart and brother to Bret (and five other brothers who would wrestle to less acclaim), and he was by many accounts the most naturally gifted grappler of the bunch. But despite his best efforts to find a career outside the ring—supposedly to keep his new family away from the wrestler's life that he grew up with—he soon decided that wrestling was his only lucrative path. He started off as a golden boy in his father's Canadian promotion, Stampede Wrestling. Brother Bret was then entrenched in the WWF as half of the Hart Foundation (along with Jim "The Anvil" Neidhart); Bret was a star, but certainly nobody would have predicted his future as a long-term Heavyweight Champion, as he was several inches too short and several degrees too plain to compare to the likes of Hulk Hogan or Randy Savage.

And Owen was, if anything, smaller and less flamboyant than his brother—he was unaffected, Real Owen playing himself—and despite his popularity in Stampede, he wasn't offered a job with one of the major American shops. He wrestled through Japan and Mexico, where his size wasn't a deterrent and his high-flying style was more commonplace. His success there would eventually lead to a job with the WWF, but rather than capitalize on his relationship with Bret, McMahon put him in a mask and called him the Blue Angel. (That beatific moniker was soon corrupted into the "Blue Blazer.") There was very little affectation; this was Real Owen with a mask. He wowed the more attentive fans with his seemingly revolutionary mix of aerial maneuvers and old-school grappling, but he was a gimmick without a backstory, form without substance, and the audience at large was unsure of what to make of him.

After only a brief run, he went back to the global circuit—Stampede, Mexico, and a cup of coffee in WCW. He landed back in the WWF, once again as plain old Owen Hart, forming the "New Foundation" with Neidhart after Bret left the Hart Foundation tag team to embark upon his singles career, and later teaming up with the unspectacular Koko B. Ware to form the team High Energy. Neither team was much of a success—the neon parachute pants probably had something to do with that.

After High Energy disbanded, Owen aligned himself with Bret in his beef against Jerry "The King" Lawler, and from there, through various feuds, the brothers' relationship took center stage. Over the ensuing months, their partnership evolved into a competition and then into an all-out rivalry, with Owen playing the angsty, underappreciated second banana: Owen finally coming into his own by playing "Owen." The sibling rivalry was Jacob and Esau shined up with baby oil. It was presumably based to some degree on real life; the angle began when Real Owen asked Real Bret why he never got the chance to fight against his brother and share in the main event spotlight. That backstage conversation evolved into a months-long on-screen campaign. The matches they

shared were always the best of the night—and among the best of the era—
but the arch familial interplay was at the forefront.

Owen had come into his own as a personality as well. Whereas Real
Owen was a mild-mannered and high-spirited jokester,[1] Fake Owen was
a sarcastic, silver-tongued jerk. When he sat in as a guest at the commentary table, he was a droll instigator of virtuoso status, especially when
contrasted with Bret and the rest of the wooden Hart clan. The Harts
were so soaked in tradition that they were nearly inert; Owen seemed to
be the only Hart who was in on the joke—and the joy—that is pro wrestling.

A number of the other Hart family members, including brother-in-law
Davey Boy Smith and the family matriarch Helen Hart, floated in and out
of the storylines; the latter tearfully threw in the towel for her son Bret
in a match against Bob Backlund upon Owen's maniacal urging.

When Bret thereafter defeated Owen to functionally put their rivalry
to an end, Owen started tag-teaming with Yokozuna with minimal explanation, and the duo held the tag team championships for five months.
He then joined forces with Davey Boy Smith, and the two had an uneasy
alliance—which mirrored to some degree Owen's partnership-cum-
rivalry with Bret—for a number of months. Both men subsequently
joined up with Bret (and Neidhart and Brian Pillman) to form a new,
larger-scale Hart Foundation. This iteration was a nationalist outfit that
proclaimed Canadian superiority and virtue in opposition to the sleazily
American WWE, much to the dismay of the audience—except, of course,
in Canada, where they were hailed as returning conquerors.

The most notorious incident in this period was Owen nearly ending
the career of Steve Austin. Owen's piledriver—this is where one man
puts the other's head between his thighs and then drops it forcefully into
the mat—actually accomplished what the move normally only insinu-
ated, and Austin was temporarily paralyzed in the ring. The match ended
clumsily, with a groggy and weak Austin unimpressively pinning Owen
so as to keep with the planned outcome. Fans could plainly see that the

---

1    His backstage practical jokes—known as "ribs" in the biz—are the stuff of legend.

finish was forced, but—tellingly—most chose to suspend disbelief; Austin was a big enough star that nobody complained about how fake it looked. It suggested the distance from reality at which the fanbase was willing to situate itself, and as such it was a painful foreshadowing of Owen's own demise.

After the Montreal Screwjob, Hart Foundation members Neidhart and Smith were allowed to follow Bret to WCW, but Owen was deliberately retained. He briefly carried his brother's torch against Michaels, but soon Michaels and his D-Generation X cohorts became full-fledged fan favorites, leading Owen, who seemed increasingly unstable, to join the Nation of Domination faction—till then the WWE's Black Power outfit— alongside burgeoning superstar the Rock as the Nation feuded against Michaels and company. It was during this period that he was hamstrung with the nickname "Nugget," a moniker that drove Fake Owen apoplectic. As the Nation dissolved, Owen began teaming with Jeff Jarrett and eventually morphed (back) into the bizarro Blue Blazer persona: Now doubly removed from his real identity, Owen was no longer himself at all.

✩ ✩ ✩

Perhaps more so than any other star of his vintage other than Mick Foley, Owen's relationship with "real life"—Owen's relationship with "Owen"— was written in such a way as to call into question the nature of wrestling reality. His relationship with his brother was inflated into an epic conflict. His accidental injury of Austin was turned into a later storyline in which Owen supposedly made the same error in "maiming" Dan Severn. And then there was the Blue Blazer angle: They took an act that he had worked years before and turned it on its head, shoehorning in his qualms with the wrestling industry at large.[2] That his death would initially be misinterpreted as a scripted pratfall is a devastating metaphor for his career as a whole.

.....................................................................................

2  It's often assumed that the parody was aiming to encompass more than just the WWE—the very act that led to Owen's death was partly a reference to Sting, a star for the competing WCW, who entered the ring from the rafters in similar fashion.

But, of course, it wasn't fake. According to CNN, "Hart was given CPR inside the ring as the ring announcer haltingly told the audience that the incident was not scripted, as professional wrestling matches openly are." The fans watching at home got the bad news from Jim Ross, who, as the lead announcer of the show, was charged with narrating the tragic event in seven-second-delayed real time during the pay-per-view telecast: "This is not a part of the entertainment here tonight. This is as real as real can be here."

When Ross first comes on-screen, he is visibly shaken and uncertain. At this point, it isn't official that Owen is dead. But more than that, Ross seems unclear about what his message is supposed to be. To acknowledge that Owen's fall is real is to implicitly acknowledge wrestling's falsehood, and for Ross—and certainly for McMahon—such a statement would threaten the heart of broadcasting.

In his death, Owen laid bare the culture of debauchery and one-upmanship that dominated the wrestling scene. The stunts had grown bigger and bigger, the quest for ratings and cheers more and more dogged; certainly there was a feeling that something like this was bound to happen. If they broke the fourth wall in telling the fans that the accident was real, it's notable that it was necessary to tell them at all.

The show went on. This was a source of great animosity toward Vince McMahon and the WWE for anyone looking to demonize them in the wake of Owen's death, but it's really a nonstarter. Owen himself had performed immediately after Brian Pillman's untimely passing, either because he thought that's what Pillman would have wanted or because that was the only way he knew to handle it. Moreover, though, it's the nature of the beast: If acts like the Blue Blazer are built on the distance between the real world and wrestling, then it follows that the intervention of real life is a prospect but not a deterrent. (And to be fair, McMahon would have been demonized even if he had stopped the card.)

Reality did intervene the next night on *Monday Night Raw*, as they did away with storylines for an Owen Hart tribute show. The matches were interspersed with eulogies from other wrestlers, who were legitimately distraught. Owen was beloved, and it showed. Here the reality vs.

unreality paradox was turned on its head. It was still pro wrestling—fake combat—but rendered pure by a unique sheen of self-awareness. When Jim Ross, on commentary, observed that Jarrett was employing Owen's Sharpshooter finisher to win his match, he said, "Jeff Jarrett's gotta be doing this for his former tag team partner"—acknowledging Jarrett's tribute but edging back from the precipice of reality by focusing only on their in-ring relationship, referencing life outside the ring only by gesturing at its in-ring shadow. (Jarrett blurred the line with less delicacy: He won the intercontinental belt in that match, the belt that had been intended for Owen to win before his death, and upon victory he held up the belt and tearfully screamed "Owen!") When Steve Austin closed the show by guzzling beers and pointing toward the sky, it was a minor variation on the routine he ran to close almost every WWE telecast of that period: a heartfelt acknowledgment, sure, but not exactly a divorce from the routine product. Even if only slightly, though, they were deconstructing the medium to honor one of the last remaining purists.

☆ ☆ ☆

There have been other wrestlers to die in the ring: Mike DiBiase ("Million Dollar Man" Ted DiBiase's stepfather) may be the only other wrestler that mainstream American fans have heard of; he had a heart attack midmatch at the age of forty-five. Larry Booker (a.k.a. Moondog Spot) likewise died of a heart attack in the ring. Gary Albright died after a "bulldog"—his head forcibly driven into the mat by his opponent—at a local show in Pennsylvania. Indie wrestler Daniel "Spider" Quirk died when his opponent fell from the ring onto Quirk's head against the concrete floor. Japanese standout Mitsuharu Misawa died after a belly-to-back suplex dropped him hard onto his neck, and female wrestlers Emiko Kado and Plum Mariko both suffered life-ending accidents in the ring. Mexican wrestler Jesús Javier Hernández—known as "Oro"—reacted too dramatically to a clothesline and landed on his head, ending his life. British behemoth Malcolm "King Kong" Kirk had a heart attack after landing a "splash" on his opponent. Ray Gunkel died in the locker room after an in-ring punch to the chest (and undiagnosed arterio-sclerosis) apparently gave him a heart attack.

These tragedies—all of them nebulous incidences to the average wrestling fan—are balanced by a handful of storylines in which death, or near-death, was scripted: Fritz Von Erich's postbeatdown collapse, Ric Flair's midmonologue heart attack, Road Warrior Hawk's leap off the Ti-tantron, referee Tim White's (numerous) suicide attempts. The list could go on to include lesser offenses: Brian Pillman pulling a gun on Steve Austin, Hulk Hogan sending the Giant (Paul Wight) off a rooftop, and, less seriously, the Undertaker's innumerable "buried alive" and casket matches.

If wrestling fans are inured to the untimely deaths of their idols, is it fair to ask if it's as much because of these plots as it is for the proliferation of actual deaths? It isn't so much an issue of taste or apathy; it's an issue of reality vs. illusion. Wrestling, with its frequently upended and dis-carded plotlines and the regular movement of performers between com-panies, has at its core an element of confusion—an inherent inanity that viewers take for granted. Finding out that a character like Yokozuna died isn't so much a tragedy as it is the next (and last) chapter in his al-ready disjointed narrative. That it occurs off-camera renders it somehow less real. Owen's death was the antithesis of this: Ross may have broken the rules of kayfabe, but Owen's death had already taken them off script. It wasn't just an instance of a wrestler dying in front of thousands of wrestling fans; it was the death of a real human being in front of thou-sands of other real people. As with McMahon's Montreal Screwjob inter-view, the curtain was pulled back to expose reality; this time, however, reality couldn't be wedged into a storyline.

Owen's widow, Martha, sued the WWE over the federation's use of footage from Owen's old matches. Apparently McMahon had promised her that he wouldn't seek to profit off Owen's death, and Martha took that to mean that he wouldn't seek to capitalize off anything Owen had ever been involved in. Her immediate objection was to Owen's inclusion on a DVD about the Hart family. Recently, Bret—who, sadly, hasn't had any contact with Martha or Owen's children in years—wrote, "Just because

Owen died doesn't mean the Hart legacy from Stu down to his wrestling sons and grandchildren has to die too." I think that's right. But if I may be so bold as to restate that from a fan's perspective: To write Owen out of wrestling history is to deny what he meant to all of us.

He wasn't as famous as his brother Bret; he wasn't as famous as he might have become. But when he died, millions of fans the world over were heartbroken. Maybe that's little solace for Owen's family, but that's something. Owen taught us that real life lay just beyond the ring. He succeeded within the parameters of wrestling's pretend world, and that alone was enough to make him a star. What made him something greater was that all the while he helped us measure the distance between that pretend world and reality. Owen acknowledged the quotation marks and thrived between them. He could wink without destroying the illusion. His death—*this is as real as real can be here*—allowed us to see how indelicately we had been treating reality, how McMahon and the WWE and all its fans had become cynical and callous, and that in doing so we were missing the point. We weren't traditionalists like the Hart clan, but we were guilty of the same misapprehension: We had forgotten the joy that is pro wrestling.

# MAIMING AND KILLING THEIR WAY TO STARDOM

One night in 1952, two literal giants of the day were in a ring in Montreal. On one side was Yukon Eric, a beloved rustic warrior from the wilds of Fairbanks, Alaska. On the other was Walter (Wladek) Kowalski, one of the sport's original monster heels. Eric was a sort of ur–Hillbilly Jim, a backwoods powerhouse with a sixty-six-inch chest and limbs like the huge logs he chopped in promotional photos. He wrestled barefoot, his jeans belted with a stretch of rope, and he often wore a sleeveless plaid shirt to the ring. He was a huge star in Canada, and a big enough name in the northeastern United States that A. J. Liebling wrote a piece about him in *The New Yorker.* If Eric was a jovial Norse god, Kowalski came from the mythos of vengeful Roman deities. Kowalski was 6-foot-7 and 290 pounds in his prime, all sinew and odd angles, a Frankenstein's monster with anti-American patina. He wrestled Orville Brown for the world championship six months after his first match—a notable accomplishment in those olden days when record and accomplishment meant a great deal—and years later, in 1972, would become the first man in recorded wrestling history to pin Andre the Giant.

Back to that night in 1952, though. The two rivals were deep into their match when Kowalski climbed the ropes to deliver his signature knee drop. His landing glanced the side of Eric's head, accidentally clipped one of Eric's cauliflowered ears—the grotesquely bloated and hardened ears were, and still are to some extent, a common repercussion of the grappling lifestyle—and tore it off the side of his head. At least in part, anyway—the legend is hard to sever from the reality. But he left Eric without at least part of an ear, and to an audience already disposed to loathe the putative foreigner, this was unforgivable. When the papers the next day confirmed the mauling, fan outrage grew to a fever pitch, and the promoter feared for Kowalski's personal safety lest angered fans try to exact ear-for-an-ear revenge upon him on the street, so it was suggested to Kowalski that he visit Eric in the hospital to give the appearance of contrition.

In real life, Kowalski (he was born Edward Spulnik but eventually legally changed his name to Walter Kowalski) was a kindhearted soul, an artist and photographer and reader of philosophy and eventually a vegan, notoriously incapable of keeping up kayfabe because he was too nice to be a heel in real life. He said he often dressed in disguise to go out in public so that he wouldn't be harassed by fans, but it was probably just as much that he didn't want to do any harassing himself. He would go on in his later years to be a teacher of the craft and a proselytizer for clean living. But he had a wry sense of humor to match the crooked smile on his ogre face.

Kowalski agreed to go to the hospital—he and Eric were friends in real life after all—but there was a reporter from the paper there covering the plight of the local hero, and when Kowalski got into Eric's hospital room, the sight of his "foe" in a ridiculous full-head bandage made him laugh. Eric laughed right along, but the sportswriter stationed outside the room reported only Kowalski's laughter and framed it as the valedictory insult of a vicious monster. The headline the next day said that Kowalski showed up only to laugh in

Eric's face. Suddenly Kowalski had a new nickname—"Killer"—and a clearly articulated purpose in life. In a world of fake injury, inflicting such real catastrophic injury could in those days be a lifelong meal ticket. It wouldn't be his only moment of semireal violence—in one match, he injured special referee Jack Dempsey, and once attacked Australian talk show host Don Lane.

Of course, those were relatively minor incidents for the wrestling profession—it was only notable that Kowalski had directly caused the original sin against Eric in front of a paying audience, and from that garnered infamy that would label his every action thereafter as the act of a madman.

One can't consider that scene and not think of Mick Foley, the Modern-Era star most famous for graphic self-disregard: He's thrown himself off the top of a steel cage and through tables and into barbed wire more times than one can—or should—count. Perhaps the most notable moment in establishing his star came in 1993 when—performing as his original character, Cactus Jack—he was wrestling Big Van Vader on a WCW tour of Europe in a brutal episode of a notoriously brutal feud. Early in the bout, Foley was (deliberately) caught in a "hangman," his head tangled in the top two ropes and his body dangling below, and when he eventually freed himself, his ear was ripped off by the unusually taut ropes. He thereafter declined reconstructive surgery so as not to miss a big match, thinking WCW would build a story around his mutilation. He was wrong, but the mishap would eventually come to define the legend of Mick Foley—a visible, real-world symbol of all the brutality he had put his body through in service of the craft.

The fame Kowalski and Foley garnered wasn't unique, though it was severe. A couple of even more drastic instances exist, though they're mostly lost to history. A lost ear—that's a good gimmick. But death? In a world in which violence is carefully balanced between gory and vaudevillian, the question stands out in relief.

On July 27, 1951, a lady wrestler named Ella Waldek was in a tag match in Ohio with Mae Young against Eva Lee and a newcomer named Janet Boyer Wolfe. Boyer Wolfe—who was purportedly being adopted by lady wrestling impresario Billy Wolfe (the widespread implication at the time was that Wolfe, a notorious seducer of his talent, was taking her into his harem despite her being underage)— had wrestled Waldek earlier that day and was complaining of a splitting headache. After a hard bodyslam from Waldek, Boyer shrunk to the corner and onto the ringside floor, where she promptly died. Waldek was distraught, but her career was buoyed: "Boy was I drawing some houses. Everybody wanted to see the stupid blonde who killed Janet Wolfe."

Ox Baker was maybe the Platonic ideal of the monster heel, a hulking brute with a bald head, a handlebar mustache, and thick eyebrows that shot upward in Hollywood Asian curls. He made his own shirts that gloated about recent victories or diabolical goals, iron-on letters on ringer tees that seem like hipster irony now but back then read as a kind of murderous commitment to the craft. His big move was a heart punch—Baker was a magnificent talker and a competent wrestler, but he was never a great athlete, so his finisher was more form than substance. But what provocative form it was. The move was so feared that it was sometimes banned for its lethality. Little wonder then that when, in June 1971, Alberto Torres died of a ruptured appendix after wrestling a tag team match against Baker, Baker's heart punch was blamed. Baker himself was crushed, but when his paychecks started going up, he couldn't help but see the potential value. A year later in Savannah, Baker was wrestling area promoter Ray Gunkel when Gunkel had a heart attack in the locker room after the match. Baker's star was born of implicit murder. Wrestling magazines put Baker's grimacing mug on their covers, proclaiming his deadliness, and the stories of ill-fated happenstance evolved into tales of gruesome in-ring murder.

Of course, none of these three deaths is particularly famous. Even if they drew big money at the time, the continuing popularity of the sport makes impossible the glamorization of in-ring death. There are a million other instances of wrestlers claiming to have inflicted the injuries of their foes, but for the most part "killing" is left to the empty threats of angry men with bad attitudes.

# YOKOZUNA

Pro wrestling has long been a land of expansiveness, a playground for literally outsize men to act out metaphorically outsize tropes and storylines for the teleological gratification of the masses. Nevertheless, when a 500-pound man makes his way down the aisle, people stop to pay notice. Or, hey, maybe they're a little bit distracted at just that moment by an argument over the relative merits of the feuding tag teams the Nasty Boys and Money Inc., as were announcers Vince Mc-Mahon and Curt Hennig when Yokozuna first set (bare) foot in the WWF ring—but once they noticed, they were suitably awed. Oozed McMahon:

"Take a look at this! Take a look at the girth! Take a look at five hundred and five pounds of Yokozuna! This man is huge!"

Led by longtime scoundrel manager Mr. Fuji, Yokozuna—né Rodney Anoa'i—was a behemoth even by the bloated standards of the WWF, for which a new plus-sized hire wasn't exactly a rare occurrence. But gargantuan wrestlers—be they tall, fat, overmuscled, or some combination of the three—never seem to lose their luster in the eyes of the wrestling audience. Or, more precisely, in the eyes of McMahon and the other heirs of Barnum who run the shows and sign the paychecks.

From almost the earliest days of the sport, in every fairground or vaudeville hall where a ring was erected and a crowd assembled, there were semiathletic butterballs on hand to shock and awe the audience with their mind-boggling bulk, put on display like their carnival sideshow forebears. These men, though—from Haystacks Calhoun and Gorilla Monsoon to the One Man Gang and King Kong Bundy—didn't just suit up for the gawking. They whooped and jeered, and once the battle commenced, they punched and chopped and (usually at the end) fell down heavily upon their opponents, the spectacle of their king-sizedness now palpably painful and almost interactive. Still freaks in a sense, they'd nevertheless upped the ante considerably. They weren't just the sideshow—they were the circus.

And in 1992, from this esteemed tradition came Yokozuna, the wrestling sumo.[1] A few things to clarify about Rodney Anoa'i up front: He was not Japanese, as was implied by the flag that he toted into the ring (he was Samoan and was announced as being from the South Pacific Islands or Polynesia, though you could hardly hear it over the traditional Japanese music that attended his arrival); at the beginning of his career, he was probably not the full 500 pounds at which he was introduced (he was rumored to have worn padded tights to increase his lower-torso bulk), though he vastly exceeded that mark by the end of his career; and he was

---

[1] The name refers to the highest rank in sumo wrestling.

not Akebono, the famed Hawaiian sumo wrestler, as was (and is) often mistakenly assumed.[2]

Yokozuna may have been none of these things, but he was monster enough to make up for it. In some ways, his own backstory was even more interesting than his fake one. Anoa'i was the nephew of Afa and Sika, the famed Wild Samoans, the Polynesian antecedents of a massive clan of grapplers, including Rikishi, Samu, Rosey, Umaga, and, by association, Dwayne "The Rock" Johnson. (Afa and Sika considered "High Chief" Peter Maivia, the Rock's grandfather, their honorary uncle.) After training with Afa and Sika, Anoa'i wrestled in Mexico and Japan to hone his craft, and did a stint in the AWA under the name "Great Kokina." Wearing the traditional (wrestling) garb of Pacific Islanders—the three-quarter-length tights and bare feet, with a Troy Polamalu–esque shock of curly, black hair—Kokina was playing to his heritage, but as the modifier made clear, the emphasis was already on his immensity.

Vince McMahon, always a fan of the physical oddity, soon came calling. And in his characteristically idiosyncratic way, he repackaged Anoa'i as Yokozuna, a sumo grand champion and nominally Japanese powerhouse that set a new bar for racial caricature. Mr. Fuji, who was already a one-stop shop for Asian stereotypes, soon traded in his black suit, bow tie, and bowler hat for a formal kimono, and he would accompany Yokozuna to the ring tossing salt from a wooden bucket. They were escorted by geisha girls for higher-profile matches. Yoko would scream in pidgin Japanese as he bullied his opponents, and his matches almost always culminated with him yelling "Banzai!" and jumping off the second rope, butt-first, onto his victim's chest.[3]

Yokozuna soon competed in the Royal Rumble and won—what with it being difficult to throw him over the top rope and all, an annual theme with the various superheavyweights in that match—thus earning

**2**  Akebono himself did eventually make a WWE appearance, squaring off against the Big Show (who had no sumo background) at WrestleMania 21.

**3**  *The Man Show* lent Yokozuna's name to a prank that was basically a drunken, bare-assed variation of that "Banzai Drop."

himself a heavyweight title shot at WrestleMania IX. (In the meantime, he would reinforce his anti-American credentials by squashing "Hacksaw" Jim Duggan, second-tier symbol of American jingoism.) At WrestleMania, Yokozuna competed against Bret "The Hitman" Hart in probably the best technical match of Yoko's career. When Hart somehow wrenched Yoko's tree-trunk legs in the Sharpshooter leg-lock, his signature move, the challenger's fate seemed all but sealed. But no: The nefarious Fuji threw salt into Hart's eyes, blinding him and leaving him open to a Banzai Drop and defeat at Yokozuna's hands.

Yokozuna was the champion, but his reign wouldn't last long enough for him to savor it. Backstage politics were the real victor of the day: Hulk Hogan had returned to the WWF from a leave of absence.[4] The previously ascendant Hart was viewed anew as merely a stopgap champion, and Yoko too was simply a transitional champion, a means of taking the strap away from one good guy and giving it to another.[5]

When Hogan stormed to the ring to protest the match's decision and to attend to his "friend" Bret (because in those days just before the Attitude Era took hold, all good guys were de facto friends), Mr. Fuji presumptively challenged Hogan to a match, right then and there. Hogan accepted, temporarily (and incongruously) abandoning Bret's cause and ongoing blindness, and defeated Yoko in a matter of minutes. Hulkamania was seemingly restored, and despite his function as the most transitional of champions, Yokozuna continued on as the first monstrous opponent on Hogan's dance card. The two titans feuded on until the King of the Ring event. There, Hogan and Yoko battled, and in parallel to WrestleMania, the hero seemed poised to win. And again, it wasn't to be:

...............................................................................................

**4** From the point when he lost the belt to the Ultimate Warrior, Hogan's WWF schedule was dictated by his movie career, such as it was, and his seeming general disinclination to wrestle full-time. Nonetheless, he was always the top dog when he was present in the WWF, and his wins and losses in championship matches more or less coincided with his erratic employment schedule.

**5** A role played decades earlier by the Iron Sheik, who ferried the belt between golden boys Bob Backlund and Hulk Hogan, and later, in 1994, by Backlund himself as he served as the middleman between champs Bret Hart and Diesel (a.k.a. Kevin Nash). These stories repeat themselves even as the participants change roles. Backlund once teamed with Jerry Brisco to take Georgia tag titles from Toru Tanaka and . . . Mr. Fuji. It's inescapable.

A Japanese "photographer" situated outside the ring leaned in for a shot—presumably he was put there by Fuji—and the camera exploded in Hogan's face. The Hulkster was disoriented, and once again Yokozuna pulled out a victory—and regained the championship—thanks to Mr. Fuji's conniving. As can probably be surmised from the relative oddity of Hogan losing the title, Hogan was again leaving the WWF to "pursue other interests." Yokozuna and Fuji boasted about putting an end to Hulkamania once and for all.[6] When Hogan had beat him to regain the title, Yokozuna seemed secondary to the wattage of Hogan's star. Whether he had grown into something bigger is questionable, but he was all they had.

☆ ☆ ☆

After winning the title this time, Fuji and Yokozuna decided to celebrate in high style, by hosting a bodyslam challenge on the deck of the USS *Intrepid*—an incredibly hokey scene that culminated in a newly heroic Lex Luger, who had until then been a preening narcissist,[7] arriving via helicopter and slamming the sumo giant, thus igniting Yoko's next feud. Bobby "The Brain" Heenan, who was the color commentator for the telecast, insisted that the bodyslam was really more of a hip toss, and he had an argument. Whatever it was, it wasn't wildly impressive. Despite Luger's chiseled physique, Yoko was probably more than 600 pounds by this point and unwieldily assembled.

As a villain, Yoko was a pure product of America's bizarre cultural moment in the 1980s and early '90s, when our uncertain geopolitics left Hollywood to ponder the potential ascendance of the Asian workforce with its usual lack of deftness. I refer, of course, to movies like *Gung Ho* and *Rising Sun*, which were premised on the notion of the Japanese as menacing exotics with queerly dainty methods, here to destroy America

---

**6**   And although that wouldn't have been true of many other Hogan sabbaticals, this time the boast bore some vague resemblance to the truth. During this next break he decamped for rival fed WCW, and he didn't return to McMahon's organization for nine years.

**7**   Nickname: the "Narcissist."

from within. Sometimes geopolitics breaks kayfabe, as with the Sgt. Slaughter-as-Iraqi-sympathizer storyline of 1990. Yokozuna was a part of this tradition as well, if a few years behind the curve, and so in juxta-position to such a foreign threat, all Lex needed was a new pair of stars-and-stripes briefs to formalize his rise to Hogan's place in wrestling's pantheon of true patriots.

Yokozuna and Luger feuded until the Survivor Series, when Luger's "All-Americans" team took on Yoko's "Foreign Fanatics." The xenopho-bic megamatch ended awkwardly, with Yokozuna retreating and All-American Undertaker pinning the overmatched Fanatic Ludvig Borga (yes, the Deadman is apparently a true patriot). The fallout was a new feud between Yokozuna and the Undertaker that culminated in a casket match[8]—an Undertaker staple—that Yoko managed to win, but only with heaps of outside interference.[9] For a monster, he was not proving himself to be exactly unstoppable in championship matches.

At WrestleMania X, Yokozuna fought both Luger and Hart, sepa-rately. He first defeated Luger (again with assistance, this time courtesy of special guest referee Curt Hennig) but then lost cleanly to Bret (who, in the interest of competitive fairness, had fought his brother Owen ear-lier in the night). Bret (and the belt) quickly moved on. Perhaps it was a long-overdue moment of awareness on the part of McMahon and his writers; that Yokozuna, a supremely unpopular foreigner, was allowed to reign atop the WWF for as long as he did might have spoken to the thinned WWF roster during a period of talent migration to WCW, but more likely it was just an incredibly wrongheaded lapse. Unlike many other promoters, WWF has usually tended toward the hero-champion model—contra the Ric Flair–style villain-champion model—and it felt as if the WWF wanted desperately to put someone in that role, but the fans rejected Luger, and McMahon himself didn't quite trust Hart. And so Yo-kozuna was left to his minor reign of terror. Regardless, once Hart had

........................................................................................

**8** 'Taker had to construct an extra-large casket for the occasion.

**9** Fuji engaged the services of the Great Kabuki, Tenryu, Bam Bam Bigelow, Adam Bomb, Jeff Jarrett, the Headshrinkers (Samu and Fatu), and Diesel to get the job done.

reclaimed the title, the WWF spent little time in removing Yokozuna from contention.

☆  ☆  ☆

Yoko, for the first time in his WWF tenure, was a monster adrift. No longer the undefeatable champion, he was now almost strictly a spectacle, relegated to the second tier. The only highlight of the ensuing months was a rekindled feud with the Undertaker, wherein 'Taker finally avenged his earlier casket match loss. The rematch was just as chaotic as the first, only this time, for whatever reason, Chuck Norris was present as the match's "special enforcer."

Yokozuna retuned to the spotlight later as half of an odd-couple tag team with Owen Hart. By now, Yoko was heavier than ever—purportedly more than 700 pounds—and much like Andre the Giant at the end of his career, his primary role was to stand on the ring apron looking ominous (and enormous) while Owen fulfilled most of the in-ring demands. The duo dominated the tag ranks for months, but when they finally lost the belts, Yokozuna's WWF tenure was all but over. He turned on his old fiendish friends, had a run as a good guy,[10] and hung around for a couple more years, but his glory days were far behind him.

In a 1996 SummerSlam match against the emerging "Stone Cold" Steve Austin, Yoko's weight had clearly ballooned, and the ending was built around this newly acquired girth. When he climbed up to the second rope for his Banzai Drop, the turnbuckle "broke," sending Yoko crashing down onto his back and allowing Austin to steal the victory. Up until now, his immensity had been his calling card. Now it was a punch line.

Even though the WWF didn't traditionally grant its wrestlers health insurance—or, more likely, because of that—the idea of a wrestler suffering a heart attack in the ring was unappealing to say the least. Whereas

---

**10** In line with the long pro wrestling tradition of a change in facial hair signaling a change in heart, good-guy Yokozuna wore a scraggly beard.

once WWF management had outfitted Yoko to make him look meatier, now they insisted that he lose weight, and when the pounds didn't immediately fall off, they released him.

So what becomes of the monster who becomes too monstrous, the genetic freak who becomes solely a freak show? Despite some appearances, pro wrestling isn't a World's Strongest Man competition, and it's certainly not a World's Fattest Man contest. And the freak in the age of television—in which the whole world is a sideshow tent—is not one with a long shelf life. That Yokozuna lasted as long as he did in this era is an accomplishment in itself. That he held the belt for as long as he did—from Haystacks to Andre, monsters of Yoko's ilk were largely seen as division killers and were rarely gifted with championship runs—is unique. He was a grotesque, a caricature, and his career straddled an old-school wrestling world in which racial/ethnic stereotyping was the norm and a new era in which a new style of un-PC excess reigned.

Yokozuna wrestled occasionally at independent shows, including the 1999 Heroes of Wrestling event, where, massively overweight even compared to his later WWF days, he and King Kong Bundy—an earlier big man who seemed half the size of the enlarged Yokozuna—heroically lumbered to the ring to save a Jake "The Snake" Roberts–Jim "The Anvil" Neidhart match that went sour from the start due to Jake's evident intoxication. It would be his last moment of valor.

On a European wrestling tour in 2000, he suffered a fatal heart attack in his hotel room. It's safe to say that few were wholly surprised. What *was* somewhat surprising was that he was still trying to wrestle, or at least still making appearances at wrestling shows. But he was a living spectacle, and the walk to the ring was his display case. It was by then the only world he knew. In his last match, Yokozuna didn't even enter the ring: He stood on the apron, a literal sideshow now, looking ominous and enormous, and then he went back to the hotel and died.[11]

-------

11  The coroner called the cause of death a fluid blockage in his lungs and listed his weight at 580 pounds.

# LUDVIG BORGA:
# LAST DAYS OF THE FOREIGN MENACE

If Yokozuna signaled the power of geopolitical scaremongering in the wrestling world, Ludvig Borga showed that the foreign menace wasn't all that it used to be.

Borga wouldn't be tops on anyone's list of all-time great anti-American wrestlers. He's someplace southward of Colonel De-Beers, Nikolai Volkoff, and the Iron Sheik, and, hell, probably even the Quebecers, the rather bland baddies from the frozen north. But there's something about Borga that encapsulates the entire U.S. vs. Them fetish of the premodern wrestling era. Like Ivan Drago in *Rocky IV*, Borga was genetically engineered with the sole purpose of striking fear in the hearts of an American audience—but not so much fear that you ever really questioned the ending.

The origins of this type of storytelling in wrestling go back to those halcyon days when pro wrestling existed not on cable television but in low-rent coliseums and state fairs. Without the ability to attach long, developed storylines to feuds, the promoters grabbed onto the lowest common denominators: blond pretty boy vs. diabolical masked man, American vs. foreign aggressor, nice white person vs. angry black person.

The fact that this sort of lazy booking was still going on in the early 1990s, when Borga surfaced in the World Wrestling Federation, probably says as much about our culture as it does about wrestling's creative minds, but it was nonetheless standard. Borga—who was actually a Finnish man (of all things) named Tony Halme—was a legitimate toughman who, in an odd historical footnote, fought MMA legend Randy Couture in Couture's very first match in the UFC. So when Borga debuted in the WWF, entering the ring to the Finnish national anthem and slapping hapless jobbers into his "Torture Rack" finishing hold, even the most thickheaded of wrestling fans knew a confrontation with the newly patriotic Lex Luger was in the offing.

Revisiting Borga's one notable match—the All-Americans vs. the Foreign Fanatics at Survivor Series 1993—is, in retrospect, almost morbid: It included Rodney "Yokozuna" Anoa'i and Brian "Crush" Adams, who have both since passed; Luger, who suffered a spinal stroke and was paralyzed in 2007 (he has since regained some motor function); and Scott Steiner, who tore his trachea in Puerto Rico and was put into a two-week-long induced coma while doctors operated on him.

Unfortunately, the Luger vs. Borga singles tilt was not to be. Borga hurt his ankle in a match soon thereafter and was never heard from (in WWF storylines, anyway) ever again.

Halme's public life didn't end there, though. As Jonathan Snowden of Heavy.com tells it: "Halme also wrote four books and had a gold single, 'Viikinki,' from his first and only album. And, like Finland's version of Jesse Ventura or Antonio Inoki, Halme was elected to Parliament."

That he turned out to be a real-life Finnish nationalist—or, rather, nativist—is sort of beside the point, as are his alcohol-related arrests, his stint in a mental institution, and the "SS" purportedly tattooed on his calf. He was important to us wrestling fans as a symbol: Evil Personified. Or, at least, Evil Oversimplified.

# BRIAN PILLMAN

It's June 1993, and Brian Pillman is killing his idols. He's parodying "Nature Boy" Ric Flair, one of the most respected and venerable wrestlers in the world. The segment is called "A Flare for the Old," a lampoon of the Nature Boy's "A Flair for the Gold" interview segments. Pillman is dressed in a sequined robe over a pair of briefs a la Flair, and he's wearing a shaggy gray wig and glasses. Pillman and Austin had been teamed up as the Hollywood Blonds to act as "mechanics," in Austin's terminology, a couple of good workers, good athletes with strong personalities that would serve to make their opponents even more popular—like jobbers, only several notches higher. The Hollywood Blonds are the bad guys in this feud, but the fans are laughing along with their irreverence. It's safe to say that this was not exactly what WCW had planned.

Their script is mediocre—it's basically "you're old, we're young" sass talk that most viewers have heard before. But their delivery is impeccable, and the final product borderline galling. The week before, they appeared on an actual "Flair for the Gold" segment and kicked off the rivalry, but Pillman and Austin avoided the usual sort of physical confrontation that fans would expect. They weren't pompous, self-congratulatory heels like, well, Flair was; they were sneering visions of the future of wrestling. They grinned cruelly, they snarled knowingly: This might be the first time that mainstream wrestlers really didn't seem to give a fuck.

It was an act, of course, but it was as believable as anything wrestling fans had seen in years. This was Brian Pillman's oddly significant contribution to the wrestling world throughout his heyday: He didn't give a fuck, so we never knew what was going to happen. We never felt safe when Pillman was on-screen, and the wrestling establishment would never recover from the wounds he delivered, and that's a good thing. That the danger was in some ways a *real* thing—that the sneer was a reference to the disregard that he had for himself in life—is tragic, but it only makes his career the more compelling. The result was good; the acknowledgment of reality is sad. But you can't consider Brian Pillman without acknowledging reality, because reality—or the presumption thereof—was what made him great.

☆ ☆ ☆

Brian Pillman was born in 1962 under one of those bad moons that people talk about. His dad died of a heart condition when he was only two months old. When Brian was two, he was diagnosed with throat cancer, and his childhood was riddled with throat surgeries thereafter; he underwent more than forty when all was said and done. When something like that doesn't kill you, a personal determination often takes hold: The high school football coaches said he was too small to play, but he ended up the team's standout; he wasn't heavily recruited but ended up making the Miami (Ohio) squad, where he was a two-time All-American playing as a relatively minuscule defensive tackle; told he was too small to make the pros, he still had a stint with his hometown Bengals,[1] then almost caught on with the Bills, and finally played for the Calgary Stampeders of the CFL until a leg injury forced him out of the game. But that didn't deter him, and that's one of a few phrases that appears over and over again when you start reading about Brian Pillman: "The Leg Injury Didn't Deter Him," along with "Before His Time" and "Increasingly Unhinged."

After he healed up, he found his way to Stu Hart's wrestling school, where he excelled, and then to a top spot in Stampede Wrestling, and then to WCW, where he once again found his stature questioned: He was shunted into WCW's rarely compelling lightweight division of the early '90s, which wasn't so much a showcase for highfliers in the lucha libre/puroresu mode[2] as it was an orphanage for the less beefy guys on the roster, although Pillman did have one incredible match against Japanese highflier Jushin "Thunder" Liger at SuperBrawl 1995. Pillman impressed everyone with his aerial repertoire. And he was impressed upon the fans as a fresh-faced, athletically gifted comer, though, based strictly on his size, a guy not expected to reach the upper echelons of the wrestling world. As Paul Heyman put it in an interview: "He was on a totally different level than everybody else who was in the industry at the time. . . . Brian's style in 1988–1989 was more of a 1995–1996 style. He was way ahead of his time." That didn't mean he was at the top of the game, though.

It was only in turning heel and working with Austin that Pillman was allowed to start becoming something greater. He and Austin would do a big move in the ring and then they'd celebrate by pantomiming like they were operating an old movie camera, holding the handle with one hand and cranking with the other, all the while grinning diabolically. Or

---

**1**   He was roommates with defensive back and current Baltimore Ravens coach John Harbaugh.

**2**   The styles of wrestling favored in Mexico and Japan, respectively.

they'd do it outside the ring, pointing their "camera" at the real camera. It was a "Hollywood" thing, obviously, meant to incite the crowd, but subtly, they were acknowledging the scripted-Hollywood pretense of the whole endeavor. They were reminding us that this was all just a TV show and that they were just actors. The crowd booed; Pillman and Austin cackled as if to say, "You didn't want to know? We don't care."

Despite his feuds with the Horsemen, the critical acclaim the Blonds constantly received, and his occasional upper-card billing, Pillman couldn't work his way into a top spot. WCW split up the Blonds when they seemed to be on the cusp of real popularity; Austin maintains to this day that it was *because* they were getting so much response from the crowd. They were soon feuding with each other, safely ghettoized away from the main event scene. The WCW midcard must have begun to feel like an NFL practice squad to Pillman, like failure even in the face of success, and he once again started fighting his way through. By late 1995 he had begun conceiving a new character that would revolutionize his career.

And it was around that time that people started noticing that Pillman's character was becoming—here it is—increasingly unhinged. He behaved erratically. Normally, wrestlers interact with the cameras like traditional sports stars do: They address them directly during interviews but go along as if they're not there when competing or when entering or leaving the game. Pillman would find the camera on the way to ringside and grin menacingly at it, eyes bulging, as if to simultaneously undermine the pretense of the endeavor and underscore his compliance with that nonexistence. He even spat at the camera, as if directly assaulting the fourth wall with his insolence, with his very DNA. On a show in January '96, seemingly off script, he grabbed announcer Bobby Heenan by the neck, and Heenan—who had a history of neck issues—said, "What the fuck are you doing?" live on the air. Heenan later said that he reacted so harshly because he assumed it was a fan who was suddenly manhandling him. But that's exactly the point: Pillman was doing something wholly unexpected—both at that moment and in a broader sense. He was an irritant, and just what wrestling needed.

☆ ☆ ☆

WCW chief Eric Bischoff has never been called a traditionalist, and often he's blamed for losing sight of what has made wrestling work through the decades in his quest for bigger-faster-cooler. He always loved sticking it to the know-it-all wrestling fans who populated Internet message boards, and in Pillman he found his muse. It's interesting that Pillman's antiestablishment breakout occurred when he was made a part of a reunited Four Horsemen faction alongside old foes and icons of the old guard Ric Flair and Arn Anderson. There was something of Flair's wild eyes in Pillman's unruly glare, but in juxtaposition to the older generation, his eccentricity stood out as something wholly new.

During a match at SuperBrawl VI in 1996 against Kevin Sullivan—the storyline was that Sullivan thought Pillman wasn't showing proper respect for the business, and let's face it, he wasn't—in which the loser had to formally announce his respect for the victor, Pillman came out and immediately the match went off the rails. The two men started fighting before the bell in an awkwardly realistic manner, and when Sullivan managed to separate himself, he recoiled with a stagger that seemed to belie the unscriptedness of what had just transpired. Pillman grabbed a mic and addressed Sullivan—who was then the head writer, or "booker," of WCW—dismissively, half-sarcastically, almost crazily: "I respect you, booker man." Most fans had no idea what was going on. Even the smart fans who Pillman was toying with—people who knew that Sullivan was the booker and knew that Pillman's expiring contract was creating some backstage friction between the two—thought that it was off script. (Said Bischoff: "For a brief moment, that audience was watching Brian Pillman and said to themselves, 'I know all the rest of that stuff is all make-believe, but Brian Pillman really hates Kevin Sullivan.'")

In retrospect, it's easy to let Pillman's oddball act blur into the background of all the reality-altering stuff that came around after it, but the "booker man" bit was so unusual that it wasn't even widely understood for what it was until years after the fact. After SuperBrawl, he got Bischoff to release him. According to Bischoff, his leaving was part of the plan, the next phase of their assault on reality and the wrestling intelligentsia—who, it should be said, loved every bit of this storyline once it became clear. The idea was that Pillman would go to ECW, fully form his "loose cannon" personality, and then return triumphantly to WCW as if uninvited. And in the information age, he had to be actually released for the shtick to be believable. If that was the plan, it didn't go right. Pillman never returned to WCW. Either the script didn't play along with reality, or Pillman didn't play along with the script. Or, as Bischoff put it: "I'm not sure if he was working me or if we were working everybody else."

He materialized on ECW's CyberSlam event in February 1996, appearing from out of nowhere in the ring, and started talking trash about Bischoff—he was "a coffee gofer"[3] and, since Pillman was now freed from the strictures of network TV, a "piece of fucking shit"—much to the delight of ECW fans, who largely were attuned to the wrestling rumor mill. But then, in a moment that seemed inexplicable, he turned his ire directly on those fans, calling them "motherfuckin' smart marks"[4] and "sorry son of a motherfuckin' bitches" for good measure. And then he threatened to piss in the ring—an act of disrespect too far even for the bloodthirsty ECW fans, one imagines—and called Heyman "booker man" just for giggles. The crowd that was so happy to see him just moments before turned on him. On the way out, he attacked a fan, dragged him into the ring, and started gouging him with a fork he pulled from his boot. This fan was a plant, the whole thing staged, but his metaphorical assault on the hardcore fanbase of wrestling was shocking because of how irresponsible it seemed. He could cuss out Bischoff, and that was fine. But to turn his back on the fans? It was self-destruction as performance art.

While he was working in ECW, he started negotiating a contract with the WWF, regardless of whatever handshake deal he had with Bischoff. Before he could ink the contract, though, Pillman shattered his ankle in

........................................................................

**3**  A reference to his time as an assistant in the AWA.

**4**  *Smart mark*—often abbreviated as *smark*—is a term used to describe the modern meta-fan steeped in Internet rumors and insider info, an archetype situated between actual backstage insiders and oblivious fans of yore.

a car accident, which many official accounts refer to as "an accident with a drunk driver," but nobody outright denies the other prevailing story, which is that Pillman fell asleep at the wheel, wrecked his vehicle, and was thrown from the car in one of those he-wasn't-wearing-a-seatbelt-but-if-he-had-been-he-would-have-actually-died kind of wrecks, and while it's not impossible that both stories are partly the truth, it's unclear how the drunk driver factors into that second account. He shattered his ankle, but the injury wouldn't hold him back. Despite his inability to wrestle, Pillman got the first guaranteed contract that the WWF ever issued. McMahon had been signing wrestlers to contracts since his earliest days, but those deals placed the obligation in the lap of the talent, and WWF was largely free to cut ties with them at will; Pillman's was the first in which the WWF was as obligated to employ the talent as the talent was to be employed.

While he was rehabbing, Pillman debuted on WWF television holding the microphone once again, interviewing other wrestlers in the ring. In one segment with his old partner Austin (the announcers avoided specifically naming WCW or the Hollywood Blonds but ominously referred to their "shared history"), who had morphed by then into a mercenary, mold-breaking, vest-wearing loudmouth—sound familiar?—Pillman seemed perhaps a little too biased in favor of Bret Hart, Austin's upcoming opponent. Austin attacked Pillman, folding a metal chair around his injured ankle and stomping on it, graphically "reinjuring" it. I use those quotes tentatively; doctors had already determined that Pillman's ankle needed another surgery,[5] so the injury was in some sense real, but Austin's attack was show. Nonetheless, that folding-chair-aided technique is to this day referred to as "Pillmanizing" someone.

The concept of reality would only be further abused in what followed. In a remote shoot from Pillman's home, an enraged Austin showed up to further his beatdown, and Pillman, who was laid up on the couch with his leg in an enormous wrap, pulled a gun on Austin. The camera initially cut away, leaving the audience with the impression that he may have

---

**5**  Pillman's ankle would eventually be fused into one position.

used it. On the web there's a reel of the real-time footage from that night, the part where they're waiting to go live in Brian's living room, which shows Pillman and his wife going over the staging with the interviewer and the segment producer. "My cue on the gun is 'Hostage in your own home'?" Pillman plaintively confirms. His wife joins in: "And I don't start screaming till that window is broken?" The WWF shared the segment live on TV for whatever reason, and their demeanors reflect a certain anxiety about it, but looking at the video now, one is struck with an odd solemnity, like they could foresee the outcry that the angle would bring about. As former WWF producer Tom Prichard soberly put it: "I think [the network] would have preferred that a gun had not been pointed at someone on television."

Pillman segued back into an on-screen role as the cohost of a new late-night show called *Shotgun Saturday Night*, where he called matches alongside announcer Jim Ross, who had taken a fatherly interest in Pillman. That stint ended—in storyline—when Pillman again attacked a (fake) fan on camera. It wasn't so much a replay of his ECW stunt as it was a statement: Pillman wasn't done yet. He wasn't content to be a color commentator, and that was his way out.

He acted out his dissatisfaction in real life too. He wrecked three rental cars in a month. He appeared out of it backstage. Ross ordered him to take a drug test. Pillman was offended. Ross insisted he was looking out for Pillman's health. "Goddammit, I'm not going to die," Pillman said.

Pillman had long lived out his character in life; nobody could tell where his character ended and the real Pillman began, but for some reason everyone seemed confident enough that there was a difference. His last few storylines—revisiting his relationship with Austin, joining up with the Hart Foundation, around whom he'd begun his career, and feuding with Goldust[6] over the "services" of his on-screen valet and real-life wife whom Pillman had real-life dated back in their WCW

---

**6** a.k.a. Dustin Rhodes. Well, *technically* a.k.a. Dustin Runnels, but that's beside the point.

days—certainly serve as a metaphor for the closing gap between the real and the imaginary.

On October 5, 1997, hours before a WWF pay-per-view show, Pillman died in a Minnesota hotel room. There was an ESPN story about Pillman's death, and it starts right in with the ten-bell salute that WWF gave him on the show the night after he died. The wrestlers all gathered on stage to stand in tribute, and it feels like one big black shadow; in the first shot, as the first bell rings out, the camera lands squarely on Owen Hart; second bell, there's Rick Rude. The ESPN reporter, Kelly Neal, jumps to the coroner's report, about how it was heart failure but that cocaine was involved, about how that's a lot like what happened with another wrestler named Eddie Gilbert. And how another one, Louie Spicolli, mixed booze and painkillers. She misses the part where his dad died of the same heart condition right after Pillman was born, but you can hardly fault her for going for the drama. This was dramatic stuff, and Pillman almost certainly helped his death along. His widow, Melanie, for one, sure thought the culture of pro wrestling was to blame: "It was just a matter of time before it happened to someone and unfortunately it was my husband." She said he went from pharmacy to pharmacy, shy about his painkiller intake, though it was nominally legal; he probably filled scrips at thirty or forty pharmacies in the Cincinnati area. And then there was the human growth hormone: Neal says that Melanie fingered Hulk Hogan for telling Brian "he could obtain HGH from Dr. Edmund Chein at the Life Extension Institute, and a former wrestler who wished to remain anonymous says Hogan recommended Chein to many wrestlers." Which was followed by this shockingly bald-faced denial: "Through a spokesman, Hogan says he's never heard of Chein, and Chein says he does not prescribe the hormone to athletes, and has never knowingly treated any wrestler." The report ends, and they cut back to the *SportsCenter* desk, where that same image of Rude from earlier, standing on the stage, is there framed like a headshot in the upper left of the screen, and the anchor says that Rude just died too.

It's too easy to say that just as Pillman was a trailblazer in the integration of uncertainty into the wrestling world, he initiated a spate of deaths that would forever rock the wrestling world. The two things are true, but they're separate.

We say all the time about these wrestlers that they died too soon, and most of them did, but somehow there's not a case as truly disheartening as Pillman's: He hadn't accomplished the heights that so many others had, but in hindsight, he was knocking on the door. He would have been WWF champion, and probably would have been mentioned right alongside his old partner Austin when people talk about era-changing wrestlers; hell, he might have replaced Austin. He was destined for greatness in a way that that old canard doesn't do justice.

We know his leg injury wouldn't have held him back, anyway. We know he was growing increasingly unhinged at a moment when the crowd was finally clamoring for it. And we know that he went before his time. "We knew that he was hurting, but when you asked him, he would lie to you," says Ross. He was forever working the fans, and working the boys backstage, and, in the end, working himself. He was living the lie more fully than anyone else, and that's what made him amazing, and that's what killed him.

# CHRIS KANYON

One could hardly get past the headline of any of the multitude of Chris Kanyon obits in the days following his death in early 2010 without being confronted with Kanyon's "idiosyncrasy"—which is to say, his apparent homosexuality. The irony of this is that Kanyon was never a particularly eccentric on-screen personality. He was the proto-typical performer of his era in all the wrong ways: He was a midcarder with constantly mutating gimmicks and schizophrenic allegiances, simultaneously afforded television time by the bloat of late-'90s wrestling television yet perceived as criminally underused by the "smarks" of the wrestling message boards—an upwardly mobile jobber with nowhere to go. That his personal life belied his public persona—and defied the strictures of the two-dimensional character wrestling had created for him—seems to have eventually spelled his end, both in career and, sadly, in life. The wrestling world has always had a hard time handling idiosyncrasy in three dimensions.

☆ ☆ ☆

Born and raised in New York, Chris Klucsarits was a physical therapist before he jumped into the wrestling biz. He worked a few weekend shows before he committed to the craft full-time, and he, like so many others, worked initially as "enhancement talent" in the WWF—which means that he existed to be demolished by the established stars of the day. His full-time career functionally began in WCW in 1997, when he debuted as "Mortis," a cartoonish Grim Reaper, in the painful-to-watch "Blood Runs Cold" story. WCW was attempting, blatantly, to rip off the video game *Mortal Kombat* and its burgeoning popularity, and the story saw Mortis and his partner "Wrath" feud with a babyface named "Glacier" in a sort of alternate WCW universe. Despite coming to fruition after the nWo appeared, "Blood Runs Cold" was plainly a product of a cartoonish pre-nWo era, and its debut was pushed back by the sudden arrival of Scott Hall and Kevin Nash at the promotion. (What is too often overlooked about the innovation of the nWo is how unbearably bad some of the dreck it replaced on WCW TV actually was.)

Post-Mortis, Chris Kanyon (as he was now called) embarked upon a fairly lengthy feud-cum-partnership with Raven and his Flock.[1] Subsequent to that was a protracted partnership-cum-feud with Diamond Dallas Page that began with their teaming up (along with Bam Bam Big-

---

1   Imagine Pearl Jam, muscled up and less musically inclined.

elow) as the Jersey Triad. Their affiliation continued for months as the two exchanged punches right up until WCW was yanked off the air in 2001.

A noteworthy sidebar to his WCW tenure: Kanyon worked as a sort of in-house trainer, teaching the basics of the wrestling trade to the procession of celebrities that climbed inside the ring for WCW during its ongoing endeavor to gain mainstream attention. Kanyon was a true student of the craft—he had studied at the legendary (now defunct) Lower East Side Wrestling Gym and under both the Fabulous Moolah and Afa, the Wild Samoan—and he was known at times as the "Innovator of Offense" for his imaginative moveset. It must have been something of an honor to mentor the likes of Dennis Rodman, Jay Leno, Karl Malone, and (sigh) David Arquette in their entrées into the sport. Surely he brought out the best in them. But it also saddles his career with some of the disgrace of those ill-fated ventures—unquestionably among the worst matches in wrestling history. When Arquette[2] actually won the WCW championship on April 26, 2000, WCW had somehow found a new way to make a mockery of an enterprise that had, in recent years, almost become a self-parody.

☆ ☆ ☆

Kanyon transitioned to the WWF roster as a part of the WCW Invasion angle after Vince McMahon purchased his rival in 2001. The two factions were portrayed as being bitter coinhabitants of the new, bigger WWF, like AOL and Time Warner but with swinging steel chairs. It was a disappointing time for fans, as the real WWF-WCW feud had considerably more angst and enmity than this fake one, but Kanyon was something of a standout of the Invasion/Alliance era. He was bequeathed the WCW U.S. Championship, and he had a decent little run as the "Alliance MVP," playing a bristly loudmouth who would come into the ring and, in his thick Queens accent, ask the audience, "Who betta than Kanyon?"

........................................................................................................

**2** With whom Kanyon had worked on the set of the pitiable wrestling film *Ready to Rumble*.

The question wasn't rhetorical. That period of wrestling television was fat with call-and-response catchphrases, and this one was no different. The "desired" reply from the audience in this case was, of course, "Nobody!" The real answer, obviously, was lots of people. When the crowd wised up and started shouting "Everybody!" back at Kanyon, he cunningly changed the question to "Who's *not* betta than Kanyon?" and reveled in the perceived endorsement bestowed by the double negative.

Mortis aside, all of his gimmicks over the years seemed oddly self-conscious, or at least bizarrely referential. He was a ring technician as the "Innovator of Offense"; he was a ladies' man as "Champagne" Kanyon; he was an egocentric poseur as "Positively" Kanyon. He was whatever he thought he should be, without ever really bothering to change who he was. "Who betta than Kanyon?" begged an answer that was probably too obvious.

The implicit self-deprecation in his catchphrase probably didn't suit him in the long run, though. His WWE career fizzled, and he was released in February 2004. It wasn't a unique or unexpected fate for a grappler of his level and vintage. He later claimed to have been improperly fired and subsequently blacklisted from the WWF, but what is being blacklisted in the world of pro wrestling, when any transgression can be forgiven in the name of making a splash or a dollar? Kanyon's sin was that he never made either.

☆  ☆  ☆

At an indie show in 2006, Kanyon outed himself as gay. There's some dispute as to his authenticity—he eventually backtracked, saying it was part of the character he was playing, and he later went on to recant that disavowal. More likely the waffling was evidence of an increasingly unsettled emotional state. He appeared a couple of times on *The Howard Stern Show*, where they played up his homosexuality and the seeming incongruity—or, to be honest, the incredible obviousness—of a gay man in the pro wrestling business. Despite Stern's fascination, this was not exactly wrestling's Stonewall moment. Many of his WWE coworkers have since said that they didn't know Kanyon was gay but that it wouldn't have bothered them.[3] That's beside the point: However accepted he might have been within wrestling, it's worth wondering if he did irreparable damage to his career by bringing his personal life into his storyline. The era of kayfabe may have been over, but when the spotlight is on, we expect our fighters to keep their reality to themselves. All successful wrestlers are closeted in one way or another.

In any case, if Chris Kanyon was gay—and he almost certainly was—it's easy to see how being closeted in an overly agro locker room could lead to powerful feelings of alienation and disenfranchisement. And small wonder that such feelings ballooned after his release, when the WWE was the only major wrestling outfit left, and as his increasingly erratic public profile cemented his estrangement from the company.

☆ ☆ ☆

This rift was fortified in early 2009, when Kanyon, alongside Raven (Kanyon's old in-ring foe, whose real name is Scott Levy) and Mike Sanders, sued the WWE. The pro wrestling industry is built on a profitable but morally suspect framework that designates all the wrestlers as "independent contractors," meaning that power rests lopsidedly in the hands of the wrestling company. Wrestlers can be fired at will, are denied health insurance, and are burdened with innumerable other inconveniences like having to provide their own travel and having to file tax returns in every state in which they perform.

Various calls over the years for wrestling talent to unionize have largely gone nowhere, for obvious reasons. It would be a sorry system even if the industry weren't centered on its "independent contractors" risking life and limb on a nightly basis. But with the WWE as a monolithic near-monopoly, the workers' power is almost entirely diminished—as was the WWE's argument, first broached in the Territorial Era, that it

---

**3** Some of McMahon's top lieutenants, it should also be noted, have purportedly been gay.

couldn't afford to make concessions that its major competitors weren't making. A suit like Kanyon's was a long time coming. But the status quo makes it dangerous for any current or potential employees to sue—if they lose, the resultant hostility will render them unemployable. So the threesome who lodged the complaint were minor players—in WWE terms, anyway—and they hadn't been under WWE employ for years.[4] The statute of limitations took precedence over the legitimacy of the claim, and the lawsuit fizzled.

So, sadly, did Kanyon's career. He did a short stint in TNA and wrestled in a number of the "major" independent shows, more or less fading into wrestling oblivion. He had gone up against the greatest villain in all of wrestling—the all-powerful Corporation, the WWE—and he had lost. Insofar as the average wrestling fan was aware of the lawsuit, it was seen not only as an assault on tradition but as another betrayal of wrestling's immutable code of secrecy: It doesn't do much for the idea of wrestling as a self-contained universe to point out that all these oiled musclemen in singlets are actually contract laborers.

In a metaphorical sense, Kanyon's professional career had a reverse life trajectory. As Mortis, he started off as death in caricature, a one-dimensional villain who later evolved into a regular guy and, as he outed himself, into a fully formed, multilayered human. Human frailty is an all-too-real thing, however. Kanyon was diagnosed with bipolar disorder, and in early 2010 he threatened suicide. On April 2 of that year, he was found by his brother, having lethally overdosed on pills. He was forty years old.

Supposedly he had been making plans to put his craftsmanship to good use and open his own wrestling school; the potential for a strong second act seemed real. But after his dreams of wrestling stardom dissipated, his self-perpetuated segregation from the wrestling mainstream left him ever more despondent. His death was a sad end to an imperfect career.

---

**4** It still remains to be seen if history will judge them the Curt Floods of the squared circle, but it doesn't seem likely.

# UNIONS IN WRESTLING

In October 2011, at the close of an episode of *Raw*, on-screen chief operating officer (and wrestler) Triple H stood in the center of the ring to address his employees and, in a comically formal proceeding, request their vote of confidence. The preceding months had been more than a little unruly. And despite Triple H's insistence that he was working with the audience's best interests in mind, each nominal faction of on-screen talent—the good guys, the bad guys, the female wrestlers, the referees—explained that they felt their workplace had become unsafe under Triple H's leadership. After erstwhile announcer Jerry "The King" Lawler (who had been pancaked through a table by Mark Henry a couple of weeks before) said his piece, he formally walked out on his "boss" and was followed by the wrestlers, the announcers, and the ringside cameramen. Triple H was even abandoned, in the end, by announcer Jim Ross, whom the COO had reinstated only weeks before. (Ross later explained his decision on Twitter by saying, "When a coach loses his locker room, something has 2 b done.")

It wasn't the first time workers' rights had become a going issue in the pro wrestling world.

In May 1999, the WWF had a mock labor uprising on *Monday Night Raw*. The members of the Corporate Ministry were in the ring, filling it roughly from rope to rope. It was a valedictory moment for the new diabolical faction, which had formed just four days earlier, an unholy amalgamation of the Undertaker's pseudosatanic Ministry of Darkness and Shane McMahon's Corporation. They were interrupted, as in-ring orations so often are, by four familiar faces: Mick "Mankind" Foley, the Big Show, Test, and Ken Shamrock, all former associates of the Corporation.

They each held an oversized two-by-four—more a blue-collar metaphor than a physical threat—and announced the formation of an opposition group called the Union. Their beef was not strictly physical; yes, they wanted to beat up the Corporate Ministry, but the Union's complaint was broader. Since the Corporation had formed, its members had been mistreating their foes and steering opportunities toward cronies. Now, by negotiating a merger with Undertaker's Ministry, the new faction looked like it could dominate WWF matchmaking for the foreseeable future. The Union's goal wasn't just to settle a fight but also to protect its members' jobs. Who knows what events in (real-life) labor relations inspired wrestling writers to go all Marxist, but the on-screen "movement" landed with a thud. The Union feuded with lesser members of the Corporate Ministry while bigger stars the Rock and "Stone Cold" Steve Austin remained above the fray. Before long, the entire storyline was scrapped after Foley went out with an injury.

That either of these stories was even allowed to exist, however, is shocking. The wrestling industry has never seen—nor permitted—any form of unionization by the talent.

Despite the fact that WWE wrestlers are, by definition, full-time employees, WWE designates them as independent contractors. This is "so they don't have to pay social security and the wrestler has to pay 15 percent self-employment tax," former WWF mainstay Jesse "The Body" Ventura told Howard Stern in 2012. "How are they self-employed when you're signed exclusively, you can't work for nobody else, they tell you when and where you'll work? They can totally control your life, and yet they'll call you an independent contractor." To some degree, wrestlers' contracts are this way for historical reasons. In the Territorial Era of the 1970s and '80s, wrestlers were indeed independent contractors and operated as such, but the WWF/WWE absorbed that template when it expanded its territory nation- and worldwide. Now there's no doubt that wrestlers' status as "independent contractors" should be seen as a capitalist strong-arm tactic. WWE and its shareholders are surely aware that they're no longer operating a regional sideshow. Likewise, they're aware, if not by common sense then by the writ of their own contracts, that the wrestlers they employ are not "independent contractors" any more than LeBron James or Peyton Manning are independent contractors for the Miami Heat and Denver Broncos.

Not that it matters in real life. The walkout and the Union angle were remarkably liberal on-screen performances in an industry fully controlled by right-leaning, antiregulation capitalists.

Notably absent from the walkout were the headline good guys—Cena, Punk, Randy Orton, Sheamus, and Kelly Kelly. It's hard not to notice the similarities between this development and the storyline years before, when, despite a common foe in the Corporate Ministry, the Rock and Austin didn't associate themselves with the Union. They were already situated atop wrestling's pecking order, and factions like the Union would serve only to elevate less-prominent performers. As is often the case in real life, the top dogs felt little need to unionize. They found no common cause with the Union's plea for better working conditions.

For all the on-screen labor unrest, however, the real wrestling industry hasn't faced a serious unionization threat. Jesse Ventura tried to organize a union in the 1980s but, according to *The New York Times*, "found it hard to find wrestlers willing to join him." When he later sued the WWF to reclaim royalties he thought were owed him (Ventura eventually won a more than $800,000 judgment), it was revealed in the proceedings that Hulk Hogan ratted out his unionization scheme to Vince McMahon. It's hard to imagine a more blatant example of a top star protecting his status by sabotaging collective action.

There are rumors that famed wrestler and G.I. Joe figure Sgt. Slaughter tried to unionize—or at least agitated for better working conditions—prior to his 1984 departure from the WWF. (And, inevitably, there are rumors that his return as an anti-American villain was payback.)

In 2008, three wrestlers—Raven, Chris Kanyon, and Mike Sanders—sued WWE for "cheating them out of health care and other benefits" and insisted that the "independent contractor" designation was a sham since WWE had "virtually complete dominion and control over its wrestlers." A federal judge threw out the case, supposedly because the statute of limitations had expired, but this case and others over time have proven that WWE has little to fear from legal proceedings.

Raven and company were essentially blackballed for turning on their employer, but at least their case brought the issue to light. While promoting *The Wrestler*, director Darren Aronofsky spoke at length about pro wrestling's labor issues: "The problem starts with the fact that they're not organized and they're not unionized," he said. "There's really no reason why these guys are not in SAG. They're as much screen actors as stuntmen. If not more. They're in front of a camera performing and doing stunts, and they should have that protection. . . . Or, if they're not even on TV, the ring is a theater. So they're not just screen actors, they're theater actors. They're performers. They should have health insurance and they should be protected."

Former longtime WWF champ Bret Hart has become a vocal pro-union voice in recent years. "I don't think that wrestlers will get any type of support until they get a union," he has said. "I think that any wrestler that says that they don't need a union is just a sheep that doesn't have enough brains to know that they do need a union." Of course, this comes from a guy who probably could have done more to help the formation of a union in his heyday than anyone.

When John Cena appeared on *Larry King Live* in 2007, King asked if he thought wrestling needed a union. Unsurprisingly, Cena demurred: "I believe that professional wrestlers, WWE-specific and across, they all know what they're getting into. Nobody is forcing them to get into the ring. It's a job that they all want to do." According to Cena, the question of unionization "won't ever be answered, because I don't think it'll ever be asked."

Well, at least not in real life.

# CHRIS BENOIT AND
# EDDIE GUERRERO

March 14, 2004, was a day wrestling fans will remember
forever and that the wrestling establishment would like to forget. It was
WrestleMania XX at Madison Square Garden—the company's two-
decade anniversary return to the site of the original 'Mania, the mecca
of pro wrestling in the United States. Eddie Guerrero beat Kurt Angle to
retain the WWE Championship[1] and, in the last match of the night,
Chris Benoit defeated Shawn Michaels and Triple H to win the World
Heavyweight Championship. After Benoit's win, his real-life buddy
Guerrero came out to the ring and the two champs celebrated together
while confetti dropped from the rafters. The crowd went wild. Three of

..................................................................................................................
1   This match featured the infamous moment in which Eddie unlaced his own boot to
allow himself to slip out of Angle's dreaded ankle-lock finisher.

the era's biggest stars—Triple H, Michaels, and Angle—had been felled, backseated at the biggest show of the year in favor of two undersized also-rans.

Guerrero and Benoit were booked as the good-guy underdogs, sure, but their win evinces a stranger, more surprising reality: They won despite the fact that—nay, *because*—they were favorites of the wrestling egghead commentariat. These fans—the meta fans, the Internet intelligentsia—understand the backstage workings that average fans don't. They treasure history and reality as much as the storylines, and they prize the qualities that mainstream wrestling's decision-makers frequently overlook: charisma over size, in-ring ability over physique. And, of course, they all consider themselves smarter than Vince McMahon and all the promoters who have come along to challenge him. Sometimes, they have a point.

Guerrero and Benoit were favored by the "smart marks" because they traveled through Japan and Mexico to hone their craft, and because they went to ECW and showcased their "pure" wrestling styles in stark opposition to the hardcore brawls that ECW was known for. Back in those days, while the golden-tanned beefcakes of the WWF and WCW were broadcast to every cable TV household in America, Benoit and Guerrero were known only to the lucky few who stayed up late to watch ECW and the guys who traded videocassettes of independent and foreign promotions. To name-check either of them was a sort of secret handshake for wrestling fan purity, a gnostic cult growing in the shadow of the WWF's mainstream religion.

In hindsight, their fame was sort of a Pyrrhic victory. Benoit and Guerrero became legendary for precisely the same reason they hadn't yet become superstars: They didn't fit the mold. They were as highly skilled as they were undersized compared to most WWF wrestlers of the '90s (or most other decades, for that matter). They were great conveyors of theatrics during their matches but, particularly in the case of Benoit, they weren't compelling actors in backstage sketches and prematch promos. Neither had a face that could grace the cover of *Tiger Beat*. Hell, for the bulk of their careers, neither face would even move copies of *Pro Wrestling Illustrated*.

What seemed to make Benoit and Guerrero great was the fact that they weren't given an easy path to stardom. They were both hired by WCW when, during the Monday Night Wars, WCW expanded its flagship show to three hours and needed talent to fill the time. Guerrero and Benoit were poached by the WWF after they overachieved in WCW. Even then, their ascent to the top of the card was never assured, and the paths they took there were anything but linear. Despite the fanfare that accompanied their signings, the WWF didn't seem eager to bet the bank on either of them.

This, then, is the core of the "smart" wrestling fan's adoration for Benoit, Guerrero, and their ilk: In an unreal world of fake rivalries, fake villains, and fake odds to be overcome, Benoit and Guerrero were real-life heroes who deserved success but were held back by the most dastardly foe imaginable—the establishment, the guardians of the pro wrestling status quo. When both men were pushed to the top in early 2004, they were beloved by the average fan because they were scripted to be underdog heroes, overcoming great odds to achieve their lifelong dreams. But at the same time, they were even more beloved by the smart fans because this whole thing was so unlikely. Benoit and Guerrero were never supposed to be scripted as the big winners in the first place.

☆ ☆ ☆

The first thing you need to know is that Chris Benoit doesn't exist. That's what WWE would have you believe, anyway. His matches are scrubbed from DVDs, his name largely whitewashed from the WWE record books, despite the fact that he's a five-time U.S. Champion, a "triple crown" champion.[2] He was WCW Champion and (WWE) World Heavyweight Champion, and was slated to become the champ of the WWE-owned ECW brand, but that never happened, because—well, we'll get to that later. The important thing is that he's WWE's forgotten man; the

---

**2** Meaning he held the primary title, secondary title (Intercontinental or U.S. Championships), and tag team titles at various times.

only evidence of his existence are old VHS tapes at yard sales, old wrestling magazines at flea markets, and "out of stock" DVD listings on amazon.com.

Eddie Guerrero, on the other hand, is a name steeped in legacy. His father, Gory Guerrero, was a legendary wrestler in Mexico and the southwestern United States, and his sons all had wrestling careers of significant repute—the modern viewer might recall that Hector achieved a special kind of pro wrestling ignominy for portraying Lazer Tron[3] in WCW and the dancing turkey the Gobbledy Gooker in the WWF, and Chavo Sr. appeared on WWF television in his dotage as the second to his son, Chavo Jr., who was Eddie's nephew (even though he was only a couple of years younger than Eddie). But in the Territorial Era, and in the fraternity of wrestling, the Guerrero name was famous. Chavo, who frequently teamed with Eddie during his heyday, is still an active wrestler, and Eddie's widow, Vickie, is an active player on WWE television.[4]

Eddie was born in El Paso, where his father promoted shows, and as a teenager he and Chavo Jr. would wrestle during intermissions. After a spell on scholarship for collegiate wrestling at the University of New Mexico, Eddie started his professional career in the CMLL promotion in Mexico, where he benefited from his lineage and excelled because of his talent. He was paired with El Hijo del Santo—literally "the son of El Santo," "El Santo" being Mexico's most famous wrestler, with whom Gory had famously teamed. Eddie later teamed with Art Barr, a sort of minor league Ponce de León of the North American wrestling circuit, one of the first prominent gringo stars in the Modern Era to find a place for himself in the Mexican wrestling ranks and popularize the Mexican style in the United States.[5] Barr and Guerrero became fast friends, and

---

**3**  He actually wore a Lazer Tag chest sensor as part of his costume.

**4**  Their eldest daughter is in the WWE developmental territory too.

**5**  His most prominent American exposure, in early WCW as the "Juicer," a wrestling version of the movie character Beetlejuice, was only slightly less embarrassing than Hector's mainstream roles, but his ability in the ring stood out even so. Barr was released from WCW when a guilty plea he'd taken in an Oregon rape case became publicized via a fax campaign. His first nickname in Mexico was the "American Love Machine." It's unclear if irony was intended.

they were soon the most bankable heels in Mexico, known as "La Pareja del Terror." They later expanded their posse into a group called Los Gringos Locos,[6] which relied, obviously, on Guerrero's American birthright, despite his obvious lineage not just from Mexico but also from the Mexican wrestling world. It was a tension that would play out again in his career, though often in reverse, as he would be cast, either literally or implicitly, as a Mexican nationalist through much of his career.

Art Barr died with his young son in his arms—of undetermined causes—at his home in Oregon on November 23, 1994, at the age of twenty-eight. Guerrero and Barr had purportedly just been offered a contract from ECW. Eddie took up Barr's Frog Splash finishing move in homage to his fallen partner. He took it to New Japan, then to ECW, and then to WCW.

☆ ☆ ☆

The thing you always hear about Chris Benoit's childhood is that he idolized the Dynamite Kid. That automatically puts him squarely within a unique quadrant of fandom; most kids of his generation would have hewed toward the Dynamite Kid's tag team partner, Davey Boy Smith, the taller, better-looking, brawnier of the two—and the one, not coincidentally, who went on to a high-profile career in America as a singles wrestler. The Dynamite Kid was little, particularly for the strictures of WWF television in those days, and although he was immensely talented, talent as such isn't always what the average fan registers; you can tell when a match is lousy, maybe, but not so much who's at fault for the ineptitude.

Benoit met his idol as a kid and told him he was going to be just like him. His dad got him a weight set to reward his ambition, and Benoit

---

6  The group also included Konnan and Louie Spicolli—the beloved American indie wrestler who died after overdosing on painkillers and wine in 1998, months after finally getting a WCW contract, and who performed in Mexico under the name of "Madonna's Boyfriend."

started training in his teens as a wrestler—driving hours to the Hart family's Dungeon to learn the craft. "Dynamite" Chris Benoit debuted in Stampede Wrestling in November 1985, when Chris was eighteen. The nickname was more indicator than modifier; he didn't idolize Billington by that point so much as he channeled him, move for move, down to his physique and the very way he carried himself. After Stampede closed its doors, Benoit followed the Dynamite Kid's path to Japan, where he eventually donned a mask as the "Pegasus Kid" and achieved a not-insignificant level of notoriety.

In 1994 in ECW, the Benoit mythos was first really allowed to blossom. He was nicknamed the "Crippler" after he fake-injured Rocco Rock (half of the Public Enemy tag team), and the moniker was solidified when he legitimately broke Sabu's neck in a match. It was a matter of miscommunication rather than brutality—Benoit slammed Sabu with the intention of him landing on his chest, but Sabu twisted to try to land on his back and ended up falling on his head. Nevertheless, Paul Heyman ran with it, and Benoit's mantle as one of wrestling's Legitimately Dangerous Persons was established. His in-ring style was as unrelenting as Billington's, but it's worth noting that Benoit wasn't the real-life bully that Billington had been. For Benoit, the Dynamite Kid ring style was a tribute but more importantly a brutal affectation, a means of proving his legitimacy to the fans. If his style wasn't intended to wreak havoc on the bodies of himself and his opponents, it was nonetheless a side effect.

In 1995, Benoit's U.S. visa expired,[7] and he went back to New Japan wrestling, which led—via a talent exchange program—to WCW. Benoit had wrestled a couple of matches there before, but his re-debut, as part of the New Japan posse, befits his career. Along with Guerrero and Chris Jericho and Rey Mysterio Jr. and others, he was part of an accidental insurgent movement in the wrestling world, a meteor shower of under-sized, mega-talented grapplers from the outer edges of the wrestling

---

7  Paul Heyman and his shifty office management skills are usually blamed for this lapse.

world—Japan, Mexico, ECW—whose primary purpose was to fill up programming time as WCW expanded its television presence. Their introduction was propelled more by necessity than desire. Wrestling in America is equal parts athletic endeavor and morality play, its stars as much character actors performing teeth-clenched monologues as acrobats, and when Guerrero and Benoit debuted in WCW, they were only given half of the wrestler's playbook from which to operate: They didn't ever talk. Despite their purity and devotion to the craft, they were hardly more "pro wrestlers" in the modern sense than was a manager or announcer or valet. They were empty space occupied.

☆ ☆ ☆

Of the troupe brought in to fill *WCW Monday Nitro*'s first hour with mostly story-free product over which the announcers could hype the more significant happenings of the later parts of the show, Benoit and Guerrero—along with diminutive flyer Rey Mysterio Jr.—were the ones most fans would have picked out for stardom. Nevertheless, success didn't come easily. Benoit was the first to graduate to the A-team, as he was picked to be a member of a reformed Four Horsemen stable, alongside Brian Pillman and mainstays Ric Flair and Arn Anderson. Benoit was the brooding, silent bruiser of the bunch, often seen leering in the background of Horsemen promos in a rumpled suit and collarless dress shirt.

When Pillman left WCW in 1996, Benoit was fitted into his feud against Dungeon of Doom ringleader—and backstage booker—Kevin Sullivan. Despite his involvement in the "booker man" stunt with Pillman—or perhaps lending credence to its veracity—Sullivan was about as old-school as anybody in those days, and above all he insisted on the wrestlers keeping up the facade of kayfabe. So when the storyline began to turn on Benoit stealing away Sullivan's valet, Woman (also known by her real name, Nancy), Sullivan demanded that Benoit keep up the act in real life by traveling with Nancy as if they were an item—this despite the fact that Sullivan was actually married to Nancy in real life.

As such things often go, life imitated art,[8] and Benoit and Nancy were soon an item. (Eventually, Nancy divorced Sullivan and married Benoit.) Unsurprisingly, Sullivan and Benoit's matches were gruelingly violent, even taking into account that these were two of wrestling's most famous stiff workers. Benoit said that he respected Sullivan for never taking any liberties with him in the ring. That's one of wrestling's most sacred bylaws: Your safety is consistently in the hands of your opponent, so any liberty taken in the ring—any potato punch to the noggin, any submission hold applied too tightly—threatens the very foundation of the pro wrestling art. And Sullivan was too old-school to take a cheap shot at Benoit. Even so, it's hard to watch their matches and not see the violence as more than allusion; if Sullivan wasn't exacting revenge, he was definitely seeking therapy in violence.

And yet, in those days in WCW, with so many established superstars entrenched in the upper card and with top-tier talent still migrating over from the WWF, the glass ceiling for home-grown talent was very real.[9] In one of WCW's few smart decisions, Benoit and former tag team player Booker T were matched up in a best-of-seven series,[10] which managed to elevate both men to the cusp of significance. But as Benoit's star rose, his dissatisfaction with his place in the company only increased.

On January 16, 2000, at the WCW pay-per-view Souled Out, Bret Hart was scheduled to face Sid Vicious for the WCW championship, and Benoit was scheduled to face Jeff Jarrett; Hart was pulled from the card after suffering what turned out to be a career-ending concussion from a kick from Goldberg, and Jarrett was having concussion-like symptoms from a headbutt Benoit had previously delivered him from off the top of a steel cage. Benoit was shifted into Hart's spot and won the title in the main event. It was supposedly an attempt to assuage his dissatisfaction,

---

**8** In pro wrestling, wrestlers begin dating their on-screen valets about as frequently as they're paired up on-screen with their real-life girlfriends; in many situations, the genesis of the relationship is indeterminate. It's wrestling's chicken-and-egg conundrum.

**9** Which is not to say that pre-WCW careers were meaningless, just that for those who started at the bottom, any sort of status advancement was near impossible.

**10** The seventh match ended in a no-contest, and so the series actually went to eight.

but it was too little too late. Benoit jumped ship to the WWF the next day, and his championship reign was invalidated based on a technicality.[11]

☆ ☆ ☆

When Eddie Guerrero returned to WCW in 1995 (he, like Benoit, had briefly worked there previously), he may have been a notch above the other first-hour luchadores, but he was firmly stuck in the past. He wrestled predominantly with friends and foes from his pre-WCW days, like Konnan, Dean Malenko (son of Russian scourge Boris), Benoit, Chris Jericho, and his nephew Chavo. Their kinship made for electric matches, but the distance between them and the top of the card seemed ever-expanding. Even though he had feuds with the Horsemen and with Diamond Dallas Page, those were self-evidently placeholder beefs for the upper-carders. He feuded with Konnan over the U.S. Championship, and later with Jericho and Rey Mysterio over the cruiserweight title, but the belts did little to distract from the fact that this was a world separate from that of the ruling class.

But whereas Benoit kept his dissatisfaction to himself, Eddie acted out both off-stage and on, demanding a push from showrunner Eric Bischoff[12] and walking out on the company after airing his grievances in a reality-bending worked-shoot promo. When he returned several months later, he embraced his rebellion, ironically, by affirming the affiliation that had kept him buried on the card: He formed a faction called the Latino World Order, a deliberate rip-off of the nWo that was more or less an uprising of the Mexican wrestlers stuck at the bottom of the lineup. Rather than help any of them break out, though, it only reiterated their interdependence. Despite the fact that they were getting more airtime and cutting in-ring group promos like the nWo, it was harder than

........................................................................................

11 In storyline terms, Benoit was stripped of the title when video replay showed that Sid's foot was under the ropes as he was being pinned, theoretically invalidating the win.

12 Bischoff supposedly threw his coffee on Guerrero in response; Bischoff maintains that he simply knocked his coffee over.

ever to differentiate them from one another, their demands of fierce individuality subsumed by the insistence of their association.

On January 1, 1999, Guerrero wrecked his car and sustained life-threatening internal injuries. He was impaired at the time of the accident; he later admitted to having a serious drug problem during this period and overdosing several times. He returned to the ring seven months later.

When he returned, he formed a faction called the Filthy Animals with Konnan and Rey Mysterio that to WCW fans resembled a reconstituted LWO but which more accurately referenced his Los Gringos Locos posse from Mexico. It was Eddie's most prominent placement in WCW, and yet he was still reliving his past. In January of 2000 he asked for his release and got it.

☆ ☆ ☆

On January 31, 2000, Benoit and Guerrero debuted in the WWF, along with Dean Malenko and Perry Saturn—both of whom had also gone from ECW fame to WCW aimlessness—as the Radicalz.[13] They were functionally the last insurgent turncoats in the Monday Night Wars, and in some way, they were the greatest bellwether since Hall and Nash jumped ship to WCW. The Outsiders had signaled a new way of doing things, that there was a new major player in the wrestling industry, and the Radicalz epitomized the fact that that major player was in its death throes. Frustrated by their lack of promotion in WCW, these four jumped to the WWF in what was as much a political statement as a career advancement. But even though they arrived with significant fanfare, they weren't necessarily fated for greatness. If their initial employment by WCW was a matter of necessity, their hiring by WWF was a matter of opportunity. They were all symbols of WCW's lack of ingenuity and inability to promote from

---

**13** Though the *z* plural perhaps isn't now as cool as it seemed in the Attitude Era, it still persists, presumably because it renders a normal word copyrightable.

within. In hiring them, WWF management were able to cast themselves as visionaries by co-opting wrestlers underutilized by their rival.

The Radicalz, as they were originally composed, lasted roughly five minutes. During their first run-in, Guerrero gruesomely injured his elbow while performing a Frog Splash, and he was put out of action. By the time he returned, Benoit was moving on to a singles career separate from his Radicalz comrades. Guerrero soon found a level of personality that he'd only hinted at in WCW, and was cast as a borderline comedy act, amping up his Mexicanness and wooing the Amazonian Chyna (whom he called "mamacita"), going by the nickname of "Latino Heat."

Benoit, meanwhile, entered into a lengthy beef with Chris Jericho, who, it must be said, was the precursor of the Radicalz in the WWF; once an undersized and underutilized WCWer himself, he went up north in 1999 and proved that there was room at the top of the card for an untraditional critical darling, and so paved the way for Benoit and Guerrero. Their rivalry felt like a grudge match to determine who had been repressed more undeservedly in WCW. When they eventually teamed up against Triple H and "Stone Cold" Steve Austin, at stake was the redemption of their entire lot.

As his character evolved, Eddie was ever inching toward the mainstream, appearance-wise—his mullet receded, his mustache became a five-o'clock shadow, and his muscles virtually exploded. Benoit lost his mullet too, got more physically defined, and finally achieved a personality by fully embracing his strengths: He grinned, exposing his missing teeth; he scowled in agony at even his most joyful moments; and he kept the speaking to a minimum. As Eddie almost shockingly became a rounded, WWF-style superstar, Benoit became the embodiment of the very inability to achieve that; he was a mute, leering, violent menace, the sort of personality normally only seen in monstrous villains of the past. He came to exemplify everything the WWE mainstream was not, and in doing so, he excelled. Somehow these two underappreciated indie darlings had become mainstream stars.

Benoit won the Royal Rumble in 2004 and entered into a three-way title dispute against Triple H and Shawn Michaels, thus fully insinuating himself into the superstar ranks.

Eddie's lengthy team-up with Chavo as Los Guerreros became a sort of meta racial parody: They played to Mexican stereotypes, thickening their accents, driving around in hydraulics-powered hooptie cars, and proclaiming as their motto "We lie, we cheat, we steal." And yet—unlike so many other racial caricatures in wrestling history—Eddie and Chavo seemed to relish their ridiculousness. Maybe it was finally being given a chance to shine; maybe it was a realization of the path their forebears had carved out in south Texas all those years before. Regardless, the crowd was quickly cheering on these acknowledged criminals. Self-awareness gets points.

After a breakout run with the U.S. Championship, Eddie won the WWE title from Brock Lesnar at the No Way Out PPV just prior to Wrestle-Mania. His career high didn't turn out to be a personal high point. In an interview with the London *Sun*, Eddie said, "I was ready to win the belt, but not for what lay ahead of me. I wasn't prepared mentally for what happens outside the ring—because I think that's where the real challenges lie. I was taking things like attendances and ratings very personally. I'm an extremist and that's one thing I'd like to change in my life." His fears purportedly manifested in drug use—the subtext in the interview is thick with implication—though by that interview he'd found God and sobriety.

☆ ☆ ☆

On September 9, 2004, Guerrero faced Kurt Angle in a lumberjack match, an old-school gimmick in which the ring is surrounded by other wrestlers who are tasked with tossing the matched wrestlers back into the ring if they are tossed out or try to escape. The match was significant in storyline terms for its ending, when the Big Show made a surprise return and flattened practically the entire *SmackDown* roster, but in real-life terms, it matters for a different, more serious reason. According to Angle, Eddie was in such bad shape that night that he wouldn't let Angle touch him—he literally yelled "Don't touch me" repeatedly as

Angle tried to improvise different moves. If you go back and watch the match, you can see it happening. Angle and Eddie—even in his state—are too good for it to be blatant, but in rewatching, it jumps out that few of their exchanges result in any kind of physical impact on Guerrero. When he's tossed outside the ring—where he'd normally be at the lumberjacks' mercy—they mostly stay away from him, and Bubba Ray Dudley seems to run over from the other side of the ring to shield him. Angle is uncharacteristically tentative, and the referee seems to be in a constant state of unease. There's one big spot during the match—even more incredible when one considers Eddie's state—where Angle superplexes Eddie off the top rope.[14] Angle lands and writhes in outsize pain; Eddie more or less lies still, as if he's too hurt to emote. The referee ignores Angle and hovers over Eddie for a few seconds that seem like minutes. He's so ready to signal catastrophe to the backstage area that he's practically twitching. Normally when a match between two wrestlers of this caliber ends indecisively, it's a letdown, but when Big Show came out and the match evaporated, it felt like divine intervention.

Forget the stiff punches, or the hardcore bloodlettings, or the shoot interviews: This is the ne plus ultra of reality in wrestling. The enlightened wrestling fan has likely spent significant amounts of time explaining to nonviewers that even though wrestling is staged, it's not fake—that no amount of planning, no amount of scripting, no amount of physical trickery or assisted landing, no amount of ring elasticity or floor mat cushion can remotely assuage the physical assault of an average wrestling match. Every night on the road ends with ice bags or painkillers or just plain old pain, the unrelenting kind, the "you sit down in your rental car and electric voltage shoots up your spine" kind of pain, and so what, you get in your car anyway and drive to the next town and work another match tomorrow night and the fans cheer but they don't *know*. And you get two or three days off after tomorrow or the next day, and let's hope to

---

14 Unlike a normal superplex, which is performed with the aggressor standing on the second rope and flipping his opponent over from a seated position on the top, this move saw them both standing atop the top turnbuckle, increasing the height of the move by a third and probably doubling the torque.

God that's enough to get you right, because then it starts all over again. And then again next week, and then for months, and if you're *lucky*—imagine that word, here of all places—if you're *lucky* it'll keep going for years. And there's no off-season, no prolonged downtime unless, God forbid, you're seriously injured. That's reality. Fans will try to explain this to people, but wrestlers themselves are, for the most part, too proud—or too committed to the facade—to explain it to anyone, and it's this kind of pride, this commitment, that leads to a functional code of silence, even within the locker room, even among friends, and so to painkiller abuse, to alcohol abuse to take the edge off, to illicit drug use to get you going afterward, out of the fog of painkillers and beer. This is reality. Wrestling fans can explain this, but who can put into words the pain of working a *wrestling match* in which you're in so much pain that you don't want to be touched but you're too proud not to go through with it? When your livelihood is your body and your body is betraying you? Best-case scenario, working a match in that shape is a cry for help. In Eddie's case, Angle knew, the referee knew, probably a bunch of the guys playing lumberjack outside the ring had some idea, and nobody did anything. Probably Eddie was feeling better the next night or the night after that, and everybody let it drop. Because, honestly, that's what they'd want in his position.

In the intervening year after the lumberjack match with Angle, Eddie had a lengthy, compelling storyline with Rey Mysterio, after which he was again elevated to the title scene, as he was named as the number-one contender to Batista's championship. In both stories, Eddie wavered between friend and foe of his opponent, his ambition seemingly at war with his heart. Batista beat him at the No Mercy PPV in Eddie's last big match. He had the chance to hit Batista with a chair and presumably coast to victory, but he decided against it. Heart had beaten out ambition.

★ ★ ★

On November 13, 2005, Eddie Guerrero was found dead in his hotel room by his nephew Chavo. The coroner said it was heart failure due to arteriosclerotic cardiovascular disease. He'd not been well in the week prior, said his widow.[15] In truth, he hadn't been well for a while.

Angle says that when they were feuding, Eddie knew something was wrong, that some days he showed up looking "white as a ghost," that in some matches he didn't have feeling in half his body, that he was scared out of his mind not knowing what the problem was. And his answer wasn't going to the doctor but instead "praying every night, working out every day," and hoping for something to change. This is ridiculous, of course. And yet this is reality.

In the end Eddie's heart lost out to ambition. According to his widow, "Eddie just worked out like crazy all the time. It made his heart grow bigger and work harder and the vessels were getting smaller, and that's what caused the heart failure." According to Chavo, Eddie "had been working hard and was at peak physical fitness as a result, doing cardiovascular and weight training exercises every day." He prayed and he worked out; he got bigger and bigger, and his heart took on the strain of a man twice his size, and he recoiled at the success he achieved, and he broke down.

☆ ☆ ☆

The thing you always hear is that Chris Benoit never got over Eddie's death. That's what they said in the early hours after Benoit and his family were discovered dead. Some people have said it since the reality of the situation came out, but usually they're tactful enough not to footnote the story with excuses.

But that's wrongheaded. Everything in the world is explained by excuses and caveats. None of it is ever the complete story, but it's helpful in our understanding of it. For instance: Eddie died because he had heart failure, presumably because of the toll that years of steroids and painkillers and street drugs took on his heart and, not incidentally, because he never went to the doctor for help and because nobody intervened to

---

**15** After Eddie's death, Vickie was hired by WWE as an on-screen manager, presumably to give the family a healthy source of income. Improbably, she's emerged as one of the most inflammatory villains in the company.

take him to the doctor. Probably there are more reasons underlying his death, and presumably we will never know them all, but there's a functional framework for understanding what happened.

Pro wrestling is about living out our demons and our fantasies on a mythological stage. It's about finding answers to life's inherent questions, even if they're oversimplified—or precisely because they're oversimplified. This is how mythology works.

Chris Benoit's body was ravaged by the strain of twenty-plus years of wrestling, of steroid and HGH abuse, of a broken neck he'd had fused, of the relentless compulsion to prove himself. His brain was destroyed by years of diving headbutts that probably concussed him a little every time and of being hit in the head with steel chairs—Benoit is notoriously one of the only guys who would take shots to the back of his head, which is demonstrably more dangerous to your brain. His soul was ferrying the weight of Eddie's death, of Owen Hart's death, of a possibly dissolving marriage. The doctors eventually said that when he died he had the brain of an eighty-five-year-old Alzheimer's sufferer. The weight of all that pain and stress on a dementia-stricken mind. You don't have to excuse what he did to try to make some sense of it.

The night he killed himself, Benoit was supposed to win the ECW Championship. Which is to say that everything wrestling-wise was good. That nobody saw this coming.

On Friday, June 22, 2007, Benoit murdered his wife, Nancy. He tied her up and choked her to death from behind, his knee on her back. On Saturday he left an answering-machine message for his buddy Chavo Guerrero and told him he overslept and missed his flight. That was his first weak attempt at lying; I would guess that he was more in a state of denial than trying to cover anything up. On Sunday he killed his seven-year-old son, Daniel, sedating him with Xanax and suffocating him. He communicated with Chavo and other WWE personnel by phone and text throughout the next two days, and the story became that Nancy had food poisoning, that she was vomiting blood, that their son, Daniel, was vomiting too, that he had to take them to the hospital. Benoit started texting people with vague warnings and admissions: He'd send them his address and then tell them that the dogs were pinned up by the pool, that the side door of the house was unlocked. Benoit hanged himself from the pulley of a weight machine, with 240 pounds of steel that barely outweighed his muscled frame providing the lethal counterweight. It's hard not to see the irony: the breath choked from his log-thick neck by the cord that connected the weights to the pull-up bar that had made his back so incomprehensibly thick, the giving of oneself back over to that which made one. It was an abdication of heroism, an admission of the fraudulence of the whole thing. The lies about food poisoning and oversleeping were incidental compared to the lie of the superheroic existence, the lie of a strength that was all steroids and HGH, and of invincibility that was only a disguised masochism.

Benoit didn't make the pay-per-view on Sunday, and a young wrestler named John Morrison won the ECW title instead. On Monday night, WWE paid tribute to their fallen comrade with a commemorative show. The facts of the murder scene didn't start trickling out until the show was airing on the West Coast, and nobody considered that Benoit himself could be to blame.[16] WWE Chairman Vince McMahon opened the show, alone in the ring with a microphone, which not only signified the seriousness of the night but also broke the script; Vince had recently been "killed" in storylines, and Benoit's death retconned that fiction out of existence. When the truth of the situation came out, WWE understandably scrubbed all mention of Vince's pseudodemise from its website right along with the Benoit tributes. In a segment that aired on the Wednesday episode of ECW and the Thursday episode of *SmackDown*, Vince again opened things up, apologized for Monday's tribute show, and

---

**16** Among the numerous video eulogies that aired that night, the only outliers are those of Dean Malenko, who has a subtle, if telling, sense of horror coursing through his formal tribute, and William Regal—supposedly one of the people who received text messages from Benoit over the weekend—who has a stoically circumspect take on the situation that, in retrospect, is chilling. He refused to discuss Benoit as a person, despite their close relationship, only focusing on his ringwork; one can only assume that he had considered the possibility of the true tragedy.

reinstated business as usual—minus the him-being-dead thing. He promised that the tragedy would not be mentioned again. He was serious about that. The next time Chris Benoit's name is mentioned on a WWE telecast will be the first since then.

Chris Benoit was a world champion, and he murdered his wife and son and killed himself. The latter act doesn't actually erase the former, but it suffocates it. In the arena of professional wrestling, when all the world's a stage, when the crowd's response determines wins, positions, and entire careers, a reprehensible act is enough to purge reality from the record. Benoit was only ever a star because the fans screamed for him to be. Now they withdraw those screams, and Benoit's legacy is nullified. If any of this made sense, I would say it makes a certain kind of sense.

☆ ☆ ☆

Wrestlers love to tell Eddie stories. Even the bad ones—like Angle wrestling Eddie when he was half-paralyzed and in denial—are recounted with timeworn grins like so many practical jokes. Inherent in each of these stories is a sort of misty-eyed wonderment, a visceral reaction not just to Eddie's personality but also to the miracle of his success. Had he come a few years earlier, Guerrero probably wouldn't have made it to the WWF, let alone to the top of the card. Somebody could be retelling a story about life on the road, or a backstage prank, or a booze-induced argument, and there's always the same expression: They were lucky to know him, but Eddie was luck personified—he was a gassed-up Tyche, a steroidal Saint Jude, the holy revision and rejection of the impossible: He was the grappler's crude dream in the face of defeat.

Benoit, on the other hand, doesn't exist. Call him Lethe, Greek spirit of forgetfulness and oblivion. Or Saint Anthony (of Padua), patron saint of the missing—and, incidentally, of miracles.

In the end, one man is forgotten, whitewashed not just from polite discourse but also from institutional memory. You see it when other wrestlers perform his moves, the subtle attempt to recast them as something other than Benoit's. Eddie, though, can't be forgotten—he couldn't, with his widow dominating chunks of WWE television, but even without that, he's canonized. We can appreciate Eddie's overachievement without compunction, unlike Benoit's; in some ways it's a direct corollary, that in the years since Benoit's awful ending, Eddie has become, if not the anti-Benoit, the un-Benoit. His life ended tragically but not monstrously: It was a self-inflicted tragedy, an understandable one, the sad end point of modern self-determination. He died like too many wrestlers have died, but he lived like we all should want to live, or something like that.

The world wants to pretend Benoit never lived because of the way he died. They want to pretend Guerrero never died because of the way he lived. Either way, it's ritual suicide, self-mutilation in service of a dream. Eddie lived out his dream even through the pain, and Benoit lived out his dream until his pain consumed him. In that way, they couldn't be more different, but it's willful blindness to ignore the fact that they were so much alike. They were the real-life underdogs: They fought for everything they got; they transcended their roles; they defied the script. They determined to outperform life's lot for them, by any means necessary, and they succeeded, and the crowd went wild, and confetti fell from the rafters. In the end, life bit back, and everybody suffered in indescribable ways.

# EPILOGUE

The ref counts three, the timekeeper rings the bell, the announcer says good night, the houselights come up. The promoter counts the night's haul. The wrestler takes a shower, a soak, a painkiller. The fan walks to his car and drives home. The wrestler takes a ride in a rental car to the next town. It's only in that moment that the surreal recedes into reality, that the gods go back to being men. As Barthes put it, "When the hero or the villain of the drama . . . leaves the wrestling hall, impassive, anonymous, carrying a small suitcase and arm-in-arm with his wife, no one can doubt that wrestling holds that power of transmutation which is common to the Spectacle and to Religious Worship."

My dad, who's a holy man himself, once ran into Animal from the Road Warriors and the Warlord on an airplane. He didn't know who they were, but he judged from their bulk that they were wrestlers, and he proceeded to get their autographs for me on a yellow legal pad. I was mystified, not least because they were on-screen enemies but also because he said they were both nice guys. Nice guys! Even the goldenest of golden boys has a mean streak I'd have been reluctant to arouse. But they were off duty, and physiques aside, they were human. Every other fan has a story like this. Sometimes, though, the wrestler's not as keen to be hounded—they either stay in character and stalk away or they gruffly dismiss their fans: "Can't you see I'm eating?" And you can hardly blame them—dinner is a human concern, separate from the characters they play. *Gods* don't sign autographs.

In the ring, they're near-invincible symbols of good or evil, but the wrestler outside the ring is left to deal with the real-world ramifications of his on-screen sweat. The tolls of the job have changed little over the years. As Marcus Griffin puts it in closing his 1937 book, *Fall Guys*:

Disease dogs the footsteps of the modern pachyderms.... Some matmen die in the ring, others succumb from the shocks sustained while taking those trick falls and out of the ring dives, and others end up mumbling and spatting like punchy fighters who walk on their heels. Stanley Stasiak...died from blood poisoning after being cut during a bout in Worcester, Massachusetts, with Jack Sherry. Steve Snozsky...succumbed from an attack of locomotor ataxia, directly traced to injuries caused from falls taken during wrestling bouts.... Jim Browning, one time world's title holder... spent the last few months of his life half blinded from the ravages of trachoma and in intense pain from the stomach ulcers.... Mike Romano, veteran grappler who held over from the Sandow era, collapsed in a Washington, D. C. ring one night in June, 1936, while engaged in a bout.... He had died from athlete's heart, an ailment so common to other grapplers who follow the hard and strenuous schedules that participation in professional wrestling requires.

Sadly, the list continued on and on. All the subjects I've dedicated chapters to in this book are dead. And if few of them died directly in the line of duty, it's hard not to draw a straight line between the fantasy lives they led and the hard reality of their endings. It's more than a little uplifting, though, that the rash of deaths that first spurred me to chronicle them has petered out. The new generation of wrestlers largely grew up watching their heroes die and learned the appropriate lessons, and WWE, the last standing major promotion, is invested—be it out of compassion or marketing, it really doesn't matter—in making sure its employees don't wreck their lives. Now it's said that you're more likely to find a superstar playing video games in his hotel room after a match than partying in the hotel bar. But even if the epidemic of dead wrestlers has ended, wrestlers will never stop dying so long as wrestling exists. They're human, after all.

The history of pro wrestling is one of profound fakery, sure, but when balanced against the truth of the lives the wrestlers lead and the greater truth their actions represent, is the on-screen world really so diminished a reality? After all, as Lansing McCurley, sports editor of the *Philadelphia Daily News*, says in *Fall Guys*, while you may be able to fix the matches, you can't fix death: "You get great gashes over the head from ring posts and cracked bones and torn muscles. You get noises in the head and funny spells. And you get shouts and accusations of fake and in the bag and one hundred and one other epithets."

It's an ignoble existence out in the real world, a painful and deadly one. That, above anything, is what matters. So many fans were shocked into submission by the litany of deaths in the '90s that we convinced ourselves that we were appalled by the drugs, the steroids, the hard living that drove our heroes to early graves. It never gets any easier to see heroes die, even when they've led long, full lives. Because after all we've invested in them, it's always hard to see our gods as humans.

They're human in death, but in the ring, they're gods "because," says Barthes, "they are, for a few moments, the key which opens Nature, the pure gesture which separates Good from Evil, and unveils the form of a Justice which is at last intelligible." If it's all about justice in the end, I hope I've done the wrestlers and the industry a little bit of justice in this book.

The night's done, the show's over, it's time to go home.

# CREDITS

# CREDITS

# PARTIAL BIBLIOGRAPHY AND WORKS CITED

Barthes, Roland, *Mythologies: The Complete Edition* (New York: Hill and Wang, 2012). Print.

Beekman, Scott M., *Ringside: A History of Professional Wrestling in America* (Westport, CT: Praeger, 2006). Print.

Bowden, Scott, *Kentucky Fried Wrestling*, http://www.kentuckyfriedwrestling .com/.

Capouya, John, *Gorgeous George: The Outrageous Bad-Boy Wrestler Who Created American Pop Culture* (New York: Harper, 2008). Print.

Gotch, Frank, *Wrestling* (Boulder: Paladin Press, 2008). Print.

Griffin, Marcus, *Fall Guys: The Barnums of Bounce* (Chicago: Reilly & Lee Co., 1937). Print.

Jares, Joe, *Whatever Happened to Gorgeous George* (Englewood Cliffs, NJ: Prentice Hall, 1974). Print.

Klein, Greg, *The King of New Orleans: How the Junkyard Dog Became Professional Wrestling's First Black Superstar* (Toronto: ECW Press, 2012). Print.

Krugman, Michael, *André the Giant: A Legendary Life* (New York: Pocket Books, 2009). Print.

*Online Onslaught*, http://www.oowrestling.com/.

*Online World of Wrestling*, http://www.onlineworldofwrestling.com/.

*Slam! Sports: Wrestling*, http://slam.canoe.ca/Slam/Wrestling/home.html.

Smith, Red, *Press Box* (New York: W.W. Norton & Company, Inc., 1976). Print.

Solomon, Brian, *WWE Legends* (New York: Pocket Books, 2006). Print.

# NOTES

13 **The perception of Gotch:** Thesz, Lou, & Kit Bauman, Mike Chapman, Editor. *Hooker: An Authentic Wrestler's Adventures Inside the Bizarre World of Professional Wrestling.* Wrestling Channel Press, 2001.

14 **[The wrestlers] would go to the mat:** Joel Sayre, "The Pullman Theseus," *The New Yorker* (March 5, 1932): 26.

20 **They started at 4 o'clock:** Arthur Daley, "The Same Old Script," *The New York Times* (November 5, 1952).

22 **The revival of a sport that was in the doldrums:** Morris Markey, "Catch as Catch Can," *The New Yorker* (April 18, 1931): 37.

22 **The World Almanac for 1931:** Joel Sayre, "The Pullman Theseus," *The New Yorker* (March 5, 1932).

23 **But even if they're not:** Grantland Rice, "Rasslin' Gets a Toe Hold," *Collier's* (March 14, 1931): 26.

23 **No New York newspaper:** Joel Sayre, "The Pullman Theseus," *The New Yorker* (March 5, 1932): 26.

23 **A Foreign Menace:** A. J. Liebling, "From Sarah Berhardt to Yukon Eric," *The New Yorker* (November 13, 1954).

24 **For O'Mahoney's part:** "O'Mahoney," *The New Yorker* (July 20, 1935).

24 **His ignorance of the sport:** Arthur Daley, "The Same Old Script," *The New York Times* (November 5, 1952).

24 **The veteran wrestling fans recall:** John B. Kennedy, "Pillars of Sport," *Collier's* (September 19, 1931).

25 **Not the least interesting:** Morris Markey, "Catch as Catch Can," *The New Yorker* (April 18, 1931): 37.

25 **If this be play-acting:** Joel Sayre, "The Pullman Theseus," *The New Yorker* (March 5, 1932): 26.

28 **It isn't a sport; it's show business:** Jack Miley, "Jake's Juggernauts," *Collier's* (October 22, 1938).

# NOTES

28 **The trouble, according to [Pfefer]:** A. J. Liebling, "Pull His Whiskers," *The New Yorker* (July 8, 1939).

41 **It's television:** Lawrence Laurent, "Grunt and Groaners Pin Down Another TV Myth," *The Washington Post and Times-Herald* (March 10, 1956).

56 **In the documentary *Lipstick and Dynamite*:** Ruth Leitman, dir., *Lipstick and Dynamite* (Ruthless Films, 2005), Film.

97 **Abby met her at the airport:** Mike Lano, Dutch Mantel, Desperado Hero, (September 16, 1999), www.Hack-Man.com

100 **Ed McDaniel wasn't a full-blooded Native American:** Mike Shropshire, "Wahoo McDaniel," *Sports Illustrated* (July 2, 2001).

103 **Scarpa himself said fairly explicitly:** Mike Mooneyham, "Young Flair set for Charlotte debut," *The Post and Courier* (November 23, 2008).

110 **It's a testament to the degree:** "Masked Marvel Is Wrestler Henderson," *The Day* (New York: December 31, 1915).

110 **At least I could go on the streets:** Greg Oliver, "Leukemia claims 'The Spoiler' Don Jardine," *Slam! Sports* (December 17, 2006).

118 **You can practically hear Vince drooling on commentary:** Adam Nedeff, "The Name on the Marquee: Wrestling at the Chase (01.07.84)," (August 21, 2011), 411mania.com: Wrestling.

120 **In the most recent Nielsen ratings:** Bruce Newman, "Who's Kidding Whom," *Sports Illustrated* (April 29,1985).

128 **It was good business for Jones too:** Greg Oliver, "S.D. Jones dies in Antigua," *Slam! Sports* (October 26, 2008).

129 **In 2005, Jones told Canada's *Slam! Sports*:** Dave Hillhouse, "S.D. Jones: An unforgotten gladiator," *Slam! Sports* (June 12, 2005).

133 **In the South and West:** David Bixenspan, "Black Wrestlers and the World Heavyweight Title," Cageside Seats (February 4, 2011).

134 **This was at a time when most other public events:** "Sputnik wrestled against prejudice," *The Washington Times* (December 2, 2006).

137 **He was one of a few wrestlers:** www.infinitecore.ca/superstar/index .php?km_km_ict=6e16f84c6b0b68940b62ede692437cc1&threadid= 72110& page= 0#pager.

137 **He similarly referred to black wrestler:** www.salon.com/1999/05/07/ gaffes.

138 **I'm more of a nigger than you are:** www.thesun.co.uk/sol/homepage/ sport/wrestling/1084589/WWE-suspend-Michael-Hayes-after-racist-slur.html#ixzz25YXJNpll.

203 **As wrestling writer Rick Scaia puts it:** Rick Scaia, "Road Warrior Hawk, Dead at 46 . . . ," *Online Onslaught* (October 20, 2003).

229 **Davey Boy was clearly inspired:** "Hart & Soul: The Hart Family Anthology," *WWE* (2010).

234 **In 2002, while on vacation with his girlfriend:** "Wrestling deaths and steroids," *USA Today* (March 12, 2004).

290 **This country has no place:** www.slam.canoe.ca/Slam/Wrestling/2012/05/28/19806356.html.

290 **When the local government sought to regulate:** "Law Sought to Control Wrestling," Herman Blackman, *Washington Post and Times-Herald*, October 26, 1956.

290 **Half an hour after the people:** "Promoter Answers TV Complaints," Herman Blackman, *Washington Post and Times-Herald*, October 27, 1956.

328 **Halme's public life didn't end there:** Jonathan Snowden, "The Strange Life and Times of MMA's Legendary Finn," Fight Day (January 2001).

364 **His soul was ferrying:** "Benoit's Brain Showed Severe Damage From Multiple Concussions, Doctor and Dad Say," ABC News (January 8, 2009).

# INDEX